Spiritual Dimensions of Healing

The paper used in this publication meets the minimum requirements of
American National Standard for Information Sciences—
Permanence of Paper for Printed Library Materials, ANSI Z39.48-1984.

Spiritual Dimensions of Healing

Stanley Krippner
Patrick Welch

IRVINGTON PUBLISHERS, INC.
New York

Copyright ©1992 by Irvington Publishers, Inc.

Irvington Publishers, Inc.,
Executive offices: 522 E. 82nd Street, Suite 1, New York, NY 10028
Customer service and warehouse in care of: Integrated Distribution
Services, 195 McGregor St, Manchester, NH 03102, (603) 669-5933

An earlier version of this book was published under the title
Zwischen Himmel und Erde
by Chiron Verlag, Dusslingen, Germany, 1987

Library of Congress Cataloging-in-Publication Data

Krippner, Stanley, 1932-
.Spiritual dimensions of healing / Stanley Krippner, Patrick Welch.
  p.   cm.
Includes bibliographical references and index.
ISBN 0-8290-2462-X : $19.95 (Without audio cassette)
ISBN 0-8290-3162-6 : $39.95 (With audio cassette)
1. Shamanism. 2. Mental healing. I. Welch, Patrick. II. Title.
IN PROCESS
615.8'52—dc20   92-159
                                         CIP

First Printing 1992
1 3 5 7 9 10 8 6 4 2

Printed in the United States of America

Dedication

With gratitude to Rolling Thunder, the intertribal medicine man who brought us together.

There has been a weaving together of sky consciousness with earth consciousness.... Those who walk in the wilderness will sense that balance directly.

Joan Halifax (1987)

Contents

One

Healing The Spirit

Donna Eden, a California photographer, was vacationing in Fiji with her daughters in 1978. Surrounded by tropical plants, flowers, and beaches, Eden experienced life differently than in the technological American setting she had left behind. She enjoyed the slow pace and the graceful people. In retrospect, she views Fiji's simplicity and natural setting as her two greatest spiritual teachers.

Eden met native healers in Fiji who spoke about healing in ways that were new to her, yet familiar in a way she finds difficult to explain. They spoke of the necessity to include spiritual teachings in their treatment of clients, and of "healing energies" that one could enlist in the aid of oneself or others.

On returning to the United States, Eden succumbed to "culture shock" as she became caught up in the rush and pressure of American life. One day she observed the words "Touch for Health" on a woman's T-shirt. Eden asked, "What is that?" The woman told Eden that she planned to take an instructor's course in "Touch for Health" the following week. Impetuously, Eden responded, "Me too!"

Eden placed a telephone call to the Touch for Health Foundation headquarters in Pasadena, California, to register for the course, only to discover that her name was already on the roster.

Two weeks later, Eden finished the instructor's course on a Tuesday and began to teach her first class the following Friday. She was unsure of herself, but excited about the opportunity; the response to her was favorable. Within a few years, Eden had a waiting list of people who wanted to see her for treatment. She also began to teach Touch for Health in various parts of the United States as well as in Europe.

The pathways of "body energy" identified by Touch for Health practitioners serve as a basis for "laying-on" of hands, massage, acupressure, and imagery. Eden says that she felt "at home" in Fiji and, in a similar way, felt a sense of "rightness" with Touch for Health. Within a few years, Eden had changed her vocation from that of a photographer to that of a spiritual healer.

Shirley Harrison

Both of us became interested in spiritual healing as a result of personal encounters with spiritual practitioners. In June, 1965, one of us (Krippner) was hospitalized for internal bleeding. A friend of his telephoned Shirley Harrison, a well known "psychic sensitive" living in Maine. Harrison's daughter answered the phone, telling her, "Mother has flown to New York City. She said that Dr. Krippner needed her and that she had to be near him." A few minutes later, Harrison phoned from a Manhattan hotel stating, "Stanley is seriously ill. He has bleeding ulcers and will be operated on before Monday evening. But he will survive. The power of love will help him through this ordeal." Harrison had entered an altered state of consciousness and allowed her fingers to glide around a board which contained every letter of the alphabet. Her daughter recorded the letters because Harrison, who believed she was "taking dictation" from the spirit world, typically had no recall of the experience once it was over.

On Monday morning, Krippner was operated on for two duodenal ulcers. His duodenum was so badly ulcerated that a chunk was cut out as well as a portion of his stomach. Krippner recalled:

> A hole in my side was left open to permit the drainage of waste fluids. When the hole did not close at the expected time, Harrison visited me in the hospital. She had not brought her alphabet board with her, but wrote the letters on a sheet of paper, placed her fingers on the paper, and another friend wrote down the letters as her fingers stopped. The message stated that four stitches needed to emerge from the hole before it would heal properly. She also predicted that the healing would take place within three days.
>
> As a result of Shirley Harrison's diagnosis, I proceeded to hypnotize myself several times a day, repeating the word "heal." I also evoked images of the loose stitches that were supposedly floating around my bodily cavity. On the second day of my attempts, two double stitches emerged from the hole. Apparently they had come loose and had caused considerable irritation. On the following day, the wound closed. This episode stimulated me to study alternative forms of healing, especially those involving imagery and self-regulation.

Paul Stacy

Patrick Welch met with Paul Stacy, a spiritual practitioner, several times in 1985 and 1986. Stacy related that on a stormy day in 1979, he was struck by a lightning bolt which, he claimed, "blasted me out of my body." Stacy, still very much alive, had the experience of observing his physical body laying prone 20 feet away! His impulsive plea for help was answered by the images of his dead grandparents who appeared nearby and beckoned him to come closer. Their presence reassured Stacy that he was not alone.

Stacy then saw, at chest level, what he recalls as a circle of light in which a series of images appeared portraying scenes from men's and women's lives. Stacy intuitively felt that these episodes were *his* other lives.

One story was of special interest to Stacy, and appeared to be taking place in President Abraham Lincoln's administration. It showed an American Indian medicine man; he and his tribe were about to be expelled from their territory by the American government. The tribal warriors were preparing to defend their land, but the medicine man tried to convince them that bloodshed would solve nothing. Instead, he travelled to Washington, D.C., and arranged a meeting with the President. The meeting between Lincoln and the medicine man went well, and the President promised that federal authorities would not infringe upon the tribe's territorial rights.

Upon his return, the medicine man discovered that the members of his tribe were not convinced of the President's sincerity. Six months later the tribe was ruthlessly attacked; after this episode they forced the medicine man to leave his tribe and take refuge in the world of the White people. The medicine man dressed like a White man, but continued to work on behalf of Indians' rights. (Stacy claimed that he later investigated historical documents that verified the existence of such a man and his story.)

After observing this and other vignettes, Stacy felt that he had to make a choice of whether to remain out of his body (in the world of spirits), or return to earth with a renewed sense of direction. Stacy decided that his life's purpose was to come back to his body, to continue living with his wife and son, and to practice the values of American Indian culture.

This episode in Stacy's life affected him in the same way a "vision quest" serves native people in search of the next step in their life's plan. The experience was a solidifying force in his life; the visions and insights he encountered gave him the strength to reenter the world with a new, profound understanding he had never experienced. The use of imagery can be a transformative element in healing, enabling the body, mind, emotions, and spirit to work together. The images that Stacy perceived helped give his life meaning and the image of the medicine man became a role model for his mission.

Spiritual Practitioners

Spiritual healing is not a common practice in industrialized nations, but it once permeated all forms of medicine and counseling. We use the word "spiritual" to describe those aspects of human behavior and experience that reflect an alleged transcendent intelligence or process. This transcendent entity inspires devotion and directs behavior. We find that spiritual aspects are evident among human beings whenever there is an awareness of a broader life meaning that goes beyond the immediacy of everyday expediency and material concerns. Moslems, Christians, and Jews refer to prayer as a spiritual exercise that enables them to establish contact with Allah, God, or Jehova. Buddhists and Hindus speak of the spiritual development they obtain by engaging in such practices as yoga or meditation. Marxists often use the word "spiritual" to refer to those noble, admirable, and altruistic human traits brought about by the inevitable rise of the proletariat. Like Marxists, secular humanists disregard or deny the existence of a Divine Being but may refer to humankind's highest moral and ethical motives and actions as "spiritual." Members of a native tribe may claim to receive messages from the "spirit world," a realm of being that is not immediately apparent but which directs important life decisions and activities.

The California State Psychological Association Task Force on Spirituality and Psychotherapy adopted a definition of "spirituality" that is quite similar: "It has been said that spirituality is the 'courage to look within and trust.' What is seen and what is trusted appears to be a deep sense of belonging, of wholeness, of connectedness, and of the openness to the infinite." When 1,400 California clinical psychologists were asked by mail whether or not they felt that spirituality was relevant in their personal lives and their clinical work, 406 responded. Although the majority answered positively, fewer affirmed the personal relevance of spirituality than of the population in general. Behavioral psychologists were the least likely to affirm the relevance of spirituality in therapy while Jungian analysts were the most likely. Those therapists who felt that spirituality was relevant to their personal lives were the most likely to use it in their clinical practice (Shafranske, 1984).

We take the position that "spiritual" is not a synonym for "religious" because a religion is an institutionalized body of believers who accept a common set of beliefs, practices, and rituals regarding spiritual concerns and issues. People who have internalized these beliefs and practices are generally "spiritual." In addition, many people are "spiritual" without being "religious" in the sense of participating in organized religion. However, one can be "religious" without being "spiritual"—many members of religious institutions perform the necessary rituals and accept the creed (at least superficially), but their ethics, morals, and opportunities for day-by-day practice of their religion do not match their professed beliefs.

Modern medicine, nursing, social work, counseling, and psychotherapy address themselves to a person's physical, mental, emotional, and social problems but rarely to one's spiritual concerns. Nor are most practitioners aware of cultural and ethnic differences in spiritual perspectives. Many health care professionals are embarrassed and speechless when a patient or client asks them, "But doctor, what does it all mean?" The closer people in need of professional help move toward a consideration of such spiritual issues as the fear of death, the feeling of loneliness, and the lack of meaning in their lives, the less likely it is that they can find professional workers who can be of assistance.

This was not always the case. Michael Winkelman, a social scientist, studied the records of religious and magical practices in 47 different societies (Winkelman, 1984). A "society" is a closely integrated group of people held together by mutual dependence and in which there is a division of labor. The documentary evidence from these societies revealed that the religious and magical practitioners interacted with those human experiences that could be thought of as "spiritual." They claimed to have access to spiritual entities (e.g., deities, ghosts, spirits) as they directed the society's spiritual activities (e.g., prayer, sacred ceremonies). These practitioners were felt to employ special powers (e.g., casting spells, bestowing blessings, exorcising demons) that allowed them to influence the course of human affairs or natural phenomena in ways not possible by other members of their social group.

Winkelman found remarkable similarities among these groups, especially regarding the manner in which the nature and role of spiritual practitioners changed as their society became more complex. For example, shamans were found only in groups with no formal social classes. No shamans were observed in agricultural societies; rather, their presence was typical of hunting and gathering tribes and fishing societies. The Creek, Crow, and Kiman were among the Native American tribes that awarded considerable power and prestige to the shamans in their midst.

Once the society became sedentary and began to practice agriculture, social stratification took place. In addition to the division of labor, political and economic divisions occurred. Priests or priestesses emerged, taking charge of the group's religious rituals. The shaman's power and status were reduced. According to Winkelman, the term "shaman/healer" (or *shamanic* healer) is a more accurate description of this practitioner because healing became his or her major function. The role of the shamanic healer became specialized and formalized; official initiation ceremonies and training procedures became more common. Political development beyond the level of the local community was observed in almost all the societies in which priests were present.

The Jivaros in South America and the Ibo tribe in western Africa are among the groups in which priests were assigned a healing function. Priests also served healing functions in Japanese Buddhist and Kurd Dervish groups. In this book, we will describe the healing ministry of Christian ministers and priests, as well as religious shrines where healings purportedly occur. We will also discuss our contact with shamanic healers among the Cuna, Huichol, Mazatec, and North American Indian tribes. Paul Stacy (who told Welch about his "past life" as a medicine man) would be considered a shamanic healer because he is aware of his activities and movements when he alters his consciousness during a healing session.

Political integration became even more complex with the appearance of judicial, military, and legislative institutions. As the competition between (and within) these groups took place, the malevolent practitioner (sorcerer or witch), appeared. Originally it was shamans who cast hexes and spells on tribal enemies; these functions were taken over by the sorcerer and, for a price, were often directed against members of one's own social group. Potions and charms became the province of witches and their associates. The shamanic healer's scope of activity was now reduced not only by priests but by sorcerers and/or witches as well. There were sorcerers among the Aztecs and witches among the Navahos. In addition, we have interviewed several witches who consider healing to be one of their central activities and will describe their backgrounds, rituals, and beliefs.

Further political complexities and continued dependence on agriculture became associated with the development of another practitioner, the diviner or medium, such as those found among the Eurasian Kazakhs. At one time the shaman's repertoire had included talking with spirits; later, mediums (or diviners) began to specialize in this feat, "incorporating" the spirits and allowing them to speak and act through their voice and body. At this point, the shaman's role had been dispersed to the extent that the only functions remaining were such specialized healing capacities as the performing of healing songs and dances, dispensing herbal medicines, bone-setting and surgery, and the diagnosing of disease. Altered states of consciousness were rarely present, although they once had played an important role in the work of shamans and shamanic healers. Winkelman referred to these practitioners as "healers" (or *shamanistic* healers). Shamanistic healers no longer carried out most of the shamanic functions but reflected the shamans' intent because they held the healing of one's spirit in high regard.

Both shamanic and shamanistic healers emphasized the spiritual aspects of healing that are the focus of this book. Furthermore, shamanic healers still maintained a commitment to their community that was a central element of shamanism, and often engaged in practices to alter their consciousness and enter the world of spirits. Shamanistic healers, on the other hand, were more involved in individual work than community work. Further, altered states of consciousness and journeying to the spirit world were not a core element of their healing work as was true of shamans.

We might say that shamanic healers are one step removed from shamanism and that shamanistic healers are two steps removed from these roots. Shamanistic healers can be found in diverse cultural groups. We will describe several shamanistic healers we have interviewed in North America; their professions range from art to nursing, and some are allopathic physicians! In addition, we will provide first-person accounts of healing ceremonies conducted by mediums in Haiti, Mexico, and Puerto Rico. Shirley Harrison, who visited Krippner in the hospital, did not hold healing rituals but would be considered a medium because she claimed to receive messages from the spirit world, claiming little conscious awareness during the process.

Winkelman's classification system was found to be remarkably accurate when cross-societal comparisons were made. Shamans were found in societies with no formal classes. With only two exceptions, shamans never were found in tribal groups displaying an administrative political organization beyond the local level. No shamans were found in sedentary societies where the nomadic way of life was absent. Therefore, none of the practitioners we have personally interviewed in North America, Central America, and the Caribbean could be considered shamans from the anthropological point of view; indeed, we believe that this word represents a distinguished tradition and we have applied it sparingly in our discussions.

Worldviews and Models

Underlying the procedures of each of these practitioners was an explicit or implicit model of healing that arranged, structured, and systematized the practitioner's beliefs and assumptions. For example, the allopathic medical model holds that physicians confer the "sick role" on certain people who are then treated in an attempt to restore their health. Care by physicians and nurses, diagnosis, medication, surgery, hospitalization, and visits to the physician's office all occur on the basis of this model. An obvious benefit of the "sick role" is that patients are relieved from the stress involved in carrying out their regular activities and meeting their ordinary obligations. On the other hand, taking the "sick role" too seriously often deprives patients of the opportunity to engage in self-healing and play a significant role in their recovery.

There are models of healing that differ considerably from the allopathic medical model. Allopaths assume that a large dose of medicine is stronger than a small dose. Homeopaths believe that a highly diluted solution of medicine is more powerful than an undiluted solution. Allopaths assume that the patient must be physically present for treatment. Practitioners of radionics and radiesthesia believe in "subtle energies" and operate from a different worldview, treating many of their patients at a distance. The allopathic medical model is discontinuous; people are either ill and need treatment, or they are well and do not need to be treated. The Chinese medical model, however, is continuous; people exist on a spectrum of wellness, and require treatment to keep from becoming seriously ill.

In general, allopathic physicians can not be considered shamanistic healers because they ignore their patients' spiritual needs. However, there are exceptions; we have identified a number of allopathic practitioners who are aware of the spiritual dimensions of their patients' lives. These physicians engage in spiritual counseling, discussing the meaning and value of life with their patients. Some talk about the possibility of life after death; others pray with their patients before sending them for radiation treatment or to the operating room. On the other hand, spirituality is an essential part of the shamanic healing model and permeates each of its dimensions; spirituality is also an integral part of the healing models of native priests and mediums. Often referred to as "indigenous healers," "native healers," or "traditional healers," their practices are still viable over much of the earth.

The "living earth" concept is an important part of the worldview held by Native American shamans who always have emphasized their clients' connections with natural forces. The Algonquin Indians worshipped Nokomis, the Earth Mother, and believed that all living creatures fed from her bosom. The earth was seen as a living organism by other tribes as well, and many healing procedures were based on this concept.

The central element in the Navaho healing ceremony is

the "sand painting," a symbolic design created in the soil by the tribe's spiritual practitioners. This painting represents the spiritual and physical landscapes in which the patients and their illnesses exist. At the same time, the sand painting is felt to contain the cause of the disease and the meaning of the procedure that has been chosen by the shaman for its cure. Several other tribes in the American Southwest use sand paintings in their healing ceremonies.

Stones, plants, and sacred objects often are placed inside the painting; relationships among the elements are represented in the colored sand. The sand figures may be clouds or snakes or whatever is needed to portray the path of the disease as it proceeds through collective ritual space. Dangers and hazards have their place in the matrix as well; if they have been the cause of a misfortune or ailment, attention must be paid to them in the alleviation of the ensuing distress.

Chanting and holding a community vigil are typical procedures that bring all the elements of a sand painting together. Indisposed people then become aware of the relationship of their sickness to the rest of their life. Usually they are surrounded by their friends, neighbors, and relatives who sing and pray for a recovery (Grossinger, 1982).

A variation of the sand painting is used by Navaho shamans who paint the symbols on buckskin or on their patients' bodies. Another related practice is the "ground painting" constructed by the Southern California Diseguenos during the puberty rituals held for young men in their tribe. Practitioners convey the design of the Diseguenos' worldview by presenting the horizon as a circle. Included in the ground painting are the world's edge, various heavenly bodies, power animals (such as the coyote, wolf, and crow), and the mortar and pestle used to grind up the mind-altering plants used in the Diseguenos' ceremonies.

The Salish Indians of the Pacific Northwest design a staff for spirit dancers depicting the living elements of the world. It is decorated with paddles representing water, eagle feathers symbolizing the sky, deer hooves representing animal life, and cedar bark plant life. As we see it, these and other shamanic representations of the earth rest on the concept of the planet as a living organism.

For the shaman, tremendous power rests in each aspect of nature; this net of power animates the cosmos. The shamans' knowledge enables them to understand how the life force operates in both health and sickness. For the shaman, rocks, flowers, trees, bodies of water, four-legged and two-legged creatures, as well as those creatures who swim and crawl, display spiritual qualities. The shamanic worldview acknowledges kinship among all aspects of nature. In addition to the living earth, other common primal ancestors among Native Americans are Grandfather Fire, Grandmother Moon, Mother Earth and Sea, and Father Sun.

An example of nature/human interaction is found in a Canadian Crow legend describing a discovery by One-Child-Woman, who decided to leave her husband because of his disinterest in her. She travelled along Fishtail Creek and reached the top of a hill where she rested for a while. Suddenly, she noticed a rock with several faces marked on it, yet she knew that no human had carved the faces. One of the faces was human, another was that of a buffalo, a third was the face of an eagle, and the fourth was a horse's head.

One-Child-Woman had discovered a remarkable rock that contained the power to heal. Over the years, according to the legend, it not only healed sickness and prolonged people's lives, but led to success in battles with tribal enemies, in predicting the future, and in gambling contests. Tribal members found several similar stones and rock medicine became a part of Crow medical practice (Wildschut, 1975).

Such spiritual concepts as that of the living earth are not discussed in orthodox, allopathic medical models of healing, yet they play an indispensable part in native and alternative healing models. This worldview is revered by those practitioners who are attempting to maintain and practice the old traditions. In this book we will discuss spiritual healers we have known, and show how many of their principles and practices are not necessarily incompatible with allopathic models of medicine. The search for transcendence has characterized human activity since the days of the first shamans. This search still continues and inevitably finds its way into the work of healing practitioners as they attend to the needs of their clients (Heinze, 1990).

Two.

Models Of Healing

For several decades, social and behavioral scientists have been collecting data that reflect the wide variety of humankind's healing systems. Sicknesses and injuries are universal experiences, but each social group implicitly or explicitly classifies them as to cause and cure. Furthermore, we take the position that each person has a belief system that provides an explanation of how he or she can maintain health and overcome illness.

These personal beliefs include the spiritual dimension if the social context is supportive. For example, Chicano (Mexican-American) curanderos often attribute an illness to an agent whose existence must be taken on faith because it can not be detected with medical instruments. The "mal ojo" or "evil eye" has no place in allopathic medicine but these spiritual practitioners claim it is caused by a person staring intently at someone else, usually with envy or desire. It is often treated by forming three crosses on the victim's body with an egg while the practitioner recites the Apostle's Creed. An Apache disease, "nitsch," results from the neglect of nature entities. If an Apache does not properly salute an owl, he or she may suffer from heart palpitations, anxiety, sweating, and shaking. Shamanic prayers and songs are needed to treat this illness which, it is believed, can lead to suicide.

The psychiatrist and psychologist Jerome Frank (1973) conjectured that the first healing model was built around the prehistoric belief that the etiology of illness was either supernatural (e.g., possession by a malevolent spirit) or magical (e.g., the result of a sorcerer's curse). Treatment consisted of appropriate rituals that supposedly undid or neutralized the cause. These rituals typically required the active participation not only of the sufferer but also family and community members. Spirits were felt to facilitate the healing process.

Some perceived causes and cures were seen to operate from the world of nature utilizing herbs, exercises, and fasts. When shamanic healers and shamanistic healers coexisted within the same tribal group, the former usually directed spiritual healing procedures while the latter took charge of naturalistic remedies. For example, Mexican-American practitioners believe that only certain people have the ability, gift, or "don" to work intensively on the spiritual level. They also believe that this distinction is one of degree rather than kind. The shaman or medium can receive spirit communications but, in their absence, a curandero or other practitioner can treat spiritual problems such as those ailments thought to be caused by a hex (Trotter and Chavira, 1981).

The Pima Indian Healing Model

The anthropologist Claude Levi-Strauss (1955) has proposed that the kind of logic developed by tribal people is as rigorous and complete as that of modern science. It is not the quality of the intellectual process that differs but the mode of expression and application. For example, the cultural myths of so-called "primitive" pre-Columbian Mexican and Central American societies not only were comprehensive guides to daily conduct but also provided an explanation for the mysteries of the universe. Each mythic episode can be interpreted in several ways according to the context and the listener's understanding. The symbols used are manipulated with such economy that each serves a wide range of philosophical and religious ideas. Quetzalcoatl was the "feathered serpent" (who symbolized the transformation of matter into spirit), as well as the god of the winds, the Lord of Dawn, the spirit of the sacred ocelot (a fierce jungle cat), the real-life last king of the Toltecs, and (following the Spanish conquest) Jesus Christ.

Similar evaluations have been made by other scientists. In assessing Pima Indian shamanism, the ethnologist B. L. Fontana (1974) stated that it is "a nonwestern theory of disease which is as subtle and as sophisticated as any other such theory". The principles of Pima shamanism have been recorded in some detail as a result of a study in which an anthropologist, Donald Bahr, collaborated with a shaman, a Pima translator, and a Pima linguist. These Pima Indians lived in the state of Arizona, but the Pima culture also extends throughout parts of northern Mexico (Bahr, Gregorio, Lopez, and Alvarez, 1974).

This procedure is quite sensible, and makes native people co-investigators of the study rather than mere subjects of an investigation. Some previous anthropological studies have been flawed because tribal respondents lied to the investigators, played jokes on them, or told them what they wanted to hear. Apparently, the anthropologists did not think that the natives they were studying had the intelligence to give information that was incorrect.

Because of its sophistication, the Piman theory of disease lends itself to analysis in terms of a 12-faceted model proposed by Miriam Siegler and Humphry Osmond (1974). In the social and behavioral sciences, a "model" is an explicit or implicit explanatory structure that underlies a set of organized group behaviors. Models have been constructed to describe human conflict, competition, and cooperation. Models have been proposed to explain mental illness, personality dynamics, and family interactions.

Among the Pimas, *diagnosis* is as important as treatment

and is carried out by the shaman. A patient's body is seen as the stratified repository of a lifetime's acquisitions of strengths and weaknesses. It is the task of the shaman to make an accurate diagnosis and then to turn the patient over to other practitioners for treatment. In doing this, shamans purportedly are assisted by benevolent spirits; indeed, it is believed that shamans are recruited, trained, and ordered into action by these spirits.

Etiology, or cause of the illness, depends on the type of disease that is being treated. One type of disease is untreatable because the body's self-healing capacities will deal with it (e.g., constipation, indigestion, venomous bites) or because treatment is futile (e.g., mental retardation, infant deformities). The other type of disease is treatable; the ailment may be a "wandering sickness" (caused by impurities that "wander" through the body) or a "staying sickness" (caused by improper behavior towards such "power objects" as buzzard feathers, jimson weed, or roadrunner birds). When the Europeans arrived, it was noted that they did not fall victim to "staying sicknesses." The Pimas did not lose faith in their model, merely concluding that the objects in question were not sacred to Caucasians, hence the newcomers could not be punished for treating them with disrespect.

The *patient's behavior* provides important clues for diagnosis and treatment. Wandering sickness entails such symptoms as fever, hives, piles, or sores. Staying sickness can be identified by compulsive or erratic actions as well as by lethargy or self-destructive activities. The former ailments can be communicable in contrast to the latter .

The *treatment* for wandering sickness usually entails herbs. Once allopathic medicines were encountered, they were added to the curative agents for wandering sickness. The treatment for staying sickness involves chanting, singing, oratory, blowing the harmful agencies away from the patient, sucking the harmful agents from the patient's body, eating the flesh of the dangerous object whose violation caused the disease, or placing the patient on a sand painting. Sand painting treatment is highly recommended for "wind sickness" while a feast is considered useful for "deer sickness" or "rabbit sickness."

In the case of staying sickness, some healing implements (such as crystals, tobacco smoke, and eagle feathers) are used to connect the shaman's power (or "heart") with the patient's self-healing capacities while others (such as rattles and the shaman's voice) are directed toward the spirits. Herbalists can also appeal to spirits in the treatment of wandering sickness by requesting that they bless the various plant remedies.

Prognosis, or anticipated outcome, is hopeful if the treatment is appropriate, prompt, and powerful. If not, *death or suicide* may result, or the illness may continue. Suicide can result from staying sickness while fatal heart attacks from "horned toad sickness" are not uncommon. "Deer sickness" and "dog sickness" are dangerous as well, and often lethal.

Healing is attempted in an environment created by the shaman or other healing practitioner. It is usually out-of-doors and often around a fire. For some types of wandering sickness, the allopathic physician's office or hospital serves as the environment for treatment. Thus, the *function of the institution* is for healing whether it represents the Pima tradition or allopathy.

The *personnel* involved in healing can range from the allopathic physician or nurse to the Piman shaman or herbalist. Staying sickness is primarily treated by shamans (actually, "shamanic healers" in Winkelman's classification), while wandering sickness is treated by allopaths or by herbalists (Winkelman's "shamanistic healer" category).

In the Pima system, patients have a *right* to treatment, as well as the *duty* to cooperate with the practitioner. They also have the duty to refrain from further violation of the dangerous objects that cause staying sickness. Each person has internal capacities or "strengths" located in specific parts of the body. In staying sickness, the strength of each dangerous object interfaces with the victim's strength. Thus, the victim's strength can serve as the repository of the disease; once the shaman has located it, such treatments as massaging the muscles or sucking out the impurities can be initiated.

The patient's family has the *right* to obtain treatment for its indisposed family members. Parents have the *duty* to avoid violating the dignity of dangerous objects as this might not only result in their own illness but that of their children. Parental misdemeanors are considered to be a frequent cause of infant birth defects.

Society has the *right and duty* to have healing practitioners available for its members. Society also has the duty to obey traditional spiritual laws so that its people will be protected from plagues and epidemics.

The *goal* of this healing model is to uphold the "way" or custom of the Pima that was given to the tribe at the time of creation. The Piman tradition attempts to be of assistance in the life of individuals and to keep the society "proper." This propriety results in health and joy; failure to follow the traditional commandments results in sickness.

The Allopathic Medical Model

The allopathic medical model stands in sharp contrast to the Pima healing model. *Diagnosis* is usually made by the physician. It follows logical procedures that may be carried out with or without input from the patient; it rarely asks for extensive input from the family, and almost never involves input from the patient's community. *Etiology* is considered to be natural rather than supernatural or magical.

The *patient's behavior* is connected to the diagnosis through symptoms (the patient's reported experiences) and signs (the results of examinations of the patient's body). The treatment of symptoms and signs sometimes proceeds in the absence of a known etiology. For example, a physician will often prescribe medication to lower a patient's fever before identifying the cause of the fever.

Treatment is usually medicinal or surgical. It is specific for each disease, but when a diagnosis is unclear, it may proceed by trial and error. Treatment is oriented toward specific objectives and is adjusted to the response of the patient.

Prognosis (the physician's perspective on the course of one's disease) is based on diagnosis. The physician will discuss such matters as the chances of recovery, the probable length of time needed for recovery, and the chances of a relapse. The physician offers hope but often can not promise a cure. *Death* is seen as a failure of the diagnostic and treatment system, or simply as the inevitable result of aging or of a serious disease that is unresponsive to the best treatment currently available. *Suicide* typically is seen as an extreme outcome of a psychiatric disturbance.

The *function of the institution*, whether it is the physician's office or a hospital, is to provide care for patients. Some physicians are based at a hospital while others may work at an office. *Personnel* in the allopathic medical system include physicians (who treat the patients), nurses (who assist physicians in caring for the patients), and various rehabilitationists (who teach patients how to regain lost or damaged bodily functions).

The allopathic medical model holds that patients have the *right* to assume the "sick role." While assuming this role, they can receive care and are not expected to assume their ordinary responsibilities. Patients have the *duty* to obey their physician, nurse, and/or rehabilitationist.

The patient's family has the *right* to seek help. Family members also have the right to sympathy and to receive information about the patient's condition and progress. They have the *duty* to cooperate with the medical personnel in carrying out the treatment. The patient's society has the *right* to be protected from ill people who are a danger to others. It has the *duty* to provide medical care in one form or another.

The *goal* of this model is to treat patients for illness. Allopaths attempt to restore patients to the greatest degree of functioning possible, and if not, to prevent the illness from getting worse. A secondary goal is the accumulation of medical knowledge so that more diseases can be cured and so that treatment can become increasingly effective.

The Model of Healing in Curanderismo

Curanderismo, or Mexican-American folk healing, is a coherent, comprehensive system of healing that primarily derives from the synthesis of Mayan and Aztec teachings with Mexico's heritage of Spanish Catholicism. However, traces of Arabic medicine and European witchcraft can be discerned as well. Its underlying concept is the spiritual focus of the healing and the typical curandero and curandera who subscribe to this worldview place the religious element at the center of their practice. There are several specialists in curanderismo; for example, the "adavina" diagnoses the illness but does not treat it.

Diagnosis is made on the basis of the history of the malady, the symptoms, and retrospectively by the response to treatment. Diagnosis may involve natural, psychological, and supernatural procedures. On the natural level, a practitioner can observe the client and ask questions. On the psychological level, a curandera may claim that she can "see" her client's "aura" or energy body; the size, color, and shape of this "aura" can be an important diagnostic sign. Some curanderas claim that diagnosis can be carried out at a distance through "mental telepathy." On the supernatural level, the nature of a client's problem is often revealed to the practitioner in dreams by a spirit guide. Initial diagnoses often are carried out by the clients themselves or by family members and neighbors.

Etiology can also be natural, psychological, or supernatural. The role of bacteria and viruses is taken for granted as a possible causal factor. Another common natural cause of a client's difficulty is "empacho," indigestion due to a ball of food being lodged in the intestine or food sticking to the wall of the stomach. Psychological causes are felt to be behind "bilis" (caused by anger or fear), "envidia" (caused by jealousy), "susto" (by shock following an accident or the violation of a taboo), "mal aire" (by imbalances in relationships or in personal qualities), and "caida de mollera"—a perception that an infant's fontanel is too low due to his or her mother's neglect. Supernatural etiologies abound; "embrujada" or bewitchment involves the participation of demonic spirits while "mal puesto" results from a hex. Sometimes there is a combined etiology; empacho can be brought about when a mother forces her child to eat too much or to consume food the child dislikes.

The *client's behavior* is used to make a diagnosis; for example, when crying, diarrhea, vomiting, and sunken eyes accompany a fallen fontanel, the diagnosis of caida de mollera is confirmed. One form of envidia is mal ojo which occurs when someone with an evil eye stares at the victim because of envy or desire. Symptoms include fever, headaches, vomiting, and drooping eyes. Gas, constipation, a bitter taste in the mouth, and "a dirty white tongue" accompany bilis while susto is characterized by restlessness during sleep, listlessness, depression, loss of appetite, and indifference to one's dress and personal appearance.

Treatment generally is carried out by specialists. Herbal treatments are supervised by the "albolaria," "medica," and "herbalista" while the "senora" prescribes home remedies. The client's "vibrating energy" may need to be modified by incantations or manipulation. Suggestion, confession, and persuasion are employed; the practitioner may increase clients' self-esteem by getting them involved in group activities and church functions, or asking them to visit a holy shrine. The "magica" combines herbs with spiritual practices such as prayers, chants, sprinkling holy water, burning incense, and lighting candles. A curandera is basically a shamanistic healer, hence does not typically perform exorcisms; this task is left to an "espiritista" or medium who is more adept at enlisting the help of benevolent spirits and ridding the client of malevolent ones. The etiology must be accurately made in order to insure the proper type of treatment.

There are important regional differences in curanderismo. For example, its model of health emphasizes "balance" in relationships and behavior. But a "balance" of emotional "humors" and the avoidance of an excess of either "hot" or "cold" foods is important as well. An exception is found in southern Texas where "hot" and "cold" humoral treatment is virtually absent. The role played by witchcraft in illness also varies from location to location.

Prognosis is favorable if the treatment regimen is closely followed. However, failure to comply may lead to a worsening of the condition or, in the case of such problems as caida de mollera and mal puesto, to *death*. The *function of the institution*, whether it is the curandera's home, the home of the client, a church, or a hospital, is to reflect the divine order and, in so doing, to facilitate the client's recovery.

The *personnel* will vary depending on location; a practitioner who is referred to as a "curandera" in San Jose may correspond to a "senora" in San Antonio, a "medica" in New Mexico, and a "parchera" in parts of Guatemala. Most practitioners of curanderismo are women, but the proportion varies geographically. Curanderos and curanderas typically are "called" to their profession by spiritual entities; they apprentice themselves to a friend or relative until they are considered ready to practice. Most of them are part-time practitioners who do not charge a specific fee but are given a small offering or gift.

The *client's rights and duties* are to work closely with the curandera, following the directions carefully, especially those of a spiritual nature. The *family's rights and duties* are of great importance because family allegiance and obligation are overriding cultural values. Family members generally accompany the client to the curanderismo sessions and assist the client's compliance with the regimen. The *society's rights and duties* are to support the client's recovery because the entire community is concerned and affected when a member becomes ill.

The *goal* of the curanderismo model is to assist the recovery of the client, restoring his or her "balance" within a social framework that preserves the traditions of the family and the Mexican-American subculture. Suffering and illness are seen as an inevitable part of life, and as part of God's plan to instruct human beings and lead them to salvation. Illness is not seen as a punishment from God but as a challenge (Kiev, 1968). Curanderismo demonstrates the subtle difference between "healing" and "curing." The former attempts to facilitate the restoration or development of the client's physical, mental, emotional, and spiritual capacities. The latter attempts to overcome a disease or dysfunction. If a person dies, "curing" has failed, but if that person had been spiritually restored before his or her death, the attempt at "healing" is considered to have been a success.

The allopathic model, the Pima model, and the curanderismo model are all comprehensive, yet each presents its adherents with very different worldviews. The Pima and the curanderismo models are— in part— spiritual because they demonstrate an awareness of a broader life meaning that transcends the immediacy of everyday physical expediency, as well as an "other worldly" transcendent reality that interfaces with ordinary reality. An individual allopathic practitioner might work spiritual aspects into his or her worldview and practice, but this effort is not intrinsic to the medical model as it is widely taught and promulgated. Spirituality, however, is part and parcel of Piman shamanism and of curanderismo; either model of healing would change radically if it were to lose its spiritual components.

These diversities are important to us because we (the authors) differentiate between "disease" and "illness." We conceptualize "disease" as a mechanical difficulty of the body resulting from injury or infection, or from an organism's imbalance with its environment. "Illness," however, is a broader term implying dysfunctional behavior, mood disorders, or inappropriate thoughts and feelings. These behaviors, moods, thoughts, and feelings can accompany an injury, infection, or imbalance— or can exist without them. Thus we speak of a "diseased brain" rather than an "ill brain," but of "mental illness" rather than of "mental disease." E.J. Cassell (1979) goes so far as to claim that allopathic medicine treats disease but not illness; "physicians are trained to practice a technological medicine in which disease is their sole concern and in which technology is their only weapon." Shamans have been described as "technicians of the sacred" (Eliade, 1964), but their technology involves the entry into "other worlds" so that the spiritual aspects of their clients' problems can be addressed.

Three

Shamans

Shamans have not been taken seriously by most allopathic practitioners despite the fact that many of them, such as Pima shamans, have developed sophisticated models of healing over the centuries. Furthermore, many of these models have been flexible enough to survive their contact with allopathic medicine, and even to incorporate some of its practices. Few allopathic practitioners have deliberately incorporated shamanic wisdom into their practices, raising the question not only of their open-mindedness but of their flexibility.

With the exception of its herbal knowledge, shamanism generally has been ignored or scorned by the medical and academic world. Nevertheless, shamans were the world's first physicians, first diagnosticians, first psychotherapists, first religious functionaries, first magicians, first performing artists, and first story-tellers. Shamans can be defined as tribally assigned magico-religious professionals who deliberately alter their consciousness in order to obtain information from the "spirit world." They use this knowledge and power to help and to heal members of their tribe, as well as the tribe as a whole (Krippner, 1988).

From a psychological perspective, shamans are socially designated practitioners who purport to self-regulate their attention so as to gain access to information not ordinarily available to the members of the tribal group whose illnesses they are called upon to treat. Shamans were originally active in hunting and gathering tribes and fishing societies, and still exist there in their most unadulterated form. However, shamans and shamanically-oriented healers can also be found in agricultural and even urban settings today.

Selection and Training

Shamans enter their profession in a variety of ways, depending on their tribal tradition. Some inherit their status; others may earn it, buy it, or have it thrust upon them. They may display body signs upon birth (such as an extra finger or toe) or behaviors (such as epileptic seizures) that culturally determine their social role. They may be "called" by spirits or power animals in dreams or in daytime reveries. They may survive a serious disease and interpret their recovery as a "call to heal." Sometimes several of these factors operate in combination to attract shamans to their profession.

Among the Inuit Eskimos, it is necessary to dream of spirits in order to be called to shamanism. Once the spirit appears in the dream, the dreamer spits blood, becomes ill, and withdraws from society. While alone, he sees a "tunerak" which looks like a human being but is actually a spirit. At first, this tunerak takes possession of the individual, compelling him to wander about naked. Gradually, the shaman-elect gains control of the spirit; he makes a drum and begins to assume his shamanic role (Oswalt, 1967).

A person may be called at any age, depending on the tradition of the shaman's tribe. The summons may come in childhood as the result of a dream, a fever, or a visitation from a purported spirit entity. It may come in adolescence during a vision quest. In some cases, the call may come late in life, giving shamans opportunities to continue their service to the group in ways that utilize their life experiences. A Navaho man usually is not admitted into training until he can be called "hastiin" or elder. This term is applied when he is in his middle years and has established himself as a reliable worker, a dedicated parent, and a capable community member (Topper, 1987).

The strange and erratic behaviors of a tribal member may be interpreted by the community as a "call," thereby channeling potentially disruptive actions into behavior patterns that are perceived to be beneficial. For at least a decade, the apprentice shamans of the Ammassalik Eskimos in Greenland perform a series of rituals in the summertime until they see an emaciated bear rise from the sea. The bear devours the apprentice alive, the initiate loses consciousness, then is vomited up. The apprentice regains consciousness, performs additional rituals to acquire his helping spirits, and finally notifies his family that he is ready to perform his first public ceremony (Kaweit, 1988). Allopathic physicians rarely begin their career so dramatically; they prepare for their profession through standard educational procedures, and usually focus their efforts on the welfare of individual patients rather than on a larger social group.

In some societies there is no specific training period, while in others the process may continue for several years. The teachers may be older shamans or even purported spirit guides (e.g., one's ancestors, power animals, souls of the dead, nature spirits). The spirit guides frequently are reported to give instructions in the neophyte's dreams. Among the skills to be learned are contacting souls of the dead, diagnosing and treating illness, interpreting dreams, practicing herbology, hexing tribal enemies, mastering techniques to alter one's consciousness, prophesying, story-telling, supervising of shamanic rituals, and predicting weather patterns. Not all tribes assign all of these functions to shamans, but there are remarkable similarities among shamanic societies (Boyer, Boyer, and DeVos, 1982).

A person's soul is conceptualized differently around the world. Some Eastern cultures conceive of the soul as collective, losing its individuality after death; Christianity and Islam stress the individuality of the soul as well as its eternal nature. Reincarnation is widely accepted among native people in Africa and the Americas. A common cross-cultural concept is that one's soul is that part—or those parts—of the psyche that survive death in some form. Depending on a tribal society's belief system, souls of the dead need to be contacted for different purposes. If they are lost they need to be recovered. If a person dies without leaving a will, that person's soul needs to provide information to determine property distribution; if a dead person is causing trouble, his or her soul needs to be appeased.

The Cuna people of Panama believe that the world is filled with both good and evil spirits. The soul can be captured by a "purba" or evil spirit. In the event of such an abduction, the "nele," a spiritual practitioner, boards his spirit canoe, pursues the purba, and does battle in order to retrieve the soul. In the Pacific Northwest, "soulcatchers" have long provided the shaman with a technological apparatus that can be used to retrieve a client's soul.

Magic of one sort or another is often learned by shamans, whether it be sleight of hand, taking advantage of coincidences and naturally occurring events, or the purported utilization of anomalous phenomena such as "extrasensory perception." In most shamanic societies, a variety of chants, dances, songs, epic poems, mythic stories, and/or symbols must be mastered and utilized when appropriate. Some tribes arrange a special feast or celebration when the initiate passes each phase of his or her training, and most have rituals to observe the completion of the training and the practitioner's assumption of the shamanic role. The young Navaho shaman obtains his or her initial start as a substitute for an older shaman who does not want to take a case because of the patient's poverty or poor physical condition. As their reputation grows, so does the clientele and the fee of the newcomers (Rogers, 1982, p. 26).

Personality Dimensions

It would be erroneous to claim that shamans represent a single constellation of traits, or that there is a typical shamanic personality. Some shamans, perhaps, have bordered on psychosis, living in a fantasy world that is honored by their tribe so long as their role is effectively filled and their duties are conscientiously performed. Others undoubtedly have been men and women of great talent, mastering a complex vocabulary and an extensive storehouse of knowledge about herbs, rituals, and the purported spirit world.

Many social scientists have observed the links between shamanism and changed states of consciousness, concluding that these represent schizophrenic conditions. Julian Silverman has postulated that shamanism is a form of socially sanctioned schizophrenia, noting that the two conditions share "grossly non-reality-oriented ideation, abnormal perceptual experience, profound emotional upheavals, and bizarre mannerisms." Silverman (1969), a psychiatrist, has claimed that the only difference between shamanic schizophrenia and schizophrenic conditions in industrialized countries is the degree of cultural acceptance of the individual's psychological resolution of a life crisis. Silverman claims that the social supports available to the shaman are usually unavailable to the schizophrenic in Western culture. George Devereux (1961), a psychoanalyst, took the position that shamans are neurotics. For Devereux, the shaman's reliance on dreams and fantasy could be seen as defense mechanisms to protect a fragile personality structure.

L. B. Boyer and his associates attempted to gather data regarding this controversy. They administered the Rorschach Inkblots to 12 male Apache shamans, 52 non-shamans, and several Apache men who claimed to possess shamanic powers but who had not been accorded that position by members of their tribe. Psychologists have collected a great deal of information about underlying personality structure through studying and comparing people's descriptions of these inkblots (Boyer, Klopfer, Brawer, and Kawai, 1964).

An examination of the responses to the inkblots demonstrated that the shamans showed as high a degree of reality-testing potential as did the Apaches who were not shamans. If the shamans had been schizophrenic, they would not have been able to describe the inkblots in the same way as other tribal members. However, the "pseudo-shamans" did not do as well on this dimension and demonstrated impoverished and stunted personality development.

When an ambiguous, unclear inkblot was described, shamans and non-shamans gave similar descriptions with a few exceptions. The shamans demonstrated a keener awareness of peculiarities, a greater sense of childlike humor, more responses of a philosophical nature, and a greater proportion of responses involving sex, color, and the human body. The authors concluded that the shamans were less neurotic than the other two groups.

The conclusions reached by Boyer and his co-workers were that "shamans are healthier than their societal co-members....This finding argues against [the] stand that the shaman is severely neurotic or psychotic, at least insofar as the Apaches are concerned." The Apache "psuedo-shamans," on the other hand, did show more signs of mental illness than did members of the other two groups.

Richard Noll (1985), a psychologist, took a complementary approach to the controversy, collecting shamans' reports of their experiences in altered states of consciousness. He compared these reports to symptoms of mental illness listed in the third edition of the American Psychiatric Association's *Diagnostic and Statistical Manual.* Noll reported that the shamans' experiences did not match the criteria for schizophrenia or other serious disorders from the psychiatric manual. Instead, he proposed that shamans may be especially adept at fantasy production.

Fantasy-Proneness

Two specialists in psychological hypnosis, S.C. Wilson and T.X. Barber (1983) have found that a small percentage of the American subjects they tested often confused memories of real-life events with memories of fantasies. While about 24% of ordinary people sometimes make this type of confusion, 85% of "fantasy-prone" individuals do so. Although members of this fantasy-prone group are easier to hypnotize, they are neither more nor less neurotic or psychotic than other people.

Some unique blend of genetic inheritance and early experience makes these individuals extremely prone to "see" visions, "hear" voices, and "touch" imaginary companions. They claim to have an excellent recall of their early life episodes. Wilson and Barber found that these abilities characterize about 4% of the general American population, although it might differ from culture to culture. Their work has been repeated with larger samples of subjects by other psychologists who have obtained similar results (Lynn and Rhue, 1986).

As children, fantasy-prone individuals lived in a make-believe world much of the time. They pretended or believed that their dolls and toy animals were alive, had feelings, and demonstrated unique personalities. One woman stated, in an interview, that she took a different toy to bed with her every night so that she would not hurt their feelings. While children, they believed in elves, guardian angels, and fairies, sometimes thinking that they had played with them. They often had imaginary companions (people or animals), became one of the characters in books they were reading, or would imagine they were someone else. One subject told the interviewer that she imagined she was a princess living in a castle; she told her friends about this experience and they ridiculed her. However, most fantasy-prone individuals soon learned how to conceal this information from their peers.

As an adult, the fantasy-prone individual often "smells" or "sees" what is being described in a conversation, takes the time to engage in fantasy (often having a special place where he or she engages in this pastime), and frequently has sexual fantasies so vivid that they lead to orgasm. Nine out of ten reported anomalous experiences, such as clairvoyance, telepathy, and precognition, while most reported out-of-body experiences or automatic writing. More than two-thirds told the examiners that they believe they possess the ability to heal sick people; three out of four claimed to have encountered apparitions, ghosts, or spirits.

While engaging in fantasy, a person sets a theme; then an imaginative scenario unfolds that has some of the characteristics of a story or a dream. If fantasy-prone individuals were raised in a tribal group, it is likely that many of them would become shamans. Fantasy-prone individuals often claim to see "auras," talk to dead people, receive guidance in their dreams, and spend considerable amounts of time in a private world that is not shared by their peers. Life experiences that led to fantasy-prone behavior included isolation, restriction, or encouragement by others to engage in make-believe games. All of these traits and circumstances resemble shamanic practitioners.

The characteristics of Wilson and Barber's fantasy-prone group are also the characteristics of shamans, including their finding that "subjects with a propensity for...fantasy are as well adjusted as...the average person. It appears that the life experiences and skill developments that underlie the ability for...fantasy are more or less independent of the kinds of life experience that lead to psychopathology" (Wilson and Barber, 1983). In other words, there are some individual cases that suggest a link between mental illness and shamanism, but the bulk of anthropological and psychological research data does not support this claim.

Altered States of Consciousness

"Consciousness" can be defined as an organism's total pattern of perceiving, thinking, and feeling at any given time. An organism's "ordinary" state of consciousness is that characterizing the organism's day-by-day behavior and experience; it serves as a baseline by which "altered" states can be determined. Altered states are experienced to differ from this baseline by the organism or are noted to differ from the baseline by an outside observer.

Some anthropologists claim that the first Siberian shamans were nature healers; during a later "feudal" phrase of social evolution, spirits were invented that necessitated the development of altered states of consciousness to deal with them (Hultkrantz, 1978). Most other scholars, however, favor the idea that altered conscious states are basic to shamanism. Erica Bourguignon (1968) studied 488 societies, 57% of those represented in an ethnographic atlas. She found that 89% were reported to have one or more institutionalized, culturally patterned altered state of consciousness, concluding that the capacity to experience altered states is a basic psychobiological human potential.

L. G. Peters and Douglass Price-Williams (1980) compared 42 societies from four different cultural areas to determine commonalities among shamanic altered conscious states. They identified three: voluntary control of entrance and duration of the altered state; ability to communicate with others during the altered state; memory of the experience at the conclusion of the altered state. Shamans in 18 of the cultures they studied engaged in spirit "incorporation," 10 in out-of-body experience, 11 in both, and 3 in some different altered state. Peters and Price-Williams compared these altered states to rites of passage in which an episode characterized by panic or anxiety gives way to an experience yielding insights that produce a new level of personality integration.

Shamans use a variety of procedures to induce altered

states. These include ingesting mind-altering plants, chanting, concentrating, dancing, drumming, jumping, fasting, running, visualizing, engaging in sexual activity, and going without sleep. Rarely is one procedure used in isolation. For example, mind-altering plants are often ingested in the evening; sleep deprivation, restricted nighttime vision, and the accompanying music add to the experience's profundity. Naturally occurring altered states, such as dreaming and daydreaming, are also utilized. Andrew Neher, an anthropologist, has demonstrated how drumming can produce brain activation by coinciding with the theta EEG frequency (about 4 to 8 cycles per second) through auditory stimulation (Neher, 1961).

The Ojibway Indians shocked Jesuits priests on their arrival in North America by their traditional healing procedures. It was customary for Ojibway "wabeno" (shamans) to heal by means of drumming, rattling, chanting, dancing erotically (while naked), and handling live coals. The wabeno then rubbed their heated hands over the patient while chanting the songs previously learned in their vision quests (Grim, 1983).

Among the Dieguenos and Luisenos Indians of southern California, potential shamans are selected as early as nine years of age on the basis of their dreams. It is important that a prospective shaman in these tribes have a visionary experience that results from ingesting such mind-altering plants as datura or jimson weed during the preceding ceremonials. During this altered state, the individual receives a guardian spirit in the form of a power animal as well as healing songs and other knowledge about cures and dream interpretation (Rogers, 1982).

Altered states of consciousness play a major role in the symbolic manipulation that shamans utilize in healing. The drum often symbolizes the "World Tree" the shaman climbs to the Upper World (or descends to the Lower World) during the altered state. The blowing of smoke in four directions can symbolize an appeal to spirits in the "four quarters" of the universe. Directionality is also important in the elaborate Navaho sand paintings which the shamans destroy after they have served their purpose. Symbology is also apparent in the vision quests of the Plains Indians that helped future warriors achieve contact with their guardian spirits. The anthropologist Marlene Dobkin de Rios (1984) describes these quests as attempts at "personal ecstatic learning." Hence, tribal shamans played an important role in preparing, instruction, and guiding the initiates, and in interpreting the visions.

There are shamanic healing methods that closely parallel contemporary behavior therapy, chemotherapy, dream interpretation, family therapy, hypnotherapy, milieu therapy, and psychodrama. It is clear that shamans, psychotherapists, and physicians have more in common than is generally suspected. After studying Otomi shamans in Mexico, James Dow (1983) concluded that the similarities between shamanic healing and Western psychotherapy outweigh the differences. However, for shamans the spiritual dimension of healing is extremely important while the contemporary physician and psychotherapist typically ignore it. Shamans often retrieve lost souls, communicate with spirits, emphasize the interconnectedness of their patients with the community and the earth, facilitate spiritual purification for those who have violated social taboos, explain dreams and visions, and stress the importance of spiritual growth, life purpose, and being of service to humanity and to nature. All of these functions are performed by spiritual practitioners but few attain importance or even respectability in the world views of Western physicians and other health care specialists.

Four

Shamanic Healers

When groups of people settled in one place, and when "higher" and "lower" social and political roles emerged, the role of the shaman was no longer tenable. Shamans played an indispensable role in highly mobile societies in which people's living conditions were subject to unexpected and sudden changes. Shamans' freewheeling ways allowed them to evoke visions that would promote the tribe's adaptation. Sedentary societies, however, institutionalized and dogmatized religion, taking the power away from the shaman and placing it in temple, rituals, and creeds. The shaman's duties were severely curtailed by priests and priestesses who assumed formal political status insofar as institutionalized religion was concerned. We use the term "shamanic healer" to describe practitioners who usually work part-time and whose political status is informal rather than formal. These shamanic healers still engage in disciplined alterations of consciousness that supposedly facilitate their access to the spirit world, especially to power animals (Steward, 1959).

Winkelman's data indicate that shamanic healers differ from shamans in several other ways. Shamanic healers lead fewer group activities and their initiation is less likely to be accompanied by ceremonies and rites. Their social status is lower than that of the shaman; they are less likely to communicate with spirits; and they are more likely to rely on sleight of hand to demonstrate their power or to demonstrate that they have obtained results in healing sessions. Shamans abound in hunting and gathering tribes, as well as those engaged primarily in fishing; shamanic healers are usually found in agricultural societies.

Maria Sabina

One of us (Krippner) visited the hamlet of Huautla de Jiminez in Oaxaca, Mexico, with Winkelman in 1980, observing that a variety of practitioners served the spiritual needs of the Mazatec Indian communities. Winkelman's category of "priest" is represented by the local Roman Catholic priests. Shamanic healers are referred to as "sabios" ("wise ones") if they are male and "sabias" if they are female. Winkelman's category of shamanistic healers corresponds to the "curanderos" and "curanderas" who specialize in herbal medicine. The diviners and mediums ("espiritistas") incorporate spirits and engage in divination practice. Sorcerers and witches ("brujos," "brujas," "hechiceros," and "hechiceras") cast spells and sell potions, promising good luck to their clients and misfortune to their client's adversaries.

Krippner and Winkelman were able to arrange a rare interview with Maria Sabina, the legendary shamanic healer who, in 1955, had shared her knowledge of the Mazatec sacred mushroom healing ceremonies with the mycologist R. G. Wasson (1974). Born in 1894, Maria Sabina's father died when she was very young, and she originally ate the mind-altering psilocybin mushrooms to overcome hunger. On one occasion when Maria Sabina used the mushrooms, she had a mental image of death standing near her sister during an illness. "Higher spiritual beings" told the young woman how to cure her sister and soon Maria Sabina became a well-known "curandera" or herbalist.

Dona Maria (as she was called, as a term of respect) told her clients that Jesus Christ worked through the mushrooms, giving wisdom and curing illness. Following the death of her second husband when she was in her 40s, dona Maria began to work exclusively with the sacred mushrooms and became known as a "sabia." She told Krippner and Winkelman that the mushrooms sprout "because God wills it." In dona Maria's model of healing, several functions (e.g., making the diagnosis, identifying the cause of the ailment, determining the treatment) are performed when the sabia and her clients eat the mushrooms together. Dona Maria stated that "higher spiritual beings," usually Jesus Christ, work through the mushrooms, revealing the origin of the client's disease as well as the remedy. Before the arrival of the Spaniards, the mushrooms were felt to have been the gift of Quetzalcoatl, the feathered serpent deity representing the unity of sky and earth. Although Roman Catholic priests prohibited the use of the mushrooms, the Mazatecs took the practice underground, eventually replacing Quetzalcoatl with Jesus Christ.

Dona Maria mentioned that her great-grandfather, grandfather, great aunt, and great uncle were all sabios or sabias who ingested the sacred mushroom during "veladas" or evening ceremonies. Dona Maria had no conflict with the local Roman Catholic church; she attended Mass faithfully and helped to found a local women's society, the Sisterhood of the Sacred Heart of Jesus. Indeed, the local priest came to her defense when federal authorities attempted to prevent her from conducting her mushroom veladas.

Dona Maria's ceremonial liturgy contained a variety of Roman Catholic images, but at its core were the same odes and psalms that were uttered by the high priests of Montezuma, the Aztec ruler who was captured by the Spanish invaders in 1521. The Spanish Inquisition outlawed the veladas, which then went underground for more than four centuries. Once it was discovered that the ceremonies were still being held, Huautla de Jiminez was deluged by visitors from North America and

Western Europe. Dona Maria was sympathetic with their desire for spiritual knowledge but was also critical of them because they did not respect Mazatec traditions and ate the mushrooms without adequate preparation or the guidance of a "wise one."

When Krippner and Winkelman asked permission to take photographs, dona Maria excused herself, and returned a few minutes later in her "huipil," or hand-embroidered ceremonial gown. One American visitor, feeling the full force of dona Maria's charisma, became visibly moved and began to cry uncontrollably. Instantly, dona Maria took her aside, prayed for her, and caressed the woman's body with fresh flowers. Within a few minutes, the tears stopped and she reported a state of peace and happiness that remained with her for several days.

As Maria Sabina approached the ninth decade of her life, she retired as an active practitioner. She remarried and lived peacefully in Huautla de Jiminez until her death in 1985. Dona Maria had allowed recordings and transcripts to be made of the songs and chants that accompanied her veladas. In one of them, she gave a poetic description of herself and her role:

> I am the woman of the great rain,
> I am the woman of the sacred rain,
> I am the woman of the flowing water,
> I am the little whirling woman of colors beneath the water,
> I am the little whirling woman of colors beneath the sea...,
> I am a woman of good words.

In another, she related a visionary experience:

> I go up to heaven,
> Beneath the gaze of your glory,
> There is your paper and your Book...,

I am a woman who sounds forth with divinity,
Where the shooting stars are showering, where the
flocks of the Lord's eagles are, the sacred eagles
(Estrada, 1981).

Fernando Fernandez

Living on the San Blas Islands off the Atlantic coast of
Panama, the Cuna Indians have preserved many of their
traditional approaches to healing. The psychologist Robert
Van de Castle has conducted field research among the Cuna,
reporting that they believe that dreams can foretell an impend-
ing illness or disaster. Shamanic healers among the Cuna
employ a variety of procedures to ensure a calm sleep, among
them sweet-smelling wood carvings that can be placed in the
strings of hammocks (Van de Castle, 1971).

In 1985, one of us (Krippner) gave a workshop and taught
a course on dreamworking in Panama City. One of the
participants was Fernando Fernandez, a Cuna shamanic
healer in his early 30s. Don Fernando told Krippner about the
Cuna model of healing, pointing out that he was an "abisua,"
or "singer." Other types of shamanic healers among the Cuna
include the "inaduledi" who specializes in herbal cures, and
the "nele" who specializes in diagnosis, purportedly traveling
through the earth to the Lower World. All three work closely
with the "healing spirits" and power animals who have been
venerated by the Cuna for centuries. Another type of shamanistic healer is the "grandmother" who provides assistance
during childbirth.

Don Fernando told Krippner that there are several types
of abisuas. For example, the "kantule" is a ceremonial singer
who officiates at such special events as puberty rituals and the
ceremonies held when a child's hair is cut for the first time.
Don Fernando, on the other hand, is asked to sing when a
person is physically or mentally ill, when a woman is having
difficulty giving birth, or when an overly active animal needs

to be calmed. The abisua also may sing to assist a worker who needs to hold hot metal during construction or to aid a client who desires a romantic partner. Cuna tradition allows abisuas to sing for enjoyment when they are not engaged in healing.

Like most shamanic healers who work at ordinary jobs in their communities, don Fernando is a part-time practitioner. He lives on Ustopo, the most heavily populated of the San Blas Islands as well as the most traditional. During his studies at the University of Panama, he was asked questions about Cuna culture by one of his professors and was embarrassed not to know the answer, realizing that his professor knew more about Cuna traditions than he did. This experience motivated don Fernando to become an abisua and, in collaboration with some of his friends, to found the Society for the Preservation of the Cuna Culture. One of his interests is recording and preserving the hundreds of healing songs used by abisuas.

Cuna healing songs are complex and difficult to master. Don Fernando told Krippner that he had only learned 15 of them. The shortest healing song lasts about one hour, the longest—the song of the dead—takes about 14 hours to perform and took him a year to learn. Don Fernando allowed Krippner to tape record the "akuanusa," a song used to combat fevers. He has also learned songs to treat headaches, to overcome fear, to ease the difficulties of childbirth, to treat alcoholism, and to rid a house of unwelcome ghosts. All of these songs are considered to be examples of spiritual healing because they call upon the spirit world for assistance.

The Cuna model of healing holds that most diseases are caused by germs and other microorganisms; however, even germs have spirits. Epidemics are viewed as nature's punishments when human beings have offended the spirit world. Medicines—stones as well as plants—are also imbued with spirits. Nushu, an important healing spirit, can be contacted by shamanic healers in dreams and asked for advice.

The Cuna model holds that society has the duty to provide healing services to the community, as well as a quiet place for the client to recuperate. Families must support the advice given to clients by practitioners. The prognosis is favorable if community and family support is forthcoming and if the client follows the practitioner's advice. It is believed that people are composed of eight spirits who inhabit various parts of the body, e.g., the hands, the heart, the head. A spiritual practitioner must treat the various spirits differently, as each has its own temperament. If a client dies, one or more of these spirits will travel to the Upper World unless the person committed evil acts while alive. What Western psychiatry views as multiple personality disorder is seen by the Cuna model as one or more of the eight spirits attaining salience over the entire bodily system. This disruption can be short-term or long-lasting; even though the disruption might occur frequently, the client rarely recalls the event.

Considerable attention is paid to the prevention of disease and misfortune. If a nele believes that a dream is a premonition of sickness, the practitioner might recommend daily medicine baths for his client. Fifty spears carved from black palm trees are placed in a water-filled canoe for this ritual. In addition, powdered wood is placed in the bath to cleanse the dreamer's eyes. If no adverse incidents take place during the month of this regimen, it is concluded that the treatment prevented the misfortune. Many dream images appear on the Cuna "molas," a traditional art form made by cutting and sewing several layers of cloth so that a colorful design is produced.

Porfirio Aguirre

To some extent, the BriBri Indians of southern Costa Rica share a common heritage with indigenous people of Panama. For example, both have long traditions of shamanism. In 1989, one of us (Krippner) interviewed Porfirio Aguirre of the Talamanca region of Costa Rica, a BriBri shamanic healer and member of the tribal council of elders. In describing the BriBri heritage, don Porfirio remarked, "When God lived with us, he taught teachers and masters the principles of science, medicine, and art. God taught them how astronomy, agriculture, healing, music, and dance could be used for spiritual purposes, so that after he returned home a connection with him would remain."

Don Porfirio was a featured speaker at an international conference sponsored by the United Nations University for Peace which is located outside of San Jose, Costa Rica. Don Porfirio's presentation coupled the insistence that "only native people should live on native land" with the assertion that "we all share a divine spirit." Furthermore, he continued,

> The BriBri believe that we all have the same God
> because we all share the same sun, the same rivers,
> the same plants, and the same animals. We can all
> share because we are all one. And the most impor-
> tant task we share is to respect our Mother Earth. We
> must live in harmony and peace with her, and
> protect and nourish her. When God lived with us, he
> taught us this knowledge, and we must never forget
> it.

BriBri myths hold that God fashioned the tribe from corn on the side of a river. Thus the life of the tribe was connected with plants from its very beginning. Contemporary BriBri herbalists use plants as medicines, but "awapa" (or shamans) heal by singing, as do a category of neighboring Cuna Indian practitioners. There have been female awapa in the past, but currently only males carry on the tradition.

Because of his intelligence as a boy, don Porfirio was selected as a potential "awa" (the singular form of awapa) by his family. Once a boy is identified as a potential awa by his immediate family or relatives, he is brought to the attention of a practicing awa. If the practitioner agrees, the potential apprenticeship is outlined to the boy by his relatives. If he agrees to undertake the many years of arduous training, he visits the awa and begins to learn a healing song.

After don Porfirio's remarks to the conference participants, he led a group of native people in a ritual. Two men blew conch shells while a woman raised a platter of smoldering incense to the sun. This was done four times, once in each direction. Don Porfirio remarked, "This is not a ceremony, but a ritual," suggesting that rather than a colorful series of actions imbued with little meaning, this activity was sacred and was performed with reverence.

Earlier in the week, don Porfirio and Ugowiyuhi Dhyani Ywahoo, a Cherokee clan chieftainess, had participated in an interfaith service in a magnificent Roman Catholic cathedral. There had also been representatives of Islam, Judaism, Bahai, and Hinduism. Christianity had been represented by the local archbishop, and Buddhism by Tenzin Gyatso, the Fourteenth Dalai Lama of Tibet. Again, don Porfirio had evoked the "divine spirit" shared by all humanity.

Jose Rios

Another traditional art form is the yarn painting produced by craftspeople among the Huichols. These Indians live in the Mexican Sierras, primarily in the state of Nayarit. El Colorin, a small village, was the home of Jose Rios, also known as "Matsuwa," a Huichol word meaning "pulse of energy." Born in the late 1870s, don Jose became a successful farmer but lost his right hand in an industrial accident. This event was regarded as a call from the spirit world and don Jose (who died in 1990) began an apprenticeship that lasted for 64 years.

Don Jose met one of us (Krippner) in 1977 when he came to California at the request of a group who wanted to "find their lives," as he put it, by studying Huichol wisdom. Don Jose told Krippner that he had learned many lessons from Tatewari, the "Grandfather Fire," and Tayaupa, the "Father Sun." Don Jose added that he frequently had gone into the wilderness alone to take peyote, a cactus bud with mind-altering properties. Through peyote, he gained access to Kauyumari, a power animal identified as the "Little Deer Spirit." This ally brought "nierika" or visions that gave don Jose instructions as he proceeded through his long apprenticeship.

Don Jose stated, "When you hear me chanting the sacred songs, it is not I who sing but Kauyumari who is singing into my ear. And I transmit these songs to you. It is he who teaches us, and shows us the way. This is how it is" (Halifax, 1979). Don Jose claimed that Kauyumari had taught him how to cure disease principally through offering prayers to the spirits, by sucking impurities from his client's bodies, and by using prayer arrows to balance his client's "energy fields," invisible radiations said to surround such vital body parts as the heart, sex organs, stomach, and brain.

Krippner and his friends once arranged a party for don Jose, knowing of the healer's enjoyment of music and merriment. Don Jose appeared to be participating in the festivities when his face froze and his expression turned grave. He announced, "One of my Huichol people is ill. I must return to help her immediately." Krippner retorted, "But, don Jose, there is no flight to Mexico at this hour; furthermore, you are conducting a workshop tomorrow morning." Don Jose sighed, "You do not understand. Just leave me alone," and retreated to a corner of the room where he sat facing the wall for about 30 minutes. When don Jose rejoined the group, the twinkle had returned to his eyes. He announced, "I have been able to help the woman who was sick. Let's get back to the party." Krippner realized that this was an example of a shamanic healer's purported "magical flight" or out-of-body experience (Krippner, 1988).

Don Jose and other Huichol spiritual practitioners made frequent pilgrimages to Wirikuta, the high desert in central Mexico where they found peyote. The shamanic healers and the apprentices who accompany them refrain from sexual activity and go on a specific diet before the peyote hunt. When the first cactus is found, a practitioner shoots it with a bow and arrow, just as if it were a deer. A pledge is then given that the power of the plant will be used for sacred purposes. During the peyote ceremonies, don Jose sometimes chanted for several nights and days, seated in his "uweni" or shaman's chair so that the power that is manifested will not be dissipated. Don Jose interjected wit into many of his ceremonies. Joan Halifax, an anthropologist, recalls how he once inserted an engagement for marriage in the midst of a ceremony. The surprise engagement was between Halifax and the local sorcerer. Brant Secunda, who completed a 12-year apprenticeship with don Jose and became his adopted grandson, once related how don Jose will surprise his clients by making jokes during healing ceremonies, the ensuing laughter serving as an important part of the therapy.

For don Jose, the peyote-induced images provide a method to diagnose a client's illness; the ensuing treatment may involve herbs, prayers, fasts, or a referral to a physician. Clients have the right to obtain care from the Huichol tribe and the duty to cooperate with the practitioner. Not only did don Jose's clients ask for recovery from their illnesses but they also asked the healer to help them "find their lives" so that they could discover meaning and joy in their daily activities. If one has success at this task, don Jose's approach to spiritual healing could serve as preventive medicine as well, as problems are less likely to return if a client is engaged in meaningful work and enjoyable play.

Manuel Velasquez

In 1989 one of us (Krippner) visited Chichicastenango, Guatemala, home of the Quiche Indians, one of several tribes descended from the Mayas. Krippner sauntered to the Church of Santo Tomas (St. Thomas), erected in the 17th century on a sacred Mayan burial ground. The Indians of that era were indignant, and to placate them a compromise was eventually reached that permitted them to conduct their native rituals on the steps and in the back of the church sanctuary. The Indians had little difficulty adjusting to the faith of the conquerors as they simply adapted the new symbols, rituals, and deities to their existing liturgy and cosmology. The domains of the major Mayan deities—the sun, the moon, rain, clouds, corn, etc.—were interwoven with the Holy Trinity and the panoply of Catholic saints.

It was at Santo Tomas that Krippner met Manuel Velasquez, a local "chuuch-akau" or "father-mother-doctor." Don Manuel had agreed to give his blessings to a newly engaged couple, and performed a ritual in the back of the church sanctuary, near a painting of Jesus Christ. He lit candles in an area reserved for the indigenous rites, placing them upright in the sand. This enabled don Manuel to contact the Christian saints, asking them to bless the forthcoming union, bringing prosperity and healthy children to the couple. Once his candles had started to burn, don Manuel reached into his "morral" or handbag, bringing out flower petals, seeds, and kernels of corn which he scattered on one of the stone slabs.

Following his requests for aid from the Christian saints, don Manuel turned to the Mayan divinities. For this ritual, he went outside and stood on the front steps of the church, chanting prayers in Quiche. Don Manuel held a tin can censer filled with copal incense, lit the incense, and began to swing the censer back and forth. Then he scattered seeds and rose petals on the church steps, invoking the aid of the local spirits as well as the deceased relatives.

Tourists are not allowed to enter the church from the steps as long as a chuuch-akau is at work for fear that the beneficent spirits will be frightened and leave before their help can be obtained. On the other hand, Krippner observed Quiche Indians, wearing red headdresses and black coats, place copal wrapped in cornhusks in the fire at the church steps as a sacrifice to the local spirits.

One of don Manuel's clients told Krippner that the chuuch-akau would probably take the engaged couple and their families to a local shrine, one honoring Pascual Abaj, a major Mayan deity. Located on a hill just outside Chichicastenango, the shrine is the site of blood sacrifices (in the form of chicken decapitation) as well as the customary flower petals, pine needles, and copal incense. Don Manuel's position was hereditary but still required an apprenticeship of several years. He does not incorporate spirits, but implores special blessings, defines the needs of his clients and his community, and protests angrily to the divinities when a favor is not granted.

In addition to requesting blessings for his clients in their undertakings, don Manuel blesses crops and business ventures. As a shamanic healer, the chuuch-akau engages in both religious and magical practices to treat illnesses resulting from sorcery or from violating sacred laws. However, he delegates the use of native medicines to the "herbicidas" or herbalists, and obstetrical duties to the local midwives. Illnesses believed to come from offenses against the deities or against one's ancestors require confession of the sin and performance of a penance. Those resulting from sorcery require counter-measures in the form of divination and magic. Those resulting from natural causes require herbal medicines or purification in the form of purgatives and sweatbaths. Incantations, such as those observed by Krippner at Santo Tomas, may accompany all types of healing (Orellana, 1987).

Rolling Thunder

In 1982, one of us (Krippner) spoke at an international conference on shamanism and healing held in the Austrian Alps. The invited shamans and healers met a day before the conference was to begin so that they could discuss the content of their presentations. The conference organizers suggested that Rolling Thunder be the first to speak, as he was well-known and familiar to Europeans. Upon hearing this request, Rolling Thunder, an inter-tribal shamanic healer, responded, "Don Jose Rios is my elder; it would not be appropriate for me to speak before him." Because don Jose was the only person at the conference to have passed his 100th birthday, he was everyone's elder and, at Rolling Thunder's insistence, gave the first presentation. Although Rolling Thunder's request may seem to be insignificant, it demonstrates the importance of respecting and revering one's elders—a widespread aspect of the Native American belief system.

Rolling Thunder and Krippner were first introduced in 1970 by a musician, Mickey Hart, one of the drummers for the Grateful Dead rock band. A year later, Krippner introduced Rolling Thunder to Irving Oyle, an osteopathic physician. Following several hours alone in Hart's recording studio, the two practitioners emerged arm in arm. Oyle commented, "We compared our practices. Rolling Thunder said that when a sick person comes to him, he makes a diagnosis, goes through a ritual, and gives that person some medicine that will restore health. I replied that when a patient comes to me, I make a diagnosis and go through the ritual of writing a prescription that will give the patient some medicine to restore health. In both cases a great deal of magic is involved—- the type of magic called 'faith in one's doctor'" (Krippner and Villoldo, 1987).

In 1971, Krippner acted as program chair for a conference on internal self-regulation sponsored by the Menninger Foundation in Kansas. During the meeting, Rolling Thunder, for the first time, addressed a group of physicians and scientists. He described the "other world" from which he derives much of his healing power and knowledge and remarked, "Many times I don't know what medicine I'm going to use until the 'doctoring' is going on; I sometimes can't remember what I've used. That's because it's not me doing the 'doctoring.' It's the Great Spirit working through me."

At this conference, it happened that Rolling Thunder had

a chance to demonstrate his healing ability when a student injured his ankle during a game of touch football. Preparing for the healing session, Rolling Thunder asked Krippner to obtain a pail of water and some raw meat. Once this was provided, he prayed to the Six Sacred Directions: "To the East where the sun rises, to the North where the cold comes from, to the South where the light comes from, and to the West where the sun sets. Up to the Father Sun. Down to the Mother Moon." Rolling Thunder drew upon his pipe four times, then handed it to the injured student. The two men exchanged a few words after which Rolling Thunder began to chant a call to the Great Spirit.

Lighting a fire in the dining hall fireplace, Rolling Thunder made a sacrifice of the raw hamburger meat and made some passes over the student with an eagle wing. He pressed his mouth to the young man's swollen ankle and held it there for several minutes. After letting out sniffs, howls, and wails, Rolling Thunder vomited violently, spitting a bilious fluid into the pail. The medicine man repeated this procedure several times, fanned the ankle with the eagle wing, then asked Krippner to bury the contents of the water pail.

What was the outcome of his healing session? Doug Boyd (1974), who observed the proceedings, reported that "the color had returned to normal, the swelling had decreased, and the flesh around the wound was flexible instead of hard. The young man reported that the pain was gone." Andrew Weil (1983), a physician, looked at the injury the following morning, claiming that there had been "no objective improvement in appearance, tenderness, or mobility." However, the student told Weil that he had been deeply affected by the ritual because he had never had anyone pay so much attention to him.

Rolling Thunder used ritual, mental imagery, and herbal treatments to "doctor" his clients. Like most shamanic healers, he did not engage in his spiritual practice full time. For many years, he worked as a brakeman on the railroads in the state of Nevada. Upon retiring, he organized a small spiritual community called "Meta Tantey" or "Go in Peace." Visitors, primarily from Western Europe and North America, spent time at Meta Tantey studying Native American medicine and lifestyles. In 1984, following the death of his wife, Spotted Fawn, Rolling Thunder terminated his active healing practice.

Welch was introduced to Rolling Thunder by Krippner in 1987 at a banquet in San Francisco held in honor of the medicine man to mark the end of his period of mourning. The feeling Welch was left with from Rolling Thunder's presence was clear, focused, peaceful energy. Welch recalled: "throughout the room, a vibrant, exciting force was flowing which energized and relaxed me at the same time." After a dinner of buffalo meat and vegetables prepared by the medicine man's friends, Rolling Thunder spoke about the importance and necessity of global healing and service to the Great Spirit.

In Rolling Thunder's model, spiritual healing comes from love and respect rather than from intellectual understanding. He once said, "It begins with respect for the Great Spirit, and the Great Spirit is the life that is in all things—all the creatures and the plants and even the rocks and the minerals. All things have their own will and their own way and their own purpose. This is what is to be respected."

For Rolling Thunder, health care personnel includes physicians as well as native practitioners; he has been brought into several hospitals to teach patients how to "talk to their bodies" in order to accelerate their recovery. Rolling Thunder observed the behavior of sick people very carefully, often taking three days before deciding on the type of treatment he would offer or even if he should "doctor" them at all. For example, he would send someone with a broken bone or a ruptured appendix to a physician. Prognosis, for Rolling Thunder, depends not only on the client's condition and treatment but on whether or not his or her "inner healer" has become active.

Two Trees

A fellow Cherokee and a friend of Rolling Thunder's, Chief Two Trees lives near Old Fort, North Carolina. Knowing that political roles and religious roles generally are assigned to different people by American Indians, Krippner asked Two Trees about his title of "chief" during their interview in 1988. Two Trees responded that he is the principle chief of the Bear Clan, an intertribal confederation of practitioners for whom the bear is a power animal—a source of wisdom and strength.

Two Trees' knowledge about spiritual healing had been handed down by parents and grandparents on both sides of his family. Nevertheless, he resisted becoming a medicine man for several decades, serving in the U.S. Armed Forces and working successfully with race horses before he finally submitted to the "call" of his ancestors, realizing that "the desire to comfort fellow human beings is the highest value to which one can aspire." After he made his decision, Two Trees began to study a range of traditions, determining what each could teach him about "doctoring" clients. For example, he investigated Jordanian Huna, a healing system he claims is similar to the Hawaiian Huna used by "kahunas"—the Hawaiian shamanic healers who try to maintain their traditional practices. Huna involves the development of personal power through movement, imagery, and ritual; it holds that, among other segments, the human psyche consists of a "higher self" that holds the key to spiritual development and advancement. He also makes extensive use of the local herbs in his healing practice.

Two Trees told Krippner that the Native American worldview conceptualizes life as an upward spiral; once conflicts are resolved on the lower planes, growth can proceed on the higher planes and people are better able to communicate with their Higher Selves. The resolution of one's internal battles often can be glimpsed in one's dreams, meditations,

and imaginative imagery. Two Trees is a member of the
Society of the Tree, and sees the tree as a useful symbol for
human growth, development, and rootedness. The Society's
invocations remind Two Trees of the Biblical Book of Psalms
as well as to the Kaballah, the Hebrew "book of mysteries."

Two Trees is an instructor for the American branch of
International University in Brussels, Belgium, teaching
courses in Native American Studies. In these courses, he
discusses the American Indian concept that all forms of life
are the children of Mother Earth and the Sky God. As sons and
daughters of earth and sky, we all are related not only to all
races of people but to plants, animals, rocks, etc. Therefore,
humanity must nurture all of our relatives and find ways for
the offspring of the Earth and the Sky to live harmoniously.

Fawn Journeyhawk

In 1988 one of us (Krippner) visited the temporary ranch
of Fawn Journeyhawk, of Shawnee and Mandan ancestry,
near Phoenix, Arizona. The ranch was conceived of as a
teaching and healing center that honors the intertribal "ancestors" of the Native American traditions. From childhood,
Journeyhawk experienced unusual dreams as well as intense
visual imagery in her pre-sleep hypnagogic states, and conducted spontaneous healing ceremonies for relatives and
neighbors. As an adult, these experiences were considered to
be pathological; Journeyhawk was diagnosed as suffering
from "clinical depression with schizophrenic tendencies,"
was hospitalized, and was placed on medication. A psychiatrist told her, "Having dreams is normal; listening to them is
not. Only schizophrenics follow instructions given in dreams
and if this continues, you will lose touch with reality. I'll raise
your dosage gradually until the dreams stop. Then your illness
will be considered in remission." Indeed, the medication
inhibited Journeyhawk's recall of dreams and imagery, but
produced a drug dependency.

With the help of a psychiatrist, a psychotherapist, and a psychic, Journeyhawk conquered her dependence on drugs. Joan Norris, the psychotherapist on the team, told Journeyhawk that she had "psychic potential that needed to be understood." As her dream recall resumed, Journeyhawk was given "instructions" by a number of Native American ancestors, principally Red Tomahawk Halfmoon, Wahoo Kahoonehaw, and Stormy Winds, all who said they "are of the North" as are other elders who died at an advanced age in a "state of wisdom." When she asked their identity, they replied, "We are your higher powers," and she realized that Joan Norris' advice had been valid. Another source of instruction is the information in Journeyhawk's hypnagogic visions; it was these messages that led her and her family to travel to Arizona in 1978, but she separated from her husband in 1986 because he had become increasingly uncomfortable with Journeyhawk's behavior.

One of Journeyhawk's specialties is working with drug addicts. She contacts the "spirits" of the drug and works to overcome them. She compares the spirit of cocaine to a "seducer" who lures a person into addiction with promises of everlasting bliss and pleasure. The spirit of the addict "falls in love" with the spirit of the drug; the severance of this relationship is the focus of the treatment. According to Journeyhawk, the spirit of heroin is hard to overcome because it is "strong and selfish," while the spirit of alcohol is "strictly low-class and cheap"—the easiest addiction for her to treat. Journeyhawk's treatment is directed by the ancestors who enable her to adopt the stance of a "warrior" as she engages the spirit of the drug in bargain, barter, or battle. Sometimes she will call upon other warriors for assistance; Journeyhawk's daughters, Reenie and Loni, have been trained to assist in this work. Many follow-up activities are required of the client to actualize and integrate the progress made by Journeyhawk in her battle with the drug's spirit.

In Journeyhawk's model of healing, disease is the absence of wellness. Treatment of disease is "medicine work" as opposed to the "warrior work" involved with the treatment of addiction. She claims to have been especially successful with cancer, but also works frequently with Vietnam veterans undergoing the effects of post-traumatic stress syndrome and with persons suffering from AIDS-related diseases. Journeyhawk's process of diagnosis includes reading the client's "aura" or "energy field," asking advice from the ancestors while dreaming, and relying on her own intuition or "inner knowing." Some of her information for treatment comes from White Owl, a guide who appears in dreams but who also can provide information while Journeyhawk is awake. In the latter instance, Journeyhawk insists that the experience is not one of "channeling" because she is completely aware while the advice is being given and does not surrender her own self-identity. White Owl occasionally helps Journeyhawk treat serious cases of addiction, especially non-Native American males who have a record of manipulating and lying.

She makes frequent use of ritual and ceremony as treatment modalities, both in the form of "conscious mind journeying" (i.e., a guided imagery in which Journeyhawk takes clients to a "crystal cave" while the healers work with them) and by utilizing the drums and chants prescribed by the ancestors. The "conscious mind journey" is combined with herbal preparations and dietary regimens in the "balance work" that precedes the healing ceremony. One satisfied client, Ricki Soaring Dove, wrote Krippner, "No one who I have seen for counseling has been able to delineate and peel back the armor as effectively as Fawn was able to do." Soaring Dove also reported a significant improvement in her chronic sinus condition after Journeyhawk's treatment.

Journeyhawk uses crystals and other materials when she is so instructed. Her daughter Reenie is the group's drummer; however, the drumming is not used as a stimulus for out-of-body experience or "journeying" but to summon the ancestors to assist in the healing process. Journeyhawk's "astral travel" or journeying takes place in dreams, and supposedly enables her to move through time and space, often as a white she-wolf, her power animal.

A collection of uniquely shaped and highly polished rocks, said to have been left in Journeyhawk's lodge by the ancestors, is used as "power objects" during healing ceremonies. Another group of rocks is used to construct a "medicine wheel" (on a cloth, a table, or the ground) in many of the ceremonies. This second collection consists of rocks said to be periodically placed by the ancestors in the back yard of a seven-year-old boy whom Journeyhawk treated. Krippner examined several of the rocks and was impressed by their beauty and form. Their different shapes supposedly symbolize infinity, faith, everlasting life (including possible reincarnation), maleness, and femaleness. She has met other shamanic healers at Pow Wows, noting that such practitioners as Sun Bear have the healing of the earth as their primary goal. Journeyhawk, however, sees her own mission as healing individuals by the utilization of intertribal treatment modalities.

Twyla Nitsch

In 1967 one of us (Krippner) held his first of several interviews with Twyla Hurd Nitsch whose grandfather, Moses Shongo, was the last of the great Seneca Indian medicine men. According to Nitsch, who lives near Buffalo, New York, medicine men and women not only were healers but historians and philosophers as well. Seneca shamans were among the custodians of spiritual traditions in the powerful Iroquois Confederacy that also consisted of the Mohawks, Oneidas, Onondagas, Cayugas, and Tuscaroras.

As a medicine woman, Nitsch has always looked to Mother Earth as her most important teacher. Her approach to healing focuses on encouraging people to "quiet down," to become more aware of themselves not only as individuals but as part of society, and as part of the total universe. From Mother Earth, she learned the "Secrets of the Ages," namely that self-knowledge is the key, self-understanding is the desire, self-discipline is the way, and self-realization is the goal. She also learned reverence for the Great Mystery or Great Spirit who created the universe. Nitsch is drawn to nature because the Great Mystery's wonders can be observed in the natural environment. In the out-of-doors, one can find among all creation an interdependency, relationship, and spiritual force or "swenio."

The early Senecas believed that during silent communication the physical body can undergo healing. This process can be facilitated by the "personal stones" or "power objects" the client holds until they become warm and pulsing. Then the outside world can be shut out and a calm silence can be experienced. If colors appear, Nitsch believes that they indicate what dimension needs to be explored. For her, red indicates faith, yellow is love, blue is intuition, green is will, purple is healing, white or crystal is magnetic attraction, and pastels are creativity. These procedures help Nitsch's students and clients answer the four basic questions she constantly poses:

> Am I happy doing what I am doing?
> What am I doing to add to the world's confusion?
> What am I doing to bring about peace and contentment?
> How will I be remembered after I am gone?

She teaches her clients how to make medicine pouches in which their personal stones and other power objects can be placed. The pouches are decorated with four colors of beads because, for the Seneca, four was a number of balance. Nitsch recalls the clan legends which begin:

Many moons ago, long before there were People Beings, Natureland was inhabited by Creature People and Plant People. Great peace dwelled within these Clans. They knew who they were, what work they had to do, why they did it, and how they continued life after life. They all belonged to one great family and lived in balance with each other. Later on, People Beings entered into Natureland. They did not possess the "Gift of Balance" (Nitsch, 1979).

The clan legends relate the endless quest of People Beings to live in balance with the Creature People and the Plant People. Gradually, they began to understand that the Earth was their Mother, the Sky was their Father, the Moon was their Grandmother, the Sun was their Grandfather, and Water was their medicine. Living between Earth and Sky, between Moon and Sun, Nitsch teaches People Beings to follow the Medicine Ways in order to obtain the balance that characterizes the rest of nature.

Leslie Gray

One of us (Krippner) held his first interview with Leslie Gray in 1982 shortly after she moved to San Francisco from Washington, D.C. where she was Acting Director of the Multicultural Enrichment Program and where she had received her PhD in clinical psychology. Drawing upon her Oneida, Powhattan, and Seminole ancestry, Gray obtained her knowledge of shamanism from academic research, from studying with master shamans, and from her own visionary quests. An example of the "wounded healer" who becomes a shaman, Gray injured her neck in an automobile accident and was still in pain after consulting 11 specialists. In desperation, she visited a Cherokee medicine man and found relief. She asked the shaman if she could work with him, but he told her it was more important for her to finish her doctorate so she could help the two cultures communicate (Shaffer, 1987).

Gray continued to visit shamans and, in 1982, had a vision in which she visited the Lower World, was devoured by a dragon, spit out onto a rock altar, and reassembled as a radiant being. The vision was followed by a two-week fever, and then by several positive developments in her life. This sequence of events convinced Gray that she had been called to become a healer. Gray gradually began to understand that shamanism is being relevant today because it is "an ingenious method of overcoming the modern experience of helplessness."

Gray observes that the shaman predates the priest in history as shamans gain their power through personal experience rather than through learning "handed down" rituals. Thus, shamanic rituals are often more flexible than orthodox religious rituals because the shaman's spirit guides, power animals, and power objects will vary from occasion to occasion, depending on what is appropriate. In 1985, Krippner participated in a "smoke" with Gray. Its function was to enhance the personal power of each participant. As the pipe slowly made its way around the circle of participants, Gray chanted, prayed, and sang. From time to time, she fanned the smoke from the pipe which had been filled with a mixture of raw tobacco and herbs. Krippner focused upon a difficult issue in his life during the ceremony, attempting to find the strength within himself to deal more effectively with it.

Gray holds academic appointments at several universities and observes that a dual career is not unusual for shamans. One of her apprentices, a Yaqui Indian, also trained as a registered nurse. A colleague of Gray's, an Ojibway healer, also is a computer technician. Gray calls herself "a bridge person," one who links cultures and traditions. Clients seek out Gray because they are feeling ineffectual and powerless; some are in spiritual crisis or confusion. Gray takes them on a shamanic journey, noting

When I journey for clients, it is usually to demonstrate to them how to do it for themselves. My goal is always to teach *them* to journey, never to hook them into coming back to me for a fix.

Gray's shamanic journeying involves entering an altered conscious state, usually with the help of drumming, rattling, or chanting. For Gray, journeying can involve the Upper World, the land of the ancestors, to bring back information or knowledge, or to the Lower World, the land of the power animals, to bring back personal empowerment for living on Middle Earth. Gray sees conventional psychotherapy as lying outside the realm of spirit, operating from a model of illness and emphasizing interpretation and analysis. For shamanic counseling, on the other hand, spirit and empowerment are crucial while understanding is secondary. When working with dreams, Gray will rarely engage in dream interpretation, but will locate harmful influences and remove them, or will identify power animals and guardian spirits, utilizing their power. Gray does not even insist that her clients "believe" in what she does, noting, "All I'm concerned about is whether it works."

Elizabeth Cogburn

In 1988, one of us (Krippner) interviewed Elizabeth Cogburn, a shamanic healer who lives in Albuquerque, New Mexico. Cogburn considers herself to be a "red-faced" shaman, a term used by Northwest Indians, to signify that she has followed a "call" in contrast to the "black-faced" shaman who has followed an inherited and established outer tradition. Each year Cogburn leads a "New Song Ceremonial Community" for several dozen people who come from various parts of North America to New Mexico's Jemez Mountains at the time of the summer solstice. Living with a group of people in the wilderness serves to train people to cooperate at all levels of community life. One's ordinary habits are suspended as everyone shares in the physical work of the camp—constructing a lodge and music pavilion, preparing food, digging latrines, and creating the materials used in the ceremonies (Dubin-Vaughn, 1991).

The central focus of the ritual is the Long Dance, a metaphor for life itself. The dance lasts three days and three nights during which time neither the drumming nor the movement stops. Everything that occurs in the camp prior to the dance is viewed as a preparation. Personal conflicts, unusual dreams, spiritual practices, natural phenomena, and preliminary ceremonies are all seen as useful initiatory experiences. For example, in the Opening Talking Staff Council, Cogburn holds a Medicine Pipe and establishes through her prayers the arrival of "sacred time." She then poses a set of questions about life for the participants, for example, "How do you describe yourself?" "Will you tell us, out of your personal experience, how you create unions?" "What can you share with us from your life that might be of use to the rest of us in ours?" "To what are you devoted?"

Celibacy is practiced in the camp; husbands and wives live separately. During one 24-hour period, the men and women camp apart to conduct specific gender-related rituals. When they reunite, they engage in some sort of festive ceremony, depending on the problematic issues the two groups have identified. This will change from year to year, but flexibility in rituals is common to shamanism! Cogburn argues that the attainment of ecstasy is as basic a human need as food, drink, and sleep. She teaches that if the expression of ecstasy is denied and not directed toward life-creating functions, it will erupt in violence and lead to pathology or even war. Her Long Dance is designed to cultivate "controlled ecstasy" within the structure of well-established ritual dance forms.

Nicki Scully

One of us (Welch) participated in several training workshops with Nicki Scully in 1986. Scully, who lives in Eugene, Oregon, traces her legacy to the "huna" tradition, not only of the Hawaiian kahunas but of African cultures, especially Egyptian, that she thinks preceded them. The huna tradition proposes a three-tiered model of the psyche in which there are "low," "middle," and "high" selves. None of these should be neglected or rejected as each plays an important role in the integration of the whole human being.

In his training sessions, Welch and the other students were taken on several guided imagery sessions in which the predominant image was the Cauldron—a symbol of internal alchemy and personal transformation, to connect with pertinent deities, totem power animal allies, and "archetypal entities" that are said to assist in the healing work. Scully offered initiations in which one's "life force energy" was accessed. She then taught various ways in which this "energy" could be utilized, including techniques in distant healing and "bloodless psychic surgery" principles. Scully also taught Welch how the "life force" can be mobilized in self-healing by use of dreams and spontaneous imagery. It is Scully's position that people need to take responsibility for their own healing; therefore, her teachings focus on techniques that are enhanced by client participation.

Scully makes use of her power animals or "totem allies" in individual and group healing ceremonies. She also purports to receive guidance from "archetypal entities" such as Thoth, the Egyptian god of wisdom, and Nephthys, sister of the Egyptian goddess Isis. In 1990, Scully announced that Nephthys had told her to design a class devoted to "exploring the shadow"—those rejected aspects of one's psyche that actually have something of value to offer an individual in his or her spiritual development. Scully maintains that "It is time that each of us learns to embrace our shadow side and honor it in appropriate ways so as not to further contribute to the raging insanity of violence and destruction that has overtaken our culture and our species."

Scully places the healing of the individual within the context of planetary healing. She feels that people's illnesses can be their teachers, and they must take heed of the messages that illness brings to make necessary changes in their lives. Her contact with Rolling Thunder made her aware of the need for humans to take responsibility for the health of the planet as well as for their own health. In other words, "What we create in our personal lives is reflected in the world we create." Scully points out how pregnant women and nursing mothers need to avoid polluted foods or their children will suffer the consequences. Scully informs her students that 25,000 plant species and more than 1,000 vertebrate species and sub-species are endangered, as well as hundreds of small species such as mollusks and corals whose habitats are being destroyed. In recognition of the need for people to participate actively in reversing this disturbing trend, Scully has designed a number of initiation ceremonies specifically directed toward developing effective tools for planetary healing.

Scully has produced a number of shamanic guided visualization audio cassette tapes. "The Cauldron Journey for Healing," for example, was especially designed for those people with AIDS-related diseases or leukemia (who receive free copies from Scully, as do practitioners, hospices, and healing centers working with these groups). With a musical score by Roland Barker, performed by the rock musician Jerry Garcia, this tape was designed to carry Scully's healing work to a wider public.

Graywolf

In 1976, Fred Swinney was traveling by canoe to James Bay in the wilderness of Ontario, Canada. One night he fell asleep before his smoldering campfire and had a dream in which animal predators emerged from the woods and devoured him. Awakening in terror, Swinney cast his gaze toward the coals of the fire. Just beyond, he discerned two piercing eyes and the large gray form of a wolf. Transfixed by the animal's eyes, he was unable to move. A feeling of total surrender replaced Swinney's fear, just as if he had become a wolf himself (Villoldo and Krippner, 1987).

Upon returning to work as a marriage counselor, Swinney began to read about wolves and shamans. He discovered that his dream was a typical shamanic initiation dream, and that power animals were common allies of shamanic healers. Gradually, Swinney introduced shamanic elements into his counseling practice and changed his name to "Graywolf." One of us (Welch) interviewed Graywolf in 1989 to obtain his model of shamanic healing and counseling.

Graywolf makes a *diagnosis* that provides him with therapeutic direction for the physical, psychological, and spiritual aspects of a client at the onset of their work together. Graywolf may or may not share the full diagnosis with his client, choosing instead to allow the diagnosis to evolve. Using a Native American symbol known as the "medicine wheel," Graywolf attempts to discuss its "four directions" with the client as they begin to determine his or her location on the spiritual path.

For Graywolf, the *etiology* of a client's illness can exist on several levels, e.g., self image, diet, genetic predisposition, spiritual dilemmas, and his or her model of reality. The client's *behavior* presents Graywolf with feedback on the "here and now" existential status of a client, reflecting his or her "inner being." If an "imbalance" exists on one level, Graywolf believes that it will be reflected throughout the client's entire system.

Treatment in Graywolf's terms draws on a variety of sources—Gestalt therapy, Transactional Analysis, meditation practices, bodywork, guided imagery, "Greek Aesculapian dreamhealing," "chakra energy balancing," and such Native American approaches as the vision quest and the sweat lodge. Graywolf uses a client's dreams to elicit self-knowledge and to evoke self-healing. He believes that dreams arise from creative and intuitive processes, drawing upon events from the previous day as well as from longstanding personal mythologies and other belief systems. By taking the client on a noninterpretive "dream journey," Graywolf attempts to locate the dream's "healing gifts" in the form of colors, shapes, feelings, and images.

Regarding *prognosis*, Graywolf attempts to remain unattached to therapeutic results. Of more importance to him are his client's commitment to the healing process, honesty during the process, and belief in its overall positive outcome. *Death, dying, and suicide* can actually be natural healing experiences because Graywolf believes that death is a stage of personal transformation into the world of spirit. Suicide, for some, may be a way to alleviate suffering by trusting death as a healer.

Graywolf feels that *healing personnel* are necessary to facilitate clients' healing processes when they can not help themselves; bone-setting and surgery are two obvious examples. Guiding someone to a realization of the "inner healer" should be the *function of the institution*. Only in extreme cases should health care personnel and the institution sanction medication as a way of treating pain and other symptoms. To Graywolf, the underlying issues of an indisposition may never be uncovered if they are masked by drugs.

Rights and duties on all levels can be political impositions on self-healing if they do not reflect the needs of the client. On the other hand, ethics and values (such as love, respect, and dedication) that arrive from the client's internal sources are important to acknowledge because they have the capacity to empower the client. The healer needs to dissociate from personal gain. Graywolf told Welch, "If you realize that the person doing the healing and the person being healed are just different manifestations of a common source, then rights and duties can be superfluous and detract from the healing flow. They may impose rigidity in a situation where the purpose is to induce flow."

The *goal* of Graywolf's model of healing is movement toward experiencing wholeness. Dreamwork, for Graywolf, provides a client with a doorway into the visions of healing that exist within, visions that can bring healing to both the human being and the social system.

Michael Harner

Krippner attended a shamanic drumming workshop given by Harner in 1982 and has met with him several times over the years. A former anthropology professor at the New School for Social Research in New York, Harner has conducted field research in the Andes and the upper Amazon forests of South America as well as to various parts of Mexico and the western United States and Canada. Harner received shamanic training during some of his contacts with native people and has organized the Center for Shamanic Studies to preserve and to teach shamanic counseling methods (Harner, 1980).

Harner's guiding premise is that shamans help their clients transcend their ordinary definition of reality, including the definition of themselves as ill. Shamans show their clients that they are not alone in their struggles against illness and death; shamans share their special powers and convince clients that another human being is willing to help them, even if it means making a sacrificial gesture. Harner observes, "The shaman's self-sacrifice calls forth a commensurate emotional commitment from his [or her] patients, a sense of obligation to struggle alongside the shaman to save one's self. Caring and curing go hand in hand" (pp. xi-xii).

Harner views shamanic healing as a "supplementary healing method" for achieving well-being, noting that even the advance techniques of allopathic medicine are not always adequate to solve all the problems of people who are ill, or those wishing to avoid illness. Shamanic healing, in all the native societies Harner has visited, involves entering what he calls "a shamanic state of consciousness." Noting that anthropologists have spoken of "cultural relativism," in which one avoids prejudice regarding other social life styles, Harner observes that shamans can teach "cognitive relativism," in which one avoids making negative judgments about another's way of thinking and conceptualizing both in a shamanic state of consciousness and outside of it.

Harner, his wife (Sandra Harner), and their associates at the Center for Shamanic Studies have developed a training program in shamanic counseling. Harner notes that clients of these counselors receive help and guidance in "ordinary reality." However, one of the assumptions of the counseling service is that there are also shamanic counselors in "non-ordinary reality." These "sacred teachers" are contacted by the shamanic counselors through entering the shamanic states of consciousness that enable them to "journey." The shamanic counselor's clients come for help for various reasons, among them various types of depression and/or complaints that life has lost its meaning (often interpreted as "soul loss").

Because he believes that shamanism is basically a strategy for personal learning—and engaging in activities based on that learning—Harner, in his workshops, teaches people how to enter shamanic states of consciousness. Utilizing drumming, Harner takes his students on "journeys" to find their power animals, to identify power songs, to explore the Upper and Lower Worlds, and to heal at a distance. Those students who become "Certified Shamanic Counselors" use these skills to help their clients. Nonetheless, Harner asserts that

> The task of the shamanic counselor is simply to help
> the client narrow down the definition of the problem
> so that it is clear in the client's mind. Then, after the

problem can be precisely formulated, the client uses shamanic methods to seek help in solving it. But, again, this help does not come from the counselor in ordinary reality; rather, it comes from the client's own divinatory journey to nonordinary reality, where the real counselors are (Harner, 1988).

Other social scientists who have received shamanic training, and who give classes in attaining shamanic states of consciousness, include Joan Halifax and Alberto Villoldo. Harner, Halifax, and Villoldo approach shamanic healing in very different ways. But they all agree that the problems facing individuals, societies, and the planet can best be solved by utilizing the wisdom inherent in the shamanic healing traditions (Halifax, 1979).

Wallace Black Elk

Both of us have had personal experiences with the Sioux shamanic healer Wallace Black Elk (Krippner in 1984, Welch in 1986). Wallace is the great-nephew and spiritual descendant of Nicholas "Nick" Black Elk whose childhood visionary experience was recorded in *Black Elk Speaks*. The vision was one in which Nick was given the knowledge of the World Tree, the Lakota Sioux shamanic image of the connection between Middle Earth and the Upper and Lower Worlds. A Sioux grandfather who appeared in the vision told the boy that he would preserve the knowledge and customs of his nation by bringing the World Tree to bloom in the center of it. Nick was afraid to discuss his experience for several years, but finally revealed it when he sensed that the traditional Sioux rituals were being forgotten and neglected (Neihardt, 1932).

Nick Black Elk's worldview was that all things had been created by the Great Spirit for the good of the earth and its inhabitants. Wallace Black Elk's message is the same. Born in 1921, Wallace, like Nick, received his first vision at the age of nine and now describes his mission as similar to that of a scout. While most of his colleagues remain close to their people, following the traditional shamanic vow to relieve suffering in any form, Wallace ventures into new areas to determine if the Sioux idea of spiritual healing will be received. He is willing to share his model of healing with any group of "Earth People" interested in his message.

According to Wallace, it is the present responsibility of human beings to devote each of their acts to the preservation of the endangered Mother Earth. He has been designated as a carrier of the Sacred Pipe by his tribe, and uses it to conduct rituals whenever he finds a receptive audience. The Sacred Pipe serves as the mediator between the spirit world and the world of everyday existence. In "hanbleceya," the Sioux vision questing in which attempts are made to gain strength and aid from the spirit world, the Sacred Pipe can be a shield against danger, allowing the bearers to face their worst fears and to connect with their deepest spiritual roots. The Lakota word for the sack in which the Sacred Pipe is carried is "Cantojuha"—the "Heart Bag," a term that emphasizes the spiritual connection between humanity and the rest of nature.

Wallace insists that spiritual communication is the greatest need of earth people today. This can be accomplished through sincere singing and praying—both of which Wallace uses himself to maintain contact with the world of spirit. Referring to one of his powerful experiences, he has remarked, "The power of the Great Spirit is like lightning blasting the senses. My mind is like a color television set; with it I can see all the sacred colors: blue, red, yellow, and white." He has called the Sacred Pipe his "telephone" because it provides direct contact with spiritual powers. Wallace refers to his way of life as the "Red Road," one that follows the teachings of the Sacred Pipe. In contrast, industrialized societies follow the "Black Road," one that is alienated from the earth and from the spirit (Black Elk and Lyon, 1990).

At one of the shamanic healer's presentations in 1986,

Welch recorded a vision which Wallace felt may be prophetic. It is metaphorical of the Western world's values and pursuits which, Wallace believes, are based on jealousy and greed rather than the foundation of spiritual communication he espouses:

> There is this huge monster consuming everything with no bottom to its stomach. When the monster gets its mouth half-way around this rock, a fire is going to come out of the center of the rock and blow off the monster's head.

This prophecy seems to be commenting on the exploitive habits of industrialized societies. In the Western world's eagerness to consume, it ingests the rock, that is, the earth. But in so doing, it throws nature out of balance and nature rebels. Eventually, this power destroys the monster.

Wallace has conducted "inipi" or sweat lodge ceremonies for such diverse groups as university students, professional societies, and Indians in prison. In 1985, he conducted one of the first Sun Dances for non-Indians. William Lyon, an anthropologist who has worked with Wallace, observed that he is constantly preparing himself for his next vision quest. To obtain a new vision, Wallace will frequently modify his rituals—a characteristic of the shaman but not of the priest. For example, Lyon (1987) observed that one year the inipi ceremony included several new songs as well as a new altar array of ritual paraphernalia. Like the world around him, Wallace is adapting, changing, and updating his methods and approaches to acquiring new medicines and healing powers. Vision questing (and shamanism itself) is open-ended; it is a never-ending process as there are always new healing powers to discover.

Inipis are also used by Rolling Thunder, who once invited Krippner to participate in a ceremony. The ritual was organized to facilitate personal cleansing so that Krippner and his friends could help the medicine man during a healing session. Krippner recalled that the structure was built of saplings that had been bent and tied together, and over which animal hides had been draped. A group of nine men sat in a circle as a ladle of water was poured over rocks taken from a fire. Krippner recalled:

> As the water contacted the rocks, an explosive hiss was followed by a wave of intense heat that enveloped our naked bodies. We took turns adding water and the heat increased until I thought my skin was on fire....I realized that I could not fight the heat. It was necessary to receive the heat and ride with it. I became one with the heat, one with the hot air, and allowed every breath I took to enhance the feeling.... As the sweat poured from my body, I felt purged of anxiety, depression, and all the petty concerns that would prevent me from fully participating in the healing ceremony that was to follow (Krippner and Villoldo, 1987).

Rolling Thunder's invitation is typical of those shamanic healers who invite sincere observers to learn about their traditions. Maria Sabina felt that the entire world, not only the community of native healers, needed the "old knowledge" to facilitate healing, kindness, and peace throughout the planet. These viewpoints were corroborated by other North American shamanic healers we have met, interviewed, or worked with, e.g., Brave Buffalo, Leonard Crow Dog, Prem Das, Brooke Medicine Eagle, Oh Shinnah Fast Wolf, Richard Romero, Pablo Sanchez, Brant Secunda, Medicine Story, Luisah Teish, and Sun Bear. This open-minded and open-ended attitude stands in strong contrast to the secrecy and dogma that characterize many allopathic practitioners (as well as some non-allopathic practitioners) who give little attention to spiritual aspects of health and healing. Richard Gerber (1988), a physician with an awareness of these issues, writes,

It is the endowing power of spirit that moves, inspires, and breathes life into that vehicle we perceive as the physical body. A system of medicine which denies or ignores its existence will be incomplete, because it leaves out the most fundamental quality of human existence—the spiritual dimension.

Five

Shamanistic Healers

Any attempt at healing involves four dimensions: the environment, the practitioner, the patient, and treatment procedures that lead to health and mastery. In successful healing sessions, one or more of those dimensions is positively activated. The healer and the patient share a world-view that explains the reason for both the disease and the expected cure. Certain personal qualities of the practitioner facilitate recovery. The patient's expectations of recovery assist the healing process. The techniques and materials used in treatment are conducive to success.

Sometimes only one of these principles is activated, and that suffices to bring about change. For example, a visiting physician might administer an antibiotic to a tribal patient suffering from a bacterial infection. There may be no shared world-view, the patient may be fearful rather than expectant, the physician may behave in ways inappropriate to the tribal setting; nevertheless, the treatment eliminates the infection. In more complex cases, however, especially those involving psychotherapy, the chances for improvement are enhanced if more than one of these principles are activated.

Cross-Cultural Perspectives

E. Fuller Torrey is a psychiatrist who has conducted considerable cross-cultural research in healing. He has presented two examples demonstrating the importance of these four healing principles:

> The psychiatrist looked thoughtfully at his client. "You looked angry when you were just talking about your father. You often look angry when you talk about him. I wonder if something happened to you once that made you very angry at him." At this point the client broke down sobbing, blurting out a forgotten history of neglect and deceit by a thoughtless father toward a little girl....After several more sessions in which she was able to explore her feelings of anger she began to get better.

> The witchdoctor stared solemnly at the small shells. They had landed in a pattern resembling the shape of a large animal. He picked one shell up and examined it minutely. "You have broken a taboo of your family. It has offended the sacred bear that protects your ancestors. That is why you are sick." The client and her family breathed a sigh of relief. It was what they had suspected. Now that they knew for certain what was wrong, they could proceed with the necessary sacrifices. After these had been made the patient began to get better (Torrey, 1986).

In both cases, the practitioner was able to identify what was felt to be wrong with the client and this act had a therapeutic effect. A client's anxiety is decreased by the knowledge that a trusted and respected practitioner understands what is wrong. The naming of the problem also may activate a series of associated ideas in the client's mind producing confession, absolution, and general catharsis.

Naming a disease or dysfunction tells clients that someone understands their sickness, and that there is a way for them to get well. The anthroplogist Claude Levi-Strauss (1963) has compared shamans and psychoanalysts, concluding that the goal of both is to bring to a conscious level the client's patterns of conflicts and resistances. The naming process, the use of words to represent what is wrong, is effective not only because of the knowledge that the words convey, but because this knowledge makes possible a specific experience and establishes a shared reality. In the course of the treatment, conflicts emerge in a way that permits their free development and that often leads to their resolution.

It is common to find diagnostic categories in other cultures that do not agree with those constructed by allopathic medicine and psychiatry. Lack of a shared reality is one of the reasons why most attempts at cross-cultural psychotherapy have been ineffective. Within a specific culture there may also be differences in world-view. A practitioner from an upper socio-economic class may find it difficult to treat lower class patients. Similar problems may exist when a female practitioner attempts to treat a male, or when a healer from one ethnic background attempts to treat a patient with a different ethnic identity (Torrey, 1973).

The personal qualities of the practitioner, both in actuality and those projected on to him or her by the patient, represent another dimension of healing. The psychologist Carl Rogers (1957) observed that while intellectual training and the acquiring of information have many valuable effects on the psychotherapist, they are not correlated to that therapist's success in producing positive outcomes. Rogers found that a therapist's accurate empathy, nonpossessive warmth, and personal genuineness were the factors that related significantly to a variety of positive patient personality and behavioral change measures. In other words, a therapist enters into an interpersonal relationship when he or she sees a client, and the therapeutic outcome is linked with the quality of that relationship.

The personal characteristics facilitating native practitioners' work differ from culture to culture. R. I. Levy (1967), after observing Yakut Indian shamans, reported that they feel an "inner force" that does not offend patients yet gives shamans an awareness of their power. Although some anthropologists believe that the word "shaman" was derived from a Sanskrit word meaning "singing," most hold that the original term was the Siberian Tungus word for "inner heat." A tribal healer's "inner heat," spirit communication, and wild behavior (which may include raucous singing), would be considered deviant in industrial countries, yet are valued and cultivated in native societies.

Positive patient expectations were recognized by Sigmund Freud (1940), who stated that "primitive therapists" and psychoanalysts both utilized "expectant faith" to induce positive change in their patients. Both tribal and contemporary healing systems raise patients' hopes through the ways they create the healing environment, collect healing paraphernalia, and foster the practitioner's reputation. Jerome Frank and Julia Frank (1991), in their survey of the placebo effect, stated that efforts to heighten the patient's positive expectations may be as genuinely therapeutic as any specific techniques. The converse is also true; "voodoo death" can occur when a victim believes that an enemy's hex is powerful enough to have a fatal effect, hence the victim's death results from a self-fulfilling prophecy (Cannon, 1942).

The fourth essential healing principle comprises the sense of mastery obtained from the practitioner's treatment procedures. Physically-oriented therapies may include medicine (in the form of herbs or drugs), surgery, massage, nutrition, exercise, relaxation, or a change of temperature (hot baths, ice packs). Psychologically-oriented therapies may include suggestion (hypnosis, mental imagery, rituals, charms, amulets), behavioral conditioning, dream interpretation, and confession. Social therapies are common in both traditional and industrial societies. Among the Pueblo Indians, a patient may be adopted by a new clan, or, in other tribal societies, moved to a new compound. Psychodrama was practiced by the Plains Indians before Europeans arrived in North America. Group therapy has long been a fixture of Haitian voodoo, as has the practice of taking case histories by questioning both clients and their families. It is apparent that native healing systems utilized both general principles and specific techniques found in many therapeutic schools today.

Shamanistic Healers in San Francisco

Many contemporary "healers" can be referred to as "shamanistic" rather than "shamanic" because their practices are only distantly related to shamanism. The practitioners falling into this category hold spiritual beliefs and engage in procedures that are based on assumptions about the human spirit. They frequently engage in rituals but rarely utilize deliberately-induced alterations in consciousness in their healing sessions. Winkelman defines their type of healing as a spiritual activity practiced with the intent of providing relief for various types of illness, noting that shamanistic healers emerge in social groups where mediums, sorcerers, and other practitioners have pre-empted the use of altered conscious states from shamans and shamanic healers.

In 1986 one of us (Welch) interviewed several shamanistic healers living in the San Francisco, California area. He attempted to understand their world-views and their models of healing. His interviewees included Greg Schelkun, a sculptor who had trained with spiritual practitioners in the Philippines; Genny Davis, an artist who had trained with an Alaskan shaman and a Filipino medium; Karl Wolfe, a former business executive who had trained with Brugh Joy, a well-known "holistic" physician; and Marta Talavera, the grand-daughter of a Tarahuma medicine woman from Mexico who attempts to preserve the healing traditions of her ancestors.

These shamanistic healers took several approaches to *diagnosis* . Schelkun asks his clients why they have come to see him. They describe their symptoms and he makes a few carefully chosen inquiries about their relationships, employ- ment, lifestyle, and medications. He learns a great deal through touch and through seeing "auras" or "energy fields" emanating from their bodies. Davis works both intellectually and intuitively to sense her clients' "energy flow." She at- tempts to determine whether the "energy" is closing in, or extending outward; if the latter, she asks if it is vibrant or dissipating, and whether someone else is "draining" the client's energy. She also attempts to locate one's "inner child" and asks herself how often the client heeds its advice. Once she has determined "how much the inner child needs to scream," she will be able to assess the seriousness of the illness.

Talavera's heritage is from the Tarahumaras, a Nahuatl- speaking tribe related to the Mayas, founders of the most highly developed civilization in ancient America. The Nahuatl medical texts were destroyed by the Spanish invaders but Talavera has attempted to preserve what has been passed down orally by her ancestors over the years (Josephy, 1961). She finds the facial features of her clients useful in diagnosis, as well as clues embedded in their dreams. For example, she will ask her clients how young they felt during the dream as this may provide information on when their problems devel- oped.

Wolfe intuitively senses what he calls the "energetic field" of a client, allegedly using "co-consciousness" and "telepathic" processes. In this way, he determines the relation- ship of a client's mind, body, spirit, and emotions. He claims to establish a connection at the "transpersonal level, a place where a non-judgmental field is established." From this per- spective, Wolfe listens carefully to his clients, experiencing how they relate to the various parts of themselves. From the ensuing "dialogue," Wolfe says that he "facilitates the recognition of clients' limiting patterning and belief systems, as they open to an experience of greater self love." For example, Wolfe may investigate the relationship between the "male" and "female" aspects of his clients by asking them questions concerning their eating and work habits, their feelings while enjoying their leisure time, and their behavior while driving a car. He then visualizes what he calls the "energetic" relationship and balance of the "feminine" aspects of their bodies (which he associates with the client's left side and front) and the "masculine" aspects (which he associates with the client's right side and back). If there is a lack of balance and relationship between the "masculine" and the "feminine," Wolfe attempts to help his clients understand how the rigidity of their belief systems might be fostering their disease.

Etiology, according to Davis, may often be traced to "past life" experiences that become evident in the patterns seen in the client's current relationships and behavior. Hereditary factors and negative attitudes (due to childhood losses, shocks, and traumas) are also seen as causative. For a client with diabetes, Davis might inquire not only whether the condition runs in the family but also if the client "overloaded" with sugar and sweets as a child because he or she lacked affection. For a client with cancer, Davis might ask if it represents denial of some aspect of his or her personality. Talavera would add the violation of sacred laws and the intervention of an evil spirit to the list of causative agents. For her, illness represents imbalance with one's center, one's society, or with nature itself.

Wolfe believes that there are genetic predispositions to disease, and that people often will enter a new incarnation because of the specific "gene pool" that will predispose them to either health or illness; in this manner, Wolfe believes that some people "choose" their diseases. For Wolfe, disease is actually "dis-ease," the body's way of acknowledging an imbalance and certain clients' inability to communicate with themselves; these difficulties are also reflected in their relationship with the physical and social environment.

The *client's behavior* provides additional information to Schelkun, who finds a congruence between lifestyle and illness. Schelkun's clients describe their symptoms while he assesses their bodies' "energy level" both visually and through touch. Talavera observes a client's movements for clues about the illness and for the treatment that would be the most beneficial. Wolfe attunes his sensitivity so that he can "see" the disease in his clients' bodies, "hear" it in their voices, and "feel" it in their movements.

Treatment Procedures

Treatment, for Wolfe, can take place in groups or at an individual level. It may involve work at a distance ("telepathic rapport"), the "laying-on" of hands, movement, and playing games—a frequent concomitant of his group work. Ultimately, he attempts to teach his clients how their illnesses are serving them, and to break the pattern which produced the illness. He engages in "distant healing," especially as a follow-up procedure. Wolfe reports having first observed his healing abilities following an out-of-body experience at the age of two. When he was a child, he thought it was quite natural for him to know what other people were thinking, for him to feel "energy" flowing through his body, and for people to feel better, after experiencing his presence. Often, they would report feeling "energy" during Wolfe's "laying-on" of hands. Currently, Wolfe works to facilitate an experience of what he refers to as "the denied or repressed natural energies of the body." He tells his clients that "once you can feel it in your body, you can move with the experience in your daily life, thus developing an intellectual understanding. The experience can lead you to the understanding, but the understanding cannot lead you to the experience."

Schelkun typically directs "energy" at the client,

whether he or she is in the office or thousands of miles distant. Schelkun has his clients rest on a table, relax, then administers a "laying-on" of hands. Schelkun reports a "flow of energy" throughout his body while his clients report a variety of sensations including "heat," "cold," "electricity," and out-of-body experiences. He also engages his clients in conversation, attempting to "draw understanding out of them" by having them "communicate with their illness." He estimates that as an apprentice he worked with over 5,000 cases; since then, he has worked with some 10,000 of his own clients, both in the U.S. and in the Philippines.

Talavera's treatment procedures emphasize massage, herbal preparations, dance, and counseling. Her counseling procedures focus upon enabling clients to "speak from the heart," as the human heart is a metaphor for one's deepest thoughts and feelings. She often sees people in the woods or other natural settings, and may give them a flower or other natural object to carry with them to prevent further illness. Talavera believes that humor is therapeutic and will often play games and exchange funny stories with clients.

Davis' work involves "laying-on" of hands as well as counseling; when attempting the latter, she attempts to educate clients as to what direction they want to take in their quest for "personhood." She generally has recorded music playing in the background during a session to enhance the effects. Many of her treatment procedures include playing games and moving to the music. Davis sees herself as an "activator" who "clears away" any negative forces around the client. She bases much of her treatment on passages in the book, *A Course in Miracles,* which states

> Exempt no one from your love, or you will be hiding a dark place in your mind where the Holy Spirit is not welcome. And thus you will exempt yourself from His healing power, for by not offering total love, you will not be healed completely (Anon., 1975).

Prognosis, for Wolfe, depends upon the client's perception of the transformational power of their illness. Once it is apparent how the problem serves a client's psychological and spiritual needs, that client can determine whether to abandon or transform these needs. The client needs to choose whether or not to be healed and this choice determines the prognosis. Davis perceives a client's intellectual understanding as only the first step in his or her recovery; prognosis depends upon how quickly they can change their life patterns to reflect the intellectual insights.

Death, dying, and suicide are seen as having symbolic potential by Talavera. People who have attempted suicide might want to kill a dysfunctional part of themselves. Davis warns suicidal clients that if they kill themselves in this life, they will need to come back to complete their learning task. She feels that suicide often can be prevented if it can be viewed as a cry for attention, affection, or love. She believes that, in death, the soul leaves the physical body for its next life or next phase of development. Even so, Davis suspects that spiritual and technological advances may someday lengthen the life span indefinitely.

Wolfe observes that suicidal attempts can be a form of attempted communication, e.g., a statement that they are experiencing extreme grief. Wolfe looks upon death as a transformation of consciousness; Schelkun conceptualizes death as "another life change" in which someone "lets go of the body." Both see the soul as moving on to another dimension, sometimes returning to earth later to go through the life-span again.

The *function of the institution*. Schelkun describes the function of the hospital as important, especially for those with accidents, broken bones, and in need of medicine or rest. He would like to see clients take a more active role in regaining health once they are hospitalized. Schelkun views the hospital as the nearest institution available to most people as a place of retreat and quietude. Wolfe advises that some of his clients seek hospitalization, if it appears as if "that is the course they need to choose." If so, he feels that the institution can provide them with whatever healing experience is required.

Personnel in Davis' healing system include those individuals to whom she refers clients, e.g., "holistic" physicians, body workers, acupuncturists, and healers whom she has trained. Wolfe may send clients who appear to be severely disturbed to psychotherapists or to those physicians whom he believes are also healers. He has worked jointly with other healers, taking a combined approach to the same client. Schelkun also refers his clients to other practitioners who he feels can be of assistance. Talavera works with native shamans, curanderas, and curanderos, especially when she visits Mexico.

Rights and Duties

Davis feels that there are several *rights and duties of the client*. They have the right to competent treatment, but also have the duty to face the problem directly. Davis claims that many sick people who go from one healer to another are trying to avoid facing a serious problem. Davis also assigns clients the responsibility for maintaining their health. They need to ask themselves: What am I doing to improve my life? In what way, if any, am I at war with my body? Am I polluting my body? Are my actions polluting my family? Davis holds that human beings have the right to be healed and whole, to be alive and healthy.

One important client right, for Talavera, is the right to "gentle treatment." She believes that the counselor must deal with a person's dream "very tenderly" because a client's images may represent his or her only source of nurturance and sustenance. It would be harmful to deny the importance of an image or to explain it away intellectually as this approach could produce psychological harm. For her, the client has the duty to retain balance by strengthening his or her will, and to find one's "inner guides" to assist the healing process.

Wolfe does not feel that his clients have the right to share every insight he has but he will share what he believes they need and can integrate at the time. For example, people often ask Wolfe what the outcome of their illness may be; even if he has an impression, he may not respond because his suggestion may reduce his clients' ability to exercise their own will. He gives his clients specific assignments between visits to accelerate their recovery. He focuses on bringing clients to an awareness of their own inner resources, how they create their own reality, and then encourages them to take the power they need to creatively make their own decisions and choices.

Schelkun believes that clients have the right to receive accurate information. If clients arrive expecting to be healed in one session, Schelkun explains that the average number of appointments per client ranges between five and ten. He also believes that clients can assist in their own recovery, and teaches them various breathing exercises, "energetic" movements, and spiritual "contemplations."

The *rights and duties of the family* raise important issues for Wolfe, who does not believe that his clients need to share details about his treatment with their families. He emphasizes the importance of personal responsibility on the part of his clients; their families have the duty to support this independence, especially if it is an essential part of the healing process. Wolfe observes ways in which parents frustrate the emerging power of children, most notably in labelling their natural feelings with a term (e.g., hostility, sin, selfishness) that will affect their future emotional experiences. Davis frequently works with the entire family, and teaches her clients not to waste time blaming their parents, but to focus on self-healing instead.

When working with families, Talavera will seat everyone in a circle so that they are equal in distance from each other, and equal in their right for her attention. Schelkun says that a key duty of the client's family is to assist the client's change rather than fight it. Sometimes a family member's return to health is threatening to other family members who, in the past, have blamed the client for the family's problems. Schelkun may interview members of the family to prepare them for the changes in family relationships that can follow a client's recovery.

For Talavera, the *rights and duties of society* grow out of the fact that a client's wholeness involves his or her equilibrium with the community. The community, as a result, has the duty to assist its members when they are in need of support. Davis believes that society cannot change until individuals change, and asks her clients what they are doing to bring love to the earth and all the people on the planet. Wolfe sees few role models in society that encourage creativity and open expression, two traits that he feels are important for health and spiritual growth. He thinks that society has the duty to permit the church, the art world, and the media to provide avenues for spiritual development.

Schelkun describes himself as "an anarchist" and does not think that society has the duty to provide free medical care. Instead, each individual in society has the duty to provide assistance for one another. He advocates more individual participation in obtaining health services, e.g., through barter, trade, or service. Schelkun makes this type of arrangement for his clients who have no money—approximately one third of his entire practice. He traces his ethics to "Christian spiritualism." As practiced in the Philippines, this credo is based on loving God with one's heart, mind, body, and soul, and one's neighbor as oneself.

The *goal of the model* is described by Talavera as the promotion of wholeness on the part of her clients, and the reaffirmation of their basic humanity. For Davis, the goal is to attain "personhood," the mature development of his or her potentials by making a connection with their "higher selves." Schelkun's goals are to modify physical manifestations of illness, to enable clients to understand the reasons for their illness, and to facilitate his clients' relationship with God. Wolfe's goal is to bring his clients into a closer relationship with their inner spiritual resources and with God, and to move them to a more natural, limitless, and creative experience of themselves.

Wolfe defines a healer as someone who facilitates individuals' communications with the spiritual aspects of themselves and the world. He contends that "where there is communication, there is healing." He sees "spirit" as the "energy that connects and binds everyone and everything together" and believes that "spirit" allows human beings to become "co-creators with God." For Davis, "spirit" refers to "people's connection with their higher selves." For her, everyone is connected at some level and it is "spirit" that makes this connection possible. Talavera conceptualizes "spirit" as anything pertaining to "the other world," the unseen aspects of existence. Schelkun's concept of "spirit" is "an all-pervasive awareness of our connection with God." A sick person is "out of alignment" with God.

Wolfe's concept of God is that of "an intelligence and hologram of which we are all a part." He experiences God during moments of peace, of creativity, and of love; he does not experience God as wrathful or punitive. Davis agrees, stating, "The God of fear is not the God I worship." Talavera thinks of God as the "Great Spirit of all Nature." For Schelkun, God is "all-pervasive" and "always available." Schelkun believes that being "off track" with God manifests itself in disease.

Healers and the Medical Model

The models of healing held by these four healers are similar in some ways to the medical model, but many elements are in stark contrast. Not only is the emphasis upon spiritual dimensions of healing at variance with that held by allopathy, but a number of specific concomitants of shamanistic healing also are apparent. Their appeal to the public is due, in part, to the spiritual elements of their models. The philosopher R.C. Fuller (1989) has remarked, "The continuing presence of metaphysically charged healing systems in American culture is in no small part due to their ritual power to lift individuals beyond the everyday world enabling them to temporarily experience numinous forces and powers".

These four shamanistic healers make frequent references to life after death. Reincarnation is a concept used to explain some illnesses or to identify the origin of a psychological problem. Divine intervention is occasionally called for; prayers are felt to be a worthwhile endeavor as they may "align" the client with God. "Laying-on" of hands is commonly used as a therapeutic technique. Various "energy fields" are felt to be important in spiritual healing and the "human aura" is assumed to reflect these energies. Unique abilities such as out-of-body experience and "distant healing" are accepted as part of the healing process.

The models of healing described by these four shamanistic healers share a number of components. Illness is often seen as a "metaphor" for a spiritual problem; cancer may represent an emotion that is "eating away" at a client, and suicide may symbolize a desire to terminate a destructive lifestyle. Hereditary components of disease are admitted, but may include unresolved problems from a "former life." The value of humor in treatment is acknowledged as are herbal remedies, movement, and exercise. These healers were not resistant to referring their clients to hospitals or physicians, although they preferred those with a holistic approach that took spiritual issues into account. Clients were seen as co-therapists, assuming a major share of responsibility for their healing process and in future health maintenance. Family and societal forces were seen as capable of either fomenting illness or supporting the client's recovery.

The focus on spirituality appeared to affect virtually every aspect of these practitioners' contact with their clients.

They admitted that they could not assist each person who came to them. They insisted that their work not be seen as a challenge to allopathic medicine or as a replacement for it. Even so, when they referred their clients to physicians or worked with them, the process reflected a continuation of their concern with the spiritual aspects of life.

In our opinion, most aspects of these worldviews do not contradict the assumptions of allopathic medicine as they refer to purported levels of reality that orthodox physicians do not address. However, we are skeptical about the usefulness of viewing illnesses as metaphors or as residues from "past lives." In addition to the lack of persuasive evidence on this topic, there is the danger that some clients will blame themselves (or their "former selves") for the ailment and that the ensuing guilt will increase rather than decrease stress.

Shamanistic Healers in Massachusetts and New Mexico

Shamanistic healers practice in various parts of North America, not only in California. Few of them would use the label "shamanistic" but we have found that many of their practices resemble those used by shamans thousands of years ago. In 1983, one of us (Krippner) first visited the Center of the Light in New Marlborough, Massachusetts. Located in the Berkshire Mountains since 1979, the Center sponsors workshops and programs "in the spirit of prayer and attunement to God." Healing services are held in the non-denominational Church of Christ Consciousness which states, as its goal, "to nourish, heal, teach, and offer spiritual guidance to the human family and the earth" (Summer Catalog, 1988).

The co-founders of the Center and the Church are Eugene and Eva Graf, who have designed a two-year training program which 180 people had completed by 1988. This program encompasses training in body systems, massage, herbal medicine, diet, "laying-on" of hands, healing through the "aura," "distant healing," prayer, meditation, and visualization. The bodily component of this program, called the "Graf Body Systems," was "given by the Spirit" to Eva Graf, an author, masseuse, and practitioner of Reiki (an approach to healing that utilizes "contact points" for different parts of the body).

In 1984, Krippner was at the Center when a friend of his, Michael Robert, arrived for a healing session. Robert's infant son had been hospitalized as a result of a life-threatening infectious disease. Eugene and Eva Graf brought the community together, arranging them in a circle around a chair on which there was a photograph of Robert's son. One by one, each member of the group walked to the chair, looked at the photograph and attempted a "distant healing" of the child. Finally, the Grafs led the whole group in song and prayer. By the end of the week, Robert reported that the crisis was over; eventually his son made a complete recovery. There is no way of knowing to what extent the healing service contributed to the positive outcome of this case, if it served any purpose at all except for helping Robert cope with stress. Nevertheless, it demonstrates how spiritual healing can be viewed as an adjunct to allopathic healing rather than a replacement for it.

In 1974, Krippner had his first interview with Luke Gatto, a research biologist teaching and lecturing on the empirical use of homeopathy and radiesthesic practices. Now living in Santa Fe, New Mexico, Gatto had been a first lieutenant in the U.S. Army, teaching biological defense procedures and medical therapies for illnesses contracted from exposures to radiation and biological warfare. Following his military service, Gatto studied diet with Michio Kushi, "distant healing" with Lawrence LeShan, and naturopathy with Hazel Parcells, a well-known practitioner of radiesthesia who holds a Ph.D. in nutrition.

Radiesthesia requires a "witness," some object that represents the person seeking help, usually a few drops of the client's blood, or a few strands of hair. A pendulum is held over the "witness" as the practitioner asks a variety of questions, the movements indicating a negative or a positive response. Some observers believe that the client's "energy field" is evoking the movements, while others are convinced that it is the practitioner's unconscious intuitive beliefs about the client's state of health. In either event, the pendulum sometimes can be used to prescribe treatment as well, generally in the form of herbs, diet, and homeopathic remedies.

Homeopathy holds that disease is secondary to disharmony in a client's system, and that mental, emotional, and physical symptoms reflect this disharmony. The client can regain balance through a natural substance often taken in very small doses. Allopathy takes the position that remedies suppress or eliminate symptoms by blocking the mechanisms (or killing the organisms) responsible for them. Homeopathy believes that symptoms serve a useful purpose (such as being an outlet for stress) and are often treated with minuscule amounts of a substance similar to whatever is felt to have caused the imbalance. For example, Gatto applies sulphur for childhood eczema; homeopaths claim that their success with infants and with animals precludes client expectancy from explaining their results.

Homeopathy and radiesthesia are considered "spiritual" by many of their practitioners because both take the position that people are closely linked to other people and the natural environment through "subtle energy fields." This alleged unity accounts for the purported success of "distant healing" and the effectiveness of small doses of homeopathic remedies. These ideas usually are ridiculed by the supporters of allopathic medicine; for example, Harold Morowitz (1982) refers to homeopathy as "scientific nonsense," stating that "homeopathic medicine is in direct confrontation with some of the most firmly established branches of human knowledge".

The individuals who seek treatment from practitioners of homeopathy, radiesthesia, and other "alternative" approaches often are spiritually motivated. They identify "energy," "wholeness," "balance," and "purity" as sources of health, and may find their concerns echoed in the statements of alternative practitioners. Some alternative healing approaches seem to offer people a more intense experience of a "sacred reality" than either organized religion or allopathic medicine. The book *Dimensions in Wholistic Healing* describes the fundamental premise of healing as the recognition that every human being is part of a "larger cosmic energy system." Thus one's untapped reservoir of creative potential can provide the pathway to "greater harmony between the person, the self within, and God or the universe without."

Gatto and other advocates of homeopathic treatment point out that it was found to assist clients suffering from rheumatoid arthritis when compared to a group receiving placebo solutions (Gibson, Gibson, and MacNeill, 1980). In another study, homeopathic remedies (such as sulphur) and comparison solutions (ethanol and water) were found in nuclear magnetic resonance spectra (Sacks, 1983). These differences were even found when very small amounts of sulphur were examined. These results are preliminary and in need of further replication, but they indicate that some aspects of this type of spiritual healing are amenable to scientific study (McGuire and Kantor, 1988).

Belief in "subtle energies" or in a universal "unity" is held by many of the other shamanistic healers we have observed or interviewed such as Betty Bethards, Zephra Bogert, Michael Bova, Corrine Calvet, Dominie Cappadonna, Bruce Davis, Etel de Loache, Kenji Kambara, Ron Lavin, John Meszaros, Jean Millay, Josiane Moser, Fred Null, Tiziana de Rovere, Keith Sherwood, Robert Skutch, Shelley Thompson, Virginia Veach, Dale Walker, Ambrose Worrall, and Olga Worrall. This "oneness" is held to enable the body's systems to work together in unity, to facilitate a healer's attempts to help a distant client, and to remind humankind that it must learn to protect other species and work with them to preserve the natural endowments of the planet.

Six

Priests And Religious Healers

Michael Winkelman's research study revealed that priests and priestesses emerged in societies once agricultural activity was established. Shamans generally were found in societies without agriculture, and often evolved into shamanic healers once hunting and gathering groups settled down. Priests, as a group, did not employ procedures that altered their consciousness. Exceptions were found among the Aztecs, Creek Indians, and Zuni Indians but these societies were relatively unstratified and the roles of their priests resembled those found in pre-agricultural shamanic activity. Major activities conducted by the Aztec, Creek, and Zuni priests included rainmaking, weather forecasting, and the performing of rituals that would assure a bountiful crop; all of these roles had been assigned to shamans in simpler tribal social groups.

Winkelman reported that most priests were full-time practitioners with high social and economic status, entitling them to exercise some political, judicial, financial, and military power. Priests were predominantly men but women often served as assistants. Their activities focused upon participation in public events directed toward agricultural fertility, ancestor worship, protection, and making the prayers, offerings, and sacrifices thought to be required by various gods and spirits. Shamans were believed to be endowed with personal power by tribal members; however, when priests took over sacred ceremonies, the power was felt to reside in the ceremony itself, or in the objects utilized in the ritual.

The Arrival of Christianity

Priestly training involved learning a society's theology and mastering the rituals needed for public ceremonies. Europeans who settled in North America were puzzled by the roles played by the native practitioners they encountered. Europeans were upset by the direct communication with the gods practiced by shamans, shamanic healers, and priests; it appeared that their deities could be cajoled, humored, and appeased—just as one would manipulate another human. The Europeans were especially alarmed when practitioners were observed entering altered conscious states to talk to their gods; at best, this was regarded as superstition and, at worst, the work of Satan. European priests and clergymen were quick to regard the natives as "pagan" and "heathen." Eventually, European religions supplanted the indigenous religions in North America; the native belief systems survived in only a few areas, usually by synthesizing important aspects of their traditional beliefs with those found in the new doctrines.

Christianity was far from monolithic when it arrived in North America and proceeded to become more heterogeneous as the centuries went by. One Christian practitioner, Phineas Quimby, was a 19th century clockmaker who developed a system of healing that he called "mind cure," influenced by Franz Anton Mesmer's concept of a health-regulating "magnetic fluid" that purportedly permeated the universe. Quimby expounded the idea that disease is an "error of the mind" held by the client. Disease could be expelled if the client corrected his or her error of belief. His disciples included F. W. Evans, a prominent Methodist minister; both Quimby and Evans became leaders in a movement of "mind curing" later known as "New Thought."

Quimby's most famous client was Mary Baker Eddy, who had been an invalid until the age of 41 when Quimby apparently restored her health. After Quimby's death, Eddy established Christian Science; her book, *Science and Health with a Key to the Scripture*, was a reworking of Quimby's material, even though he received no credit. The New Thought movement spawned such sects as Religious Science, Unity School of Christianity, and Divine Science, all of which focus upon healing but take a less extreme position on disease as being an "error of the mind." Another group, the Pentecostal churches, encourage "laying-on" of hands and "speaking in tongues." Pentecostalists are theologically conservative, believing that sickness is not so much an error in thinking as a "test" of one's faith, punishment for misbehaving or, in extreme cases, demonic possession.

In some instances, religious practitioners advise against seeking medical help—a violation of the principles espoused by virtually all of the healers we have interviewed. One couple took the Christian Science Church to court because their baby had died of spinal meningitis while under the care of a church-licensed practitioner (Kitman, 1984). Another Christian Science practitioner was summoned by a mother when her daughter became seriously ill; the girl died from meningitis and the mother was charged with involuntary manslaughter (Halstuk, 1988). In another instance, a Pentecostal couple threw away their diabetic son's insulin after a visiting minister claimed he had "cured" the boy. The couple was arraigned for manslaughter after their son died, even though the father kept insisting his son would be raised from the dead (A matter..., 1973).

The English words "health" and "heal" draw their meaning from a root concept of being "whole." In the King James version of the Bible, *Mark, 5:34* describes an encounter between Jesus Christ and a sick woman. It is written that the woman was cured when she touched Christ's robe, and that he remarked, "Daughter, thy faith hath made thee whole; go in peace and be whole of thy plague." In the Revised Standard Version of the Bible, the verse is translated as "Daughter, your faith has made you well, go in peace and be healed of your disease." There are 16 biblical accounts of Jesus' individual healings, and half that many reports of exorcism. Using Jesus Christ as their model, many North American Christian priests and ministers are involved in healing ministries, although there are as many differences as similarities in the methods of their practices and the theories implicit in their models of healing.

In 1932, the International Order of St. Luke the Physician was founded by an Episcopalian priest, J. G. Banks, and his wife, Ethyl Banks. The purpose of the Order is to foster an understanding of the importance of spiritual healing among Christians. Protestant, Roman Catholic, and Eastern Orthodox clergymen, clergywomen, and laypeople participate in the Order's prayer, study, and healing groups. Spiritual Frontiers Fellowship was founded in 1956 to stimulate spiritual healing and the scientific study of parapsychology. However, alleged parapsychological phenomena (e.g., precognition, clairvoyance, telepathy, psychokinesis) are held in low regard by many conservative Christians who claim that when people deliberately try to develop these abilities, they become vulnerable to demonic influence or possession. They claim that exorcisms are often needed to rid these victims of demons and similar malevolent forces (Peck, 1983).

Two United Church of Christ Practitioners

The diversity among Christian healers is demonstrated when a comparison is made between Francis Geddes and John Sandford, two ministers ordained in the same Protestant denomination, the Congregational Church (which later became the United Church of Christ). Geddes first became interested in spiritual healing in 1970, and attended one of Lawrence LeShan's (1974) five-day seminars where he learned various healing meditations. He also studied with Dolores Krieger (1979), learning her "therapeutic touch" procedure. Since 1975, Geddes has taught healing in retreat settings for various church groups, incorporating both LeShan's and Krieger's techniques. In 1984 he became coordinator of the Pacific Center for Spiritual Formation in San Anselmo, California.

In 1959, Sandford and his wife met Agnes Sanford (1972), a well-known Christian spiritual healer whose book *The Healing Light* is one of the most popular contemporary treatments of spiritual healing. The Sandfords (1985) were so deeply moved by Sanford's healing ministry that they changed the course of their work, incorporating what they had learned from her into a "healing ministry." John Sandford founded Elijah House (a Christian counseling center in Spokane, Washington), wrote several books on spiritual topics, and produced a series of "teaching tapes" including "Healing the Effects of Cult Involvement" and "The Care and Feeding of the Spirit."

In a 1986 interview with one of us (Welch), Geddes said that he is primarily a teacher of healing although he works as a member of a church healing group and sometimes practices healing in the context of spiritual counseling. On occasion, he has attempted to locate a painful area through "therapeutic touch," passing his hands lightly over a person's body. Individuals usually come to his healing group after a medical *diagnosis* has been made; if not, this "scanning" technique produces sensations of "tingling" or warmth that indicate which parts of the body are "imbalanced" or "blocked." In his writings, Sandford does not deal with diagnosis in detail, but mentions that bodily reactions accompany the spirit's experiences during life's daily events.

According to Sandford, insofar as the spiritual aspects of illness are concerned, the *etiology* is the presence of "sinful structures." Where sin has provided an access, "demonic forces" can enter to prey upon physical weakness. The human spirit can be wounded in infancy, and even in conception if rejection and abuse by the parents is experienced. One's "inner harmony" can be broken by fear, anger, or rejection. Geddes sees two basic etiological factors, outer (e.g., viruses) and inner (e.g., a lack of balance with oneself and/or a lack of connection with God).

A *subject's behavior* often provides an important clue to Sandford; when the spirit "flows" through the body, that person can be observed to perform well in athletics or other movement activities. Sometimes disturbing dreams are evidence that one's war with oneself has raged during the night. For Geddes, a person is potentially "a vast reservoir of healing energy"; an apparent lack of this energy indicates a lack of balance and connection with oneself, with other people, and with universal forces."

Regarding *treatment*, Geddes responds to an individual's needs, but all his efforts are based on the assumption that "the presence of God produces healing." The "imbalance" evident in illness can be altered by a shot of penicillin, "therapeutic touch," prayer, the use of imagery by the healer and/or ill person, or—in cases of "distant healing"—a "merging" of the practitioner and the one who comes for healing. Geddes believes that "when a person touches the deepest reality of the universe, he or she is capable of healing." Sandford uses a variety of spiritual healing techniques including prayer, confession, repentance, nature walks, outside labor, adequate sleep, sensible diet, and—in extreme cases— exorcism, in which the client's demonic forces are expunged.

Prognosis, for Sandford, depends on how steadfast his clients are in maintaining their spiritual lives. This can be accomplished through private devotions, family or corporate prayer, cherishing the spiritual needs of other people, and heeding the dictates of their conscience to keep them aware of sinful activities. Geddes feels that the restored balance and connection can be maintained if individuals continue to reduce the distance between themselves and God. During his work with a person, Geddes sometimes has an intuitive feeling about a negative outcome, but will not share it, fearing it might become a self-fulfilling prophecy. Geddes tries to avoid dwelling on these hunches, even if they are positive; he remarked, "Wanting positive results in healing can sometimes block positive results because it becomes attached to pride. This desire may block the healing channel because of its preoccupation with future results rather than with the present healing process."

Sandford speaks of two kinds of "slumbering spirits," those who never have been drawn toward spiritual life and those who were correctly nurtured but who turned away from living spiritually. Sinful acts prevent the Holy Spirit from continuing its nurturance. For Geddes, a person's spirit is connected to God by the Creator's unconditional love; this is the power behind all forms of spiritual healing. Geddes observes that Jesus Christ commissioned his followers to carry out a healing ministry and believes that this mission is just as relevant today as in biblical times.

Other Aspects of Spiritual Healing

Sandford regards *death* as the divorce of spirit and body. When one's spirit can no longer maintain its union with the physical body, it returns to God. People who commit *suicide* believe that they have no other option in a world that has become unbearable; suicides may have their origin during pregnancy when the parents express rejection and dislike of the child even before he or she is born. Geddes attempts to help people who are dying find meaning in the time they have left. He believes that the soul is bound to God by love and returns to that love after death. Geddes believes that this connection with God is the source of spiritual healing. When one counsels with someone who is contemplating suicide, Geddes refers the person to a psychotherapist, then prays for that individual.

Geddes conceptualizes his healing ministry as a cooperative effort with nursing and medical *personnel*; he will not participate in healing with persons who have a physical illness unless they are also being seen by a physician. Geddes prefers to conduct his work in the context of a church healing group that includes people with similar goals. He believes that virtually anyone has healing potential and could benefit from the LeShan and Krieger training programs. Sometimes, during a healing session, Geddes senses the presence of God and feels he is not alone while he works. Sandford also cooperates with physicians and psychotherapists, noting that "some physicians have learned to submit their hunches to God and hear and weigh the guidance He gives them." Sometimes a physician will call upon him to conduct an exorcism. Sandford follows the advice of *Ecclesiastes 38:1-2*, "Honor the physician with the honor due him according to your need of him, for the Lord created him; for healing comes from the Most High."

Sandford insists that the hospital have a calm atmosphere to assist the healing process. The function of the *institution* is to observe the importance of the church's role in healing. Elijah House, a center for Christian counseling formed by Sandford, also emphasizes the importance of involving the client's family in the healing process. Geddes will draw on any health resource as long as he feels it helps a client; he enjoys working with physicians but has "found very few physicians who would feel comfortable working with a healer." According to Geddes, medical students generally are trained to be mechanics; spiritual concerns do not fit into the mechanical model of human beings.

For Sandford, among the *rights and duties of subjects* are the necessity to avoid what he considers "the occult," e.g., astrology, sorcery, hypnosis, magic, theosophy, mediums. Geddes would take a broader view and would emphasize positive, not negative, suggestions. Geddes encourages his clients to use their motivation to get well, to lead a healthy life, and to believe in something that will maintain their connection to universal forces. He remarked, " In spiritual counseling, I can help people find these goals but cannot provide goals for them." Geddes will work with people who hold various belief systems. Unlike some healers, he does not ask clients, "What did you do to bring on your disease?" He refers to this question as an example of "holistic health overkill" and observes that it often produces confusion and guilt rather than positive attitudes.

The *rights and duties of families* are important to Sandford; the family needs to be kept in contact with the client and, optimally, would become part of the healing process. He asks God to "send His angels to encamp about every member of the family." Sandford claims that in the family alone can the client receive the nurturance that will bring their spirit into the fullness of life. Geddes believes that the family can be a supportive network but does not feel that families have the automatic right to be given all the information obtained from the ill person. The family system may be "therapeutic or toxic," and involvement in healing will depend on the amount of loving concern or "toxicity" the family exhibits toward the person seeking help.

The *rights and duties of society*, according to Sandford, include school prayer, anti-abortion laws, anti-pornography measures, and hostility toward cults. Geddes told Welch,

The way a society deals with ill people reflects the

belief systems of that society. Westerners live in technological societies, thus their medicine is technological.

However, he believes that society should allow a variety of medical care systems to prosper, and would like equal opportunities for medical care to be publicly supported. Geddes sees little commitment of the American government, clergy, or public for medical attention to poor people.

The *goal* of Sandford's model of spiritual healing is to empower the person "to choose life." Practitioners should pray for each client's spirit to be cleansed and awakened, and to "find its roots in the fear of God" even though each person will have to fight his or her own battle. Geddes remarked, "I participate in the healing process but am not responsible for it; I can facilitate healing but cannot cure because it is God who heals." His goal is to "connect" symbolically and personally those persons seeking help, and in that bonding to turn them over to God, giving them a sense that they are not alone in the universe.

Both Sandford and Geddes see "joyful living" as a goal of their model of healing. However, Sandford refers to the "salvation" and "resurrection" to a new life promulgated by his "healing ministry," while Geddes believes that healing emerges from a person's "connection" and "union" with God. Despite some crucial differences, both these members of the clergy see themselves as theological moderates. Sandford recalls that he once berated a Christian minister who told his congregation that anyone connected with psychology was filled with demons! Both Sandford and Geddes would like to see Christian churches take a more active role in fostering and restoring the physical and mental health of those people who find church worship a meaningful activity.

There are healers in any number of religious centers in North America. Solomon Friedlander, a well-known healer, was head rabbi of the Hasidic Lisker Congregation in New

York City, while another New Yorker, Abraham Weisman, is both a rabbi and a cantor. On the Caribbean island of St. Kitts, religious congregations that attempt to alter their conscious-ness for healing purposes are called "sideways churches." The "Spiritual Baptists" of Trinidad share the penchant for cer-emonial healings of the competing Afro-Christian sects. The Eastern Orthodox tradition espouses a "sacrament of heal-ing," and encourages the education of "clergy-physicians," although they are few in number because of the length of professional training required. Seventh-Day Adventists have established a large number of hospitals and have reversed a 19th century ban on medicinal drugs. Jehova's Witnesses, however, retain a ban on blood transfusions in their medical clinics and several conservative Protestant sects as well as the Roman Catholic church will not permit abortions in their hospitals. Considerable freedom of options regarding spiri-tual healing and medical practice is given by Unitarian Uni-versalists (Numbers and Amundsen, 1986).

A Group Healing Ministry

In 1988 one of us (Krippner) interviewed Jean Tiller, a member of the "healing ministry" of the Episcopal Church's Trinity Parish in Menlo Park, California. Certified during a church service with four other members of the Episcopal or Unity church, Tiller's group now sees "healees" once a week, generally on Mondays. There is no charge for the healing sessions.

Potential clients phone the church office to make an appointment, then are sent a brochure so that they know what to expect. The healing group arrives at 9:00 AM on Monday morning and spends 45 minutes in prayer and meditation. Each healee is greeted by that month's group leader who introduces other members of the circle. The healee is in-vited—but not forced—to state the reason they have come for the healing session. The procedure is explained, and the healee reclines on a comfortable couch for about 30 minutes. The group leader prays to "the Eternal Thou" for guidance; the group members look at the healee "with soft eyes," saying their name along with the healee's name "until resonance is attained." Tiller stated,

> When we feel resonance, we close our eyes in a spirit of non-judgmental, unconditional love. We ask for two identical symbols—one for the healer and one for the healee. We call upon Christ to do the healing and we merge the two symbols into one.

There is an exception: the merging process is not attempted if the healee is experiencing deep emotional problems.

After ten minutes of silence, the group leader initiates a three- to five-minute "laying-on" of hands, praying, "We 'lay-hands' on you in the name of the Christ, asking Him to uphold you and fill you with His grace that you may know the healing power of His love." The healee is left with one member of the group as soft recorded music is played. Other group members share their symbology, then return, inviting the healee to share his or her experiences. After being encouraged to relax for the rest of the day and to return for two more sessions, the healee is given warm embraces from the group members and departs. The healee's name is entered on a list for three weeks of daily prayers.

Tiller recalled one client, a woman in her 60s, whose hip was in pain prior to surgery. During the healing session, Tiller's images were of two young, healthy women loosening the earth with trowels, prior to planting. They found a boulder under the surface and did everything they could to move the boulder. After calling upon Christ to assist them, the two figures merged into one; Christ placed his hand upon the boulder and it shattered. Christ and the merged female figure removed the pieces of the boulder, knelt, and placed two small plants in the earth. Christ stood up, moved his hand, and the plants grew rapidly, bursting into vividly-colored flowers. With the fragments of the rock, the two figures built a circular well which soon was filled with water. This process of evoking images resembles the shamanic utilization of imagination in healing, a tradition that has continued in various forms and still is an important aspect of contemporary healing.

Brother Jesse and the Rev. Martinez

A similar decision to work within the church structure also was made by Brother J. Jesse Gutierrez, trained and ordained as a Roman Catholic clinical pastoral minister. Since 1973, Brother Jesse has directed Home Again, a community of counselors, educators, and business executives who serve people who feel alienated from institutions, society, or their family. Among its services are a shelter for adolescents seeking new directions in their lives, meal services for hungry people, and crisis intervention for distraught individuals. The son of a curandera, Brother Jesse was interviewed by one of us (Krippner) in 1987.

Jesse holds healing services every Sunday morning, and makes "prayers of petition" on behalf of members of his congregation who request help for themselves or others. Brother Jesse's model of healing holds that Jesus Christ is the Great Healer, and he ends his prayers with the phrase, "...if this be Thy will." In other words, Jesse assumes that Jesus *can* perform a healing, but places his trust in God that the healing must fit into the Divine Plan before it will come to pass. It is also inherent to Jesse's model that he has no healing power himself. He stated, "If a healing occurs, the credit belongs to God." Further, he believes that he, as well as his clients, benefit from the healing session. During the week, Jesse sees clients privately, noting, "When you attempt healing with a client, you really are healing yourself."

In recent years, much of Jesse's time has been spent with

victims of complications arising from AIDS. He has organized a support group for AIDS patients, attempting to ease their suffering and enabling them to find meaning in their lives. He can not "cure" these patients, but he can provide "healing," helping them to appreciate their remaining time on earth, and to die with dignity "in the arms of Jesus Christ." Jesse believes that "life-threatening illness can be looked upon as a rare gift. Many of my AIDS patients tell me that they were able to grow spiritually to such an extent that they no longer fear death."

Jesse also holds healing retreats for people who have tested positive for HIV but who have not developed AIDS-related diseases. These retreats bring clients together with healers, bodyworkers, nutritionists, and psychotherapists who work intensively together as a loving community. Dance, song, and ritual are integral parts of these gatherings. In addition, Jesse sees several dozen clients with AIDS-related diseases, attempting to counsel them toward "wholeness, resolution, and completion."

An eclectic healing tradition is represented by Rev. Joseph Martinez (interviewed by Krippner in 1988), a practitioner of yoga and an instructor in the Integral Yoga of Sri Aurobindo. Born in the Philippines and a former Christian monk, Martinez is the founder and director of the Spiritual Healing Center in San Francisco, where he integrates yoga with Christian and esoteric teachings. Martinez performs marriages, baptisms, and funerals, and directs a ministerial program as well as a class for healers.

Martinez' model of healing holds that there are "subtle energies" in the body that can be removed through one or more of the two dozen techniques that he practices and teaches. Among these techniques are "aura cleaning," "chakra cleansing," "color healing," "creative visualization," "magnetic healing," "polarity," and "Christ Light healing"; however, the emphasis is placed upon "self-healing and self-help" because Martinez believes that the client's consciousness plays a key role in any improvement that occurs.

For Martinez, the "laying-on" of hands was the method practiced by Jesus and his disciples; it represents the channeling of power from God. The healer "lays-on" hands while concentrating on the "divine energies" that he or she seeks to transmit. Another healing method closely related to the Christian tradition is "praying in tongues." A group of healers gathers around the client and they begin to pray together, using utterances that do not belong in any known language. This type of prayer is thought to unite a group of healers in a common purpose. A third type of Christian healing is simply calling on the name of Jesus Christ or of the Holy Spirit, thus becoming a "channel" for healing power.

Martinez recommends that his clients continue to see their physician and that any cessation of symptoms be validated with standard medical procedures. For example, a client may feel a release from pain due to the temporary euphoria that sometimes accompanies a novel treatment procedure. But if the pain is due to an inflamed appendix, it should be interpreted as a warning sign rather than as an unnecessary symptom. Indeed, a client who stopped seeing his or her physician after the pain disappeared might be at risk for an attack of appendicitis.

Martinez teaches meditation, observing that the student will experience various insights and, possibly, "an opening of the heart center." He remarked,

> One of the major experiences possible in the heart center is realizing the Conscious Being of God as Love itself. As the individual experiences this, there is no longer any separation between the experience of love and the very existence of love.

Martinez believes that the most intense form of spiritual healing occurs when "the healer and the sufferer unite together with the power of God." This belief resembles those of other healers who believe in various types of "union" that can span distances through the medium of unselfish benevolence and non-possessive love.

Brother Willard, Sister Amelia, and Psychic Dentistry

It is not unusual for the personal characteristics of the practitioner and the expectancies of the client to create a powerful placebo effect that can change moods or decrease pain. This effect, conceivably, can enhance performance, stop tumor growth, or restore health on either a short-term or long-term basis. But the placebo effect has its limits; it has never been credited with the growth or alteration of bones or teeth. Therefore, the claims of Brother Willard Fuller and his wife Amelia must be considered among the most outrageous in the field of spiritual healing.

A typical healing service will include an inspirational sermon by Brother Willard accompanied by the pleasant singing of Sister Amelia. People with dental problems are then invited to form a line; Willard places his hands on both sides of their face, calling upon Jesus to "make this person whole." Invariably, several members of the audience will claim to have new teeth or at least new gold or porcelain fillings. Willard's ministerial degree is from Southern Baptist Theological Seminary but he became a Pentacostalist when he began to "speak in tongues" and felt a call to "see teeth filled by the power of God." Located in Jacksonville, Florida, the Fullers do not advise people to avoid dentists; in fact, Willard has several silver fillings himself and Amelia freely admits that she has had dental care (St. Clair, 1974).

In 1982, one of us (Krippner) attended a healing session in Morristown, New Jersey, featuring Brother Willard and Sister Amelia. Following a sermon, Willard began to "lay hands" on those members of the audience requesting assistance. Equipped with a penlight and a dental mirror, Willard and Amelia inspected each client's mouth, noting when they observed a gold filling. One out of every three persons claimed that there was gold where there was only silver or a decaying tooth before. In Krippner's case, he was surprised to discover that he now had a gold filling. But upon returning to California, he checked his dental records and discovered that his gold filling had been there all along, even though he had forgotten about it. One can only surmise how many other cases of "sudden gold" could be explained in the same way.

Fuller's detractors are not satisfied with so benign an explanation, claiming that he uses sleight of hand, that the penlight he uses has a yellow glow (making silver fillings appear gold), that it is unsanitary for him to probe people's mouths without washing his hands between clients, and that he caters to "dental phobics" who will avoid receiving dental care under almost any circumstance. Although articles about his work in the popular press attest to his successes, one investigator claims that Fuller declined to forward records of a case in which a woman supposedly regrew an entire new set of teeth following Willard's "laying-on" of hands (Randi, 1987).

In the meantime, the Fullers attribute their alchemy to "the right relationship with God"; when this relationship is correct, they can even perform "distant healing." This alleged phenomenon would be fairly simple—and cost effective—for investigators to study while Brother Willard is still engaging in an active healing ministry. Both his supporters and his detractors could obtain dental records of volunteer clients, take them to the Fullers' healing session, and obtain subsequent dental reports. Whether the results support or refute the Fullers' claims, they would demonstrate the willingness of both skeptics and advocates to put their claims—and well as those made by the Fullers—to the test.

A Shango Priest in Trinidad

In 1989, one of us (Krippner) visited Trinidad and Tobago, obtaining an interview with Aldwin J. Scott, who lives in Basto Hall near San Fernando in west-central Trinidad. At that time, Scott was serving as president of the nation's Shango Belief System, an organization that includes male and female "orisha" priests and priestesses. There is a similar orisha organization, the Orisha Movement, that also originated in West Africa and was brought across the Atlantic Ocean by the slaves. Orishas are believed to be spiritual entities who came into the world at its beginning and who have put themselves at the disposal of human beings in such undertakings as farming, hunting, crafts, divination, and healing. There is an "orisha house" (or shrine) in every part of the island, probably numbering about 150. These shrines usually have a patron orisha such as Ogun (god of thunder and patron of the blacksmiths), Oshun (goddess of the rivers), Obatala (the lord of purity), Shango (god of justice and the patron of the entire Trinidad and Tobago nation), and dozens of others, most of whom originated among Yoruba tribespeople from West Africa (Ward, 1979-1980).

Aldwin J. Scott has been a full-time healer since 1983, and includes Hindu and Christian saints in his panoply of teachers and spirits. He told Krippner, "The orisha movement is an open system that respects and accepts any worthwhile spiritual belief." Scott observed that some of his colleagues are students of the Kaballah, a system of mystical doctrines associated with Judaism. Scott is a member of the Spiritual Baptist Movement, a group once banned because of its boisterous public ceremonies and supposedly heretical teachings—as well as an implicit anti-African bias. This bias was also directed against the orisha groups, and even included a ban on the beating of drums! The position was taken that residents of Trinidad and Tobago should adhere to European versions of Christianity, and that African influences were corrupting these practices. These prohibitions have now been relaxed and Scott practices openly.

Scott described his functions as those of "a healer, psychiatrist, psychologist, and seer." The goal of his treatment is "balance," and he sees his own "balance" being constantly renewed by the interplay of his activities as both a Spiritual Baptist and an orisha priest. People from all walks of life and from various religious backgrounds (including "born-again" Christians) come to Scott for spiritual work.

Some clients meet with Scott because they claim they are having a spiritual crisis, but he usually finds that they are suffering from psychological problems as well. For example, their family life might be at risk or an intimate relationship might be heading for trouble. To be of service, Scott depends upon his intuitive faculties, "bridging the conscious and the unconscious." Scott pays close attention to his dreams, because during his adolescence he had a dream in which he was "called" to orisha worship. During his baptism he "entered into a new realm of consciousness" and by the age of 18 he was both a Spiritual Baptist and a follower of the orishas.

Altered Conscious States

Incorporation of orishas by Shango priests and priestesses depends on whether the situation warrants it. According to Scott, the practitioner can be in contact with a spiritual entity while talking to a third party. On other occasions, the entity can take possession and one is aware of what is transpiring but acts and speaks as directed. Finally, there are times of "full possession" when one is completely "out of oneself" and has no knowledge of what is taking place. The manifesting orisha depends on the circumstances and the practitioner. Obatala, for example, only manifests with persons who have a "certain spiritual purity."

During periods of mourning, Scott (and other Spiritual Baptist priests or priestesses—also called "mothers") may supervise a "spiritual travel" carried out by the bereaved person. The priest or "mother" is referred to as a "pointer" and determines the procedure to be followed. In general a 7-day (or longer) period of mourning is arranged during which the mourner fasts, is blindfolded, and lives in seclusion. In some cases, no food at all is taken, but in others—depending on the mourner's health—small amounts of herbal tea, milk, or water might be made available.

Krippner observed that these conditions are ideal for sensory deprivation and the evocation of mental imagery. And it is during these spiritual travels that the mourner obtains his or her instructions as to how to honor the memory of the deceased as well as the next direction of his or her spiritual development. For example, the bereaved person might be directed toward orisha worship or Kaballah study. Scott remarked, "What you see with the spiritual eye when you travel is different than what you are used to seeing with the physical eye." Many of Scott's colleagues pay attention to the colors that should be worn while travelling, and some of them insist that the mourner stay away from black. Scott told Krippner, "This is sheer rubbish; any color will work as long as you believe it will work."

Scott told Krippner that he once engaged in spiritual travelling himself during a period of mourning, entering into King Solomon's Temple where he encountered the scents and smells of herbs and oils of which he had no previous knowledge. During another period of spiritual travelling, he went to the Valley of Asher, observing the preparation of sacred milk and honey just as it had been described in the Old Testament.

Scott told Krippner that his first encounter with the spirit world occurred when he was about 8 years of age and visited a cemetery with some friends. On leaving the cemetery, he felt that he was being beaten with a whip. Although Scott could hear the crack of the whip, he could see nothing. Welts appeared on his arms and legs, he became ill, and had to be treated by a spiritual healer. From about the age of 12, Scott could "hear voices" giving him spiritual instructions. He astonished friends by telling them about themselves, pretending to read his palms. He did "spiritual favors" for his friends by keeping them from losing money at gambling, even though he never gambled himself.

Etiology, Diagnosis, and Treatment

Scott, who requests only a free will offering for his work, suspects that about one third of sickness is primarily physical in origin, about one third is psychological, and about one third is spiritual. Even so, psychological problems are likely to accompany both physical and spiritual dysfunctions. When there is a spiritual problem, a person might have been victimized by an evil spirit which has entered someone's body. Indeed, some of Scott's clients claim to have been "hexed" through sorcery by a possessive lover, a business competitor, or a jealous neighbor. Scott's client might complain, "I've done nothing wrong, so why am I suffering?" Scott replies that the lower spirits have no respect for people and will attempt to take energy from anyone who is available.

These lower spirits need to be exorcised through herbal baths, oils, prayers, or rituals. Some clients become convinced that the exorcised spirits are trapped in the empty herbal medicine or oil bottles, but Scott regards this belief in the same way as he would "the fairy tales of the genies."

Scott is a skilled masseur and often uses massage as a healing technique, especially for sprains, strains, and dislocated joints. He may also prescribe herbal baths or oils for various ailments. Sometimes a client's indisposition is seen as a "call" from spiritual entities for that person to enter religious training. If so, the client might be directed to become a Kaballah medium and begin to incorporate spirits during the banquets held to honor the Kaballah entities.

Scott used to incorporate orishas, especially during the annual orisha feast, but these experiences declined in frequency and intensity as he grew older. Some participants enter into altered states of consciousness during the orisha feasts, in part because of the drumming. Three drums are used during these feasts—a high range drum and a low range drum to provide the rhythm and the lead drum played by the most skilled of the drummers, to provide the syncopation.

Goats, sheep, cocks, hens, ducks, turtles, and even bulls may be sacrificed to honor the entities during the annual orisha feasts. When a sacrifice is made to Shango, the blood is carefully collected and disposed of in a particular manner. During a healing session, a hen or cock might be sacrificed on behalf of the client. The term "obeah man" is often used to refer to a healer or exorcist in Trinidad and Tobago. The word, meaning "magic" or "help," was brought to the Caribbean by the African slaves and used in a derogatory manner by the slavemasters and Catholic priests to link African practices with evil. But it is now used to refer to a person engaged in spiritual work, particularly among the Spiritual Baptists and followers of the orishas. A Hindu healer may also be referred to as an "obeah man."

When Krippner left Scott's home, he observed 17 banners flying in the breeze, each of them honoring a different orisha. He also reflected on the arbitrariness of practitioner categories. Scott officiates during regular religious services, hence he is a priest. But his previous incorporation of orisha entities resembles the activities of mediums. It must be kept in mind that Winkelman's categories were constructed from archival records of native societies; to apply them rigidly to contemporary societies is neither a tenable or useful practice. In any event, Scott's renown in Trinidad and Tobago has brought a succession of anthropologists and other investigators to his door, eager to learn more about the way that an African tradition has been preserved and adapted in the New World.

Healing Shrines

Francis MacNutt, a Roman Catholic priest and a spiritual healer himself, has explored reasons for the appeal of healing shrines to members of his faith. He believes that when priests, in general, stopped practicing the "laying-on" of hands in churches, many people began praying to the saints for cures.

The Chicago Shrine of St. Jude, Patron of the Impossible, is a popular site for visits; thousands of people claim that St. Jude has answered their prayers and improved their health or that of their loved ones. MacNutt (1977) believes that the healing ministry of the church was preserved through these shrines.

Jerome Frank observes that Christianity, from its inception, has included the notion of healing through divine intervention. Healing shrines, for Frank, contain rituals that parallel religious healing in native societies. Both involve a climactic union with patients, their families, the larger community, and the spiritual world. This is accomplished by means of a dramatic, emotionally charged, esthetically rich ritual that expresses and reinforces a shared ideology. Intense emotional arousal, occurring in a setting of hopelessness and progressive isolation of patients from their usual sources of support, may contribute to their death. If the same arousal is experienced "in a setting of massive human and supernatural encouragement so that it carries a context of hope, it can be healing" (Frank, 1973). Indeed, a few research studies attest to at least temporary relief obtained by persons attending charismatic Christian healing ceremonies (Frank and Frank, 1991).

In 1986, we interviewed Pamela Biele, a Canadian psychologist who reported an interesting experience at St. Anne de Beaupre, a Roman Catholic healing shrine in Quebec City, dating back to the 17th century. Biele recalled:

> For eight years I had been suffering from an allergy to wheat. During that time, whenever I ate wheat I would become fatigued and nervous, and would have stomach problems. Because I enjoy eating bread, I had a difficult time staying on a wheat-free diet.
>
> In 1985 I went to Quebec City on a holiday. I was not watching my diet and consequently was feeling extremely tired, experiencing stomach troubles. After a week in Quebec City, I went to St.

Anne de Beaupre with my family and two friends. We all wandered off in separate directions soon after we entered the church. After about ten minutes of wandering around, I saw a column near the left front of the church. I walked toward it and noticed people kneeling around it and praying. I decided to kneel down and read the prayer that was hanging from the column. It was a prayer for healing to St. Anne. I remember thinking about all the people that must have come to this church hoping for a cure. I was an observer that day, not feeling particularly religious or pensive. I never thought to ask for healing. I am usually doubtful that miraculous healings take place.

Suddenly, after I was kneeling there for about five minutes, I felt a pressure on my head. It slowly become stronger and stronger, pushing me down into the kneeling bench. I thought it was my imagination. I stayed there, fascinated by the sensation. My fascination soon turned to anxiety as the sensation intensified. I was afraid to stay and see what would happen, so I decided to leave. Even though the pressure was strong from above, it was easy to get up and leave.

I walked around the church, trying to figure out what had happened. I thought that there must be a logical explanation for the sensation. After about ten minutes, I thought I would go back to the spot and see if the pressure would return. I realized that now my expectation alone could bring back the feeling. I decided to go back anyway. To my surprise, about 20 feet from the column, I felt myself being pulled toward it. The pull became stronger the closer I came to the column. I knelt down and immediately felt the pressure from above. The only way I can describe the sensation is that it was like the pressure one sometimes feels on an airplane. I stayed there about five minutes. The pressure became too strong, and I became frightened.

I found my family and friends, and told them the story. We were all perplexed. However, my husband mentioned that he felt that he was being pulled higher and higher when he knelt by the column. He became uneasy and left the spot. He was too afraid to go back. Later, in the car on the way home, I fell asleep. Falling asleep in a car is unusual for me. But that day, after the church experience, my eyes felt very heavy.

That evening, and for the rest of the trip, I found that I was able to eat wheat! Earlier that day, before the experience, my stomach was acting up as usual. Afterwards, my stomach felt perfectly fine and I could eat anything I desired. I was able to eat wheat for the rest of the summer. Towards the end of the summer, I decided to really test what had occurred, and I ate a large amount of bread for two days. I became slightly fatigued, but I still had no stomach complaints.

One year later, the only feeling I have after eating lots of bread or other wheat products, is a slight tiredness. My stomach has not given me trouble since my trip to Quebec City.

Biele's experience does not match the typical account of a spontaneous recovery from an illness at a shrine. She did not consciously prepare for a healing, she offered no prayers except for the one she read silently, and she was not aware of any expectation when she entered the church. Reportedly, Biele had experienced no severe allergic reaction to wheat up to the time when we saw her. If the report is accurate and if the recovery is not coincidental, one could conjecture on the mechanisms involved. Perhaps a parsimonious explanation of the incident would be that there was a strong unconscious desire to overcome the allergy, a motive that was galvanized by the visit to the shrine.

Spiritual Values

Whether spiritual healing is accomplished in the presence of a priest or a shrine, it may well be the alternative healing phenomenon most easily observed by most North Americans. Television stations regularly feature "healing sessions"; most communities have a Christian Science, New Thought, or Pentecostal Church; a growing number of mainline denominations are holding healing services in the sanctuary. However, with such a plethora of practitioners, the opportunity for fraud and disappointment exists side-by-side with the chance of relief (English-Lueck, 1990). But there is a positive result as well; serious researchers have a splendid opportunity to investigate the sociology and anthropology of religiously-oriented healing services without locating tribal people, learning a native language, or adapting to difficult living conditions.

At the same time, it should be remembered that institutionalized religion has failed to meet the spiritual needs of many people. Our definition of spirituality links it with the presence or absence of an individual's focus on higher, broader, and deeper life meanings that transcend ordinary existence. David Elkins, a psychologist, has proposed a similar definition; for him, spirituality is "a way of being and experiencing that comes about through awareness of a transcendent dimension that is characterized by certain identifiable values in regard to self, others, nature, life, and whatever one considers to be the Ultimate." These "identifiable values" of spirituality, according to Elkins (1990), include:

1. *A transcendent dimension.* This value may range from a belief in a personal God to a belief in a "greater self." In either case, the spiritual person believes in "something more" and draws personal power from this realm.

2. *Meaning in life.* The spiritual person values a quest for meaning and is confident that his or her life has purpose. While the content of that "purpose" may vary, each spiritual individual has filled the "existential vacuum" with an authentic sense of meaning.

3. *Mission in life.* The spiritual person has a sense of purpose and vocation. It may be a "call" to answer, a "mission" to accomplish, or a "destiny" to fulfill.

4. *Sacredness of life.* The spiritual person does not divide living into the sacred and the secular; he or she is able to sacralize all personal experience, social experience, and experience with nature, filling his or her days with awe and reverence.

5. *Ultimate satisfaction.* Spiritual individuals can appreciate material possessions and objects but do not seek fundamental satisfaction from them. They know that ultimate fulfillment is found in spiritual values, and that all else is illusory.

6. *Altruism.* Spiritual people are moved to respond to the needs of others; they know that "no person is an island" and that everyone partakes of a common humanity.

7. *Idealism.* Spiritual people are committed to the betterment of the world through prayer, meditation, acts of charity, and/or social activism. They see the potential of people, of societies, and of the planet.

8. *Realism.* Spiritual individuals are aware of such tragic realities of human existence as suffering, pain, and death. This knowledge deepens their appreciation of life and stiffens their commitment to "make a difference" in the world.

9. *Fruits of Spirituality.* Spiritual persons are those whose spiritual attitudes, beliefs, and activities have borne fruit. Their compassion, courage, joy, and devotion have a positive effect upon their relationships with other people, with nature, with themselves, and with whatever they consider to be the ultimate and transcendent reality.

We would agree with Elkins' thoughtful listing and would add a tenth value, that of healing. The spiritual person may not be a shaman, member of the clergy, or health practitioner. Yet spirituality has a healing quality that makes its emissary a pleasure to be near, a privilege to have as a friend, and an empowering resource in a relationship.

Elkins and his students have conducted a nationwide survey of American psychologists, finding that 66% of their respondents rated spirituality as "very important" or "important" in their lives; yet 64% answered "none" when asked how many religious services they attended per month. Nevertheless, 65% of their sample had incorporated at least one spiritual practice into their lives, and 50% claimed to have had at least one "mystical experience."

Two other investigators, Dorothy Ley and Inge Corliss, describe spirituality as manifesting itself "as a state of connectedness to God, to one's neighbor, to one's inner self. It [is the] capacity to be energized from beyond ourselves" (Reed, 1990). Organized religion needs to examine its assumptions and practices to determine if it can do more to meet the spiritual needs of human beings of this era in history. It is apparent that there are spiritual dimensions to healing, to working, to playing, to loving, and to living that are not being addressed by most institutions in contemporary industrialized societies.

Patrick Welch and Stanley Krippner holding the German language edition of *Spiritual Dimensions of Healing*.

Michael
Winkelman

Rolling Thunder and Friend *(Photo courtesy of Frank Fried)*

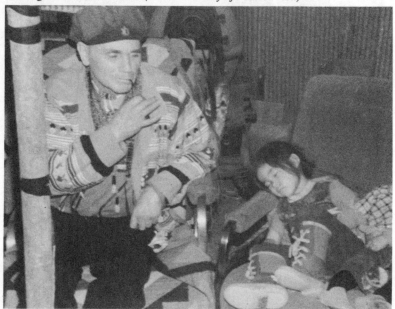

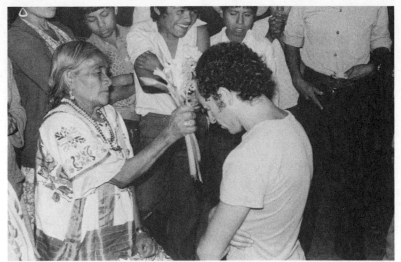

Maria Sabinea administering a floral "cleansing," Mexico.
(Photo courtesy of Bonnie Colodzin)

Mickey Hart (of the Grateful Dead rock band), Rolling Thunder,
and Stanley Krippner *(Photo courtesty of Frank Fried)*

Nicki Scully

Graywolf
(Right)

Leslie Gray
(Photo courtesy of Timothy White © 1987 Shaman's Drum)

Michael Harner *(Photo courtesy of Elvira Berndorff)*

Manuel Velasquez,
Guatemala

Karl Wolfe
(Photo courtesy of Lorin Backe)

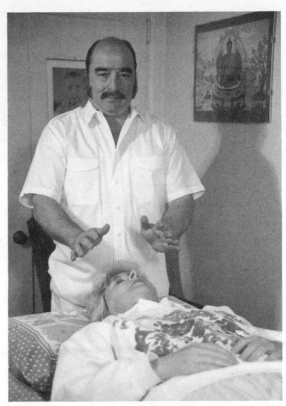

Joseph
Martinez

Jesse Gutierrez leads a healing circle in Mexico.

Mr. and Mrs. Aldwin Scott, Trinidad and Tobago

Three drums are used in voodoo rites of African derivation, Haiti

A single drum is used in
voodoo rites of Native
American derivation, Haiti

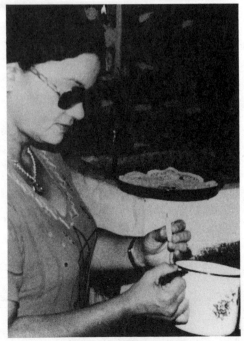

Theresa Roumier, Haiti

Voodoo altar, Haiti

Santeria Shrine, Cuba

Mario Nuñez-Molina, Patrick Welch, Señor and Señora Felix Rodrigues, and assistant, Puerto Rico.

Entrance to Santeria
Center, Cuba

Selena Fox harvesting healing herbs *(Photo courtesy of Lynnie Johnston)*

Multi-cultural Planetary Healing Ritual at Circle Sanctuary
(Photo courtesty of Lynnie Johnston)

Seven

Mediums And Spiritists

Renee Haynes, as editor of Great Britain's *Journal of the Society of Psychical Research*, attempted to differentiate between "faith healing" and "psychic healing." Haynes (1977) observed that both types of healing involve relief from an ailment, independent of medical treatment, in ways not yet fully understood by science. However, "faith healing" appears to represent an interaction between one's deeply-held beliefs and one's physiological processes. "Psychic healing," according to Haynes, appears to be based on an interaction between the healer and the client's body. "Faith healing" is initiated and sustained by "an overwhelming trust, conscious and unconscious, in the power of the healer," but "psychic healing" seems to stimulate the client's physiology directly, whether the healer uses words, gestures, or both. Haynes admitted that there is an overlap between the two types of healing in practice, but insisted that the terms should be differentiated in principle to help investigators determine if their effects were different.

We appreciate Haynes' distinctions and believe that they serve a useful purpose. We would suggest that "faith healing" can involve a deity or shrine as well as a "faith healer." In addition, we see "faith healing" and "psychic healing" as two labels used to describe particular types of "spiritual healing" that are purportedly anomalous in nature in that their methods of operation do not appear to be consistent with science's current concepts of time, space, and energy. Some observers take the position that these reports are not anomalous at all and that both "faith healing" and "psychic healing" can be explained in terms of the body's remarkable self-regulating properties, the power of suggestion, the existence of psychosomatic ailments that can respond quickly to dramatic intervention, incorrect or incomplete reporting on the part of clients, or deliberate fraud on the part of healers.

Other observers admit that anomalous healing is possible, but warn that much of it may be the work of demonic forces. One writer claims that "miracles" are the work of God, but "psychic phenomena" are works of the devil. "Psychic phenomena have been the means of drawing man into a mind trap" and "psychic power counterfeits not only the Holy Spirit's gifts to the church, but God's very qualities—omnipotence, omnipresence, and omniscience" (Hunt, 1980). Special censure is given to mediums and other practitioners who contact alleged spirits of the dead because such procedures are "forbidden in the Bible". Two other writers attribute psychic healing to demons, insisting that an increasing number of physicians and nurses "are being swayed by psychic philosophies and practices, due largely to the influence of parapsychology, psychic healing, and the holistic health movement....To be a Christian parapsychologist is to be a Christian occultist, which is forbidden" (Weldon and Levitt, 1982). Another writer is especially suspicious of mediums, observing "there is a beautiful side of evil—deceptive, subtle, adorned with all manner of spiritual refinements, but no less from the pit of hell than that which is blatantly demonic." Her advice is to "collect every book or object related to occultism in your possession and destroy them" (Michaelsen, 1982).

Mediums, like shamans, alter their consciousness but,

unlike shamans, they usually are not socially sanctioned, and work primarily with individuals rather than on behalf of the entire community. Winkelman observed that as the functions of shamans became less important in complex societies, people's contact with spirits changed from a community function to private acts and small group meetings. Whereas shamans typically controlled the spirits and easily recalled their encounter with the "other world," mediums were controlled by the spirits and typically claimed not to be able to remember the event. Mediums tended to be females in the cultures Winkelman investigated, and demonstrated little of the political and economic power held by shamans and priests. There are inevitable overlaps among these categories; the Rev. Martinez, whom we have classified among the "priests," claims to be a "channel" for ten spirit physicians who work with him during his healing sessions. It should also be noted that there are several brain syndromes whose mental consequences could easily facilitate experiences of "channeling" (Beyerstein, 1988). Hence, there are alternative explanations to those put forward by practitioners who speak of "spirit guides" that temporarily encase themselves in a human body (Ness and Wintrob, 1981).

Voodoo and Hoodoo

Slave traders of the 16th and 17th centuries brought many of their West African captives to North America. These slaves represented many different tribes, but they were all Kwa-speaking and Bantu-speaking people. In addition, they shared similar religious and magical beliefs, among them the notion that lesser deities did the bidding of the Supreme Creator. They manifested themselves as the gods of rivers and mountains, fire and iron, lightning and epidemics, war and peace. Subservient to these deities were the ancestral spirits; their duty was to see that their earthbound descendants carried out the moral precepts handed down to them. West African tribes believed that human behavior was predetermined, but that occasionally another force, the "divine trickster," would subvert the master plan.

Deities and ancestral spirits visited the living in dreams or through a medium who served as intermediary. One anthropologist studied about 500 societies around the world, discovering that spirit possession was common in 52% of them (Bourguinon, 1976). Incorporating a discarnate entity was the supreme religious experience in West African religion. Coincidentally, the heirarchy of the West African religions resembled the pantheon of Roman Catholic saints; the church's icons, rosary beads, rituals, festivals, and holy communion had their counterparts in the slaves' experience. Practitioners of religion and magic from West Africa were quick to see the correspondences; for example, Legba, the god of entrances in Dahomey (now the nation of Benin), became Saint Peter, keeper of the keys. In one of the West African languages, the word for "divinity" was "vodoun," and "voodoo" became an amalgamation of African, European, and Native American religions in what today are the American states of Louisiana and South Carolina, and the Republic of Haiti (Haskins, 1978).

One of us (Krippner) visited the Voodoo Museum in New Orleans, Louisiana, in 1982, and discussed current manifestations of the tradition with its staff. He was told that "hoodoo" is a more generalized term than "voodoo" in Louisiana and South Carolina, and is applied to magical practices, superstitions, and herbal remedies for various types of physical illnesses and psychological complaints. Among the West African slaves were shamanic healers, who brought with them their knowledge of herbal remedies, and sorcerers, who brought along their practice of magical curses, hexes, and spells.

Krippner was given a "gris-gris," or medicine bag, by a museum attendant. The name for these voodoo pouches comes from the French for "gray-gray" because they are usually used for both benign white magic and malevolent black magic (Doyle, 1990). Krippner's gris-gris bag, purportedly designed to protect him from negative influences and to ensure good health, contained a shell, dried herbs, bone fragments, and other elements from nature. The pouch was sewed from red fabric, red being a favorite color of the spirits. Gris-gris bags were (and are) available for all situations—to assure success in love or business, to cure snakebites, to win court cases, to provide luck for gamblers, and even to help preachers stay in the good graces of their congregations (even though the same preachers might denounce voodoo from their pulpits).

In 1980, one of us (Krippner) visited Port-au-Prince, Haiti, to meet several voodoo mediums and observe their rituals. Krippner was a member of an eight-person group whose guide was Therese Roumer, a well-known "mambo" (a voodoo medium). Roumer's fiance had died suddenly, and the group was invited to attend the "dessounin" or funeral ritual. The setting was a "peristyle," or voodoo temple. The mambos, "houngans" (male mediums), and their apprentices, the "hounsis," were all costumed in white garments. They announced that they were ready to be "mounted" by the "loa" (deities and spirits); in this way, the mediums could pay their respects to the "espirit" (soul) of the deceased man. An elaborate "vever," or drawing, was traced on the dirt floor with white flour; the frenzied dancing would later erase the vever, yet its preparation was an important part of the ceremony.

Krippner and his group were allowed to tape record the music, songs, and chants of the dessounin up to the time when a special drum beat called upon the loa to "mount" the mediums. As each loa took its turn entering the mediums' bodies, characteristic gestures and movements announced its appearance. The deceased man's "lagu" (ceremonial food) had been placed around the room for his soul to enjoy, and would be buried toward the end of the ceremony. At about the same time, a gourd was broken; after examining the pieces, the mambos and houngans determined that the soul of the deceased had left its body and had begun its travel to the Lower World. After a year and a day in those realms, the soul could become a minor loa, returning to the earth to give advice and comfort to the "naga" (living humans). It was important that people continued to venerate the loa, because neglect would cause the loa to disappear. Without them, the world would lose its "espirit" and nature would revert to a mechanistic, amoral state. Voodoo is unusual among North American religions in that people are dependent on the deities, but the loa are also dependent on the naga.

Krippner and his group attended a ceremony in the "hounfer" (community house) of Andre Pierre, a well-known Haitian artist. His colorful paintings depict such loa as Damballah, the loa of the heavens (whose vever is a serpent in a field of crosses), and Ghede, the loa of sex and of death (whose vever is a coffin and a cross). Each loa has an African name and an American Indian name; in the latter tradition, Damballah is Dan Petro while Ghede is Baron Samedi. Pierre is also a houngan, and led the group in a libation to the loa, spilling a few drops of an alcoholic beverage on the floor in obeisance to their presence.

Roumer held a third ceremony in her home, which also serves as a hounfer. This ritual was called an "illumination," and began with the prayer, "May there be light everywhere in all the world for everyone." Dozens of candles were lit, and a painting of Erzulie, the loa of love, presided over the proceedings. Each member of the group wrote out a question and was told that he or she might have a dream that would provide an answer. In Krippner's case, the question concerned the best way to publicize a book he had recently written. A few hours later, Krippner dreamed that the publisher would not publicize the book and that he would have to take the responsibility himself—a situation which proved to reflect reality once Krippner returned to the United States.

The major function of the mambo and houngan is medicinal. Nanan-bouclou is the loa of herbs and is called upon when a diagnosis is made. The practitioner must determine if the illness is natural or supernatural in origin as this will determine the nature of the treatment. If the etiology is natural, herbs will be prescribed or the client will be sent to a physician (if he or she can afford to pay the fees). If the etiology is supernatural, the practitioner may assign the client individual tasks (sacrifices, prayers), or may bring in the family and/or the community for a healing ritual. For example, if a sorcerer has cast a spell on a client, a "coucher" or purifying sleep may be held at the hounfer to counteract the spell. In some cases, a chicken may be sacrificed and the blood used to purify the client. Various loa may be asked to assist the client's recovery; there is no clear dividing line between the living and the dead as each supports the existence of the other (Deren, 1970).

Spiritism in Puerto Rico

Spiritualism—the practice of alleged communication with spirits of the dead—is not restricted to any one time and place. In the United States, spiritualism is commonly dated from 1848 with the purported development of mediumistic abilities by Margaretta and Catherine Fox in Hydesville, New York. In Latin America, "espiritismo" is commonly translated as "spiritism" to distinguish it from the Spiritualist Church in the United States. In 1986 we visited Puerto Rico, finding that healing practices were the major activity of the five major spiritist movements. "Santeria" had its origin in Africa and came into Puerto Rico by way of what today are the nations of Cuba and Haiti (Sandoval, 1979). In Puerto Rico, there is a small contingent of Santeria practitioners, as well as those who practice "Santerismo," an amalgamation of Santeria with local customs. "Scientific Spiritism" is European in origin, and is based on the writings of Alan Kardec, a French teacher and philosopher. "Trincadismo" is also European in origin but is based on the writings of Joaquim Trincado, a Spanish engineer and philosopher. "Folk Spiritism," the most typically Puerto Rican of the spiritist movements, is a mixture of Native American culture, curanderismo (folk healing), Roman Catholicism, and European spiritism. "Christian Spiritism" is heavily influenced by the charismatic and Pentacostal Christian churches. In fact, *all* the spiritist movements are "mixed" to some extent, borrowing from each other as well as from their antecedents in Africa and Europe. The movement is widespread; it has been estimated that at least 60% of all Puerto Ricans has visited a spiritist center at some time.

All spiritists share a belief in spirits and in mediumistic communication. Spiritists may be nominal Roman Catholics, and even attend Mass and other church functions. However, belief in reincarnation is common among the spiritists; another major difference between spiritism and orthodox Christianity is the importance that it places on direct communication between humans and spirits. This communication sometimes occurs in dreams, but more frequently the spirits speak directly through the mediums who are endowed with special "facultades" (faculties).

Spirits are ranked in terms of their moral perfection, and are conceived of as residing in separate spatial planes. For example, the lowest level is inhabited by the "ignorant spirits" who are bound to earth because of their low spiritual development, because of unfinished obligations (e.g., unpaid debts, love affairs), or because they have died prematurely (e.g., through suicide, violent crimes, or fatal accidents). It is felt that living, incarnate humans need to assist these spirits by "giving light," a practice that may include praying, lighting candles, and offering flowers. If not "given light," these "low" spirits often fall victim to "brujos" (sorcerers) who may manipulate them in harming living people.

We visited a small temple in the western part of the island that typifies Puerto Rico's indigenous folk spiritism. The walls were adorned with pictures of Jesus Christ, American Indian guides, and deceased humans who had reached a high

level of spiritual development. A father and son, Samuel and
Tomas Vilanovas, were the chief mediums in this temple
which was filled to its capacity of 30 worshippers. Tomas
wore a white tunic embroidered with the picture of a pigeon;
this design was directed by a spirit guide as was the design for
a black tunic he wore later in the service. Six members of the
congregation were mediums, including Tomas' mother who,
we were told, had supported her husband when he began his
spiritual quest many decades earlier.

When Tomas attempts to assist a member of his congregation, he looks into a bowl of water, breathes rapidly, and
enters an altered state of consciousness. He often feels a cold
sensation in his neck, then may have an out-of-body experience. The water may contain an image that Tomas can use to
determine what is affecting the client, and whether it has a
physical or spiritual cause. If it is the former, the client may be
referred to a physician, or an herbal treatment may be prescribed. In the case of the latter, it may be divine punishment,
human envy or malevolence, or an intranquil spirit who has
become the tool of a sorcerer. In this instance, Tomas may
attempt "giving light" to the spirit, or assisting its ascent to the
spiritual realm through prayers and offerings. If this does not
work, the medium may attempt persuading the spirit to leave
its victim in peace (i.e., "trabajando la causa," working the
cause). If none of this is effective, a "despojo" or exorcism
may be conducted to forcefully eliminate the offending spirit.
We observed an attempt to remove a low spirit from its victim;
a cigar-smoking medium fumigated the client with tobacco
smoke while shaking him and stroking his body with "magnetic passes." We were given a fragrant perfume to rub on our
skin as protection against the intruding spirit.

Tomas and other mediums attempt to enlist the client's
spirit guides in the healing; if the spirits have abandoned the
client, they will be asked to return. Power objects may be
given the client so that self-healing can be facilitated. Tomas
is of the opinion that most illnesses have a physical as well as

a spiritual cause and makes many suggestions regarding diet and exercise in addition to his work with the spirits. During our stay at the temple, Tomas and Samuel Vilanovas worked with a man who was suffering from pains in his legs and with a medium who claimed to have been "hexed" by an enemy. In the latter instance, all the mediums joined hands around their comrade and told the offending spirit to stop causing the man's leg pains. They believed that their efforts were successful because there was no further evidence of the malevolent spirit and the pain in the medium's leg stopped abruptly. It is believed that stern attitudes and strong admonitions often are the most effective way to deal with offending spirits. Of course, the same set of attitudes would be conducive to the psychosomatic alleviation of pain.

We also interviewed Felix Rodriguez, a medium who practices "Scientific Spiritism" with his clients. Don Felix was "called by the spirits" at the age of nine, was excommunicated by the Roman Catholic church, and rejected by his parents. Don Felix, 78 years of age at the time of our visit, believes that "the mind generates all causes of illness; these causes are in the unconscious and need to be conscious for relief." A common cause is negative thinking; another is a problem from a past life that has not been solved. Don Felix has written a book about his work, claiming that the contents were dictated by the spirits through "automatic writing" (Rodriguez, 1973). Don Felix' spirit guide works through him and assists with the diagnosis as well as treatment plans. These may include referral to a physician, magnetic passes, hypnotism, and suggestion; he remarked, "In Scientific Spiritism, we are freethinkers and use whatever will be effective." Frequently, don Felix will use a wooden knife to "direct the healing energy."

Don Felix has kept records on each of his clients so that he can follow their progress and determine what types of ailments are the most amenable to his treatment. He claims to be especially effective with people who are scheduled for hospitalization; after receiving his "spiritual operation," he claims that physicians sometimes conclude that surgery is no longer necessary. However, he believes medical doctors play an important role, and has been treated by physicians himself. Don Felix holds services in his temple two days a week; on Saturdays he counsels people and on Sunday conducts healing services, observing that many members of his congregation are Catholics and Protestants. Don Felix stated that "until the last moment of my life I will follow my mission to help needy people." His underlying belief is that "the spiritual life is more important than the material life." This philosophy, of course, is common to spiritists of various backgrounds and is what gives a semblance of unity to the movement (Rogler and Hollingshead, 1961).

We also visited Gela Ramirez, a healer who lives in the town of Lares. She told us how she was "called" to mediumship through an "energy bolt" that passed through her body, endowing her with the power to "lay-on" hands and incorporate spirits. Lares is the hometown of our guide in Puerto Rico, Mario Nunez-Molina, a psychotherapist and psychology instructor who wrote his doctoral dissertation at Harvard on the topic of espiritismo. Nunez-Molina views spirit possession as an opportunity for increased understanding and growth rather than as an example of psychopathology. In defense of his position, Nunez-Molina pointed out that mediumship does not remove the healers from community life because they continue to have similar responsibilities as non-healers. Those who adopt a pathological model of spirit possession ignore the importance of spirituality and the realm of sacred knowledge. We are in agreement with Nunez-Molina that allopathic medicine and psychiatry typically exclude these dimensions of human experience, and that their omission can be critical in the treatment of disturbances that center around loss, grief, pain, and the meaning of life.

Santeria in Cuba

In 1990 one of us (Krippner) investigated mediumship in the Dominican Republic and Cuba. In Santo Domingo, the capital of the Dominican Republic, he did not have the opportunity to participate in a voodoo ceremony but was shown drums and altars similar to those he had observed in Haiti. He found out that there are voodoo practitioners in Cuba who carry on the tradition brought to that island from Haiti; however, the main African-American spiritual practice is Santeria (Hanly, 1990).

Krippner was invited to attend a six-hour "toque" ritual held by the Children of Saint Anthony at their center in the outskirts of Havana. The first liturgy, which began about 2:00 PM, paid tribute to Elegua, the keeper of roads and crossings. There were also images of Chango, the ruler of dance and lightning, and for Babalu-Aye, lord of epidemics and healing. But the major "orisha," or deity, honored on that occasion was the hermaphrodite Obatala whose white robes symbolize purity, justice, peace, and wisdom.

In one room of the center, a beautiful shrine had been erected to Obatala which combined white fabric with strands of blue, the favored color of his consort Yemaya, orisha of the oceans and patroness of the center. In another room, musicians played the three characteristic "tambor bata" (Santeria drums): the "iya," the "olokono," and the "itotele," as dozens of participants sang and danced. One of the "babalawos" (male mediums) soon was "mounted" by Yemaya, began to adopt stereotypic female gestures, and started to attempt healings for those who requested his services, rubbing his hands over the afflicted bodily parts and embracing the supplicants.

Originally, the Cuban government perceived Santeria as anti-Marxist, but this position proved to be unpopular and Santeria was reconceptualized as a national heritage. Musicologists, ethnologists, and anthropologists now record

Santeria lore and ritual; artists and writers use Santeria themes in their paintings and novels. There are Santeria museums, Santeria dance performances, and the Children of Saint Anthony are officially registered with the government. Krippner was taken through the various rooms of the center, observing additional shrines, altars, and devotional paintings—most portraying the African orishas but some depicting their Christian counterparts (Jesus Christ is considered to be a manifestation of Obatala, the Virgin Mary of Yemaya, Saint Barbara of Chango, and Saint Lazarus of Babalu-Aye).

As the final liturgy began to wind down in the early evening (to avoid the 7:00 PM curfew), the orishas departed from their human "instruments." A "eucharist" (from the mammoth outlay of cakes and cookies) was served to each of the participants—those men and women, Marxists and Catholics, adults and children, and dark-skinned and light-skinned individuals who had come together to derive healing, meaning, and joy from an ancient spiritual tradition that had crossed the Atlantic under tragic circumstances but, in a modified form, had firmly established itself in the Americas.

Channeling Information

In 1986 we visited the Association for Research and Enlightenment (A.R.E.) in Virginia Beach, Virginia, an organization founded in 1931 to study and carry on the healing legacy of Edgar Cayce, one of America's most celebrated psychic sensitives—although the case can be made that "seer" is a better description (Bro, 1989). Once Cayce had closed his eyes and entered an altered state of consciousness, he would be given the name and location of a subject. Within a few minutes, Cayce would produce a detailed diagnosis of the ailment and would suggest a treatment. A physician, Wesley Ketchum, gave Cayce 180 names and, in 1910, announced the results before a meeting of the Boston Clinical Research Society, claiming that Cayce had made only two errors in diagnosis (Sugrue, 1970).

Cayce's recommended treatments included osteopathy, chemotherapy, hydrotherapy, nutrition, chiropractic, massage, and various folk remedies. Not all of Cayce's readings produced unqualified successes; he once gave a distant diagnosis for a girl suffering from leukemia and recommended a complicated dietary treatment. Unfortunately, the child had died the day before the reading was given (Daniels and Horan, 1987). Cayce did not "channel" messages from spirit entities but from a "cosmic mind pool." When he was in an altered state, Cayce spoke of himself in the third person. Upon his death in 1945, he left behind more 14,000 readings, 65% of them dealing with the physical ailments of his clients. The emphasis Cayce placed on meditation, reincarnation, self-healing, and "holistic" approaches to treatment put him several decades ahead of his time. In one reading, Cayce stated,

> Any manner in which healing comes—whether by the laying on of hands, prayer, by a look, by the application of any mechanical influence or any of those forces in *materia medica*—must be of such a nature as to produce that necessary within those forces...of a given body for it to bring resuscitating or healing.

The Cayce remedies have been utilized by two physicians, William and Gladys McGarey, founders of the A.R.E. Clinic in Phoenix, Arizona (although they now have separate practices). One of Cayce's most frequent and most unique prescriptions was for the application of castor oil packs for stimulating liver functions and lymphatic circulation, reducing toxemia and inflammation, and treating epilepsy and chronic headaches. Preliminary results of a study of the packs indicated that they increased the function of subjects' immune systems, fostering production of T-cells and lymphocytes; another group of subjects treated with paraffin packs showed no change in immune system function. The books and television appearances of Shirley Maclaine resulted in an avalanche of membership applications for A.R.E. The actress revealed her interest in mediums who supposedly "channeled" information about her that was both accurate and valuable.

This is a field in which fraud abounds as there is money to be made from "channeling" wisdom from ancient sages or reassurances from departed loved ones. However, fraud was never demonstrated during the long career of Paul Neary, one of America's preeminent mediums, who died in 1988. In 1986, one of us (Welch) interviewed Neary, who said that he had practiced the "laying-on" of hands since the age of 10. Neary worked as a research subject for the American Society for Psychical Research and participated in seminars sponsored by Spiritual Frontiers Fellowship. He saw his counseling as "a form of healing—spiritually, mentally, emotionally, and sometimes physically." Being "spiritual" is being "light, noble, virtuous, and moral." Neary used "light" as a metaphor for God; healing is one form of "bringing light" to those who need it. A reporter once asked Neary how he felt about his healing abilities and he responded "awed, amazed, and non-questioning" (Hammond, 1973).

Neary did very little diagnosis but he "channeled" information, claiming to have had a 90% success rate in identifying a physical problem (sometimes from photographs), motivating people to seek prompt medical treatment. For Neary, the etiology of sickness, in addition to the usual medical causes, can include negative thinking, negative lifestyles, and "karmic" patterns from past lives. He observed that "some people's thinking can cause an illness. What they are is what they attract." If guilt becomes part of a person's thought patterns if can become a "spiritual cancer" and eventually affect a person's bodily processes.

Neary's treatment included the "laying-on" of hands, "absent healing," prayer, dietary suggestions, and counseling. The basis of his healing was to "find the light and to try to project it." His clients often reported "heat," "a flow of energy," or "vibrations." Neary agreed to see a client for three healing sessions; if there was no relief by the end of the third session, he did not try again as he did not want to waste his time or the client's time. Neary believed that there are more opportunities for American children than anywhere in the world, but "they ignore many opportunities because of the quest for material possessions." Most young people care little about poverty, starvation, terrorism, and other world problems. Furthermore, they have not had the training to live their lives in a way so as to "bring in the light." The goal of Neary's model was to help people "live life to the fullest." He stated,

> Discussing the ultimate nature of the universe is a waste of time. Nobody really knows the answer. The most important way to develop our souls is to get on with life. The soul has no limitations, but the body does. We come into this world to learn about these limitations, and to become the best people we can be.

Neary's principle spirit guide was an entity named "Belnap." We have also listened to the spirit guides of such mediums as Mary Baker, Eileen Garrett, Barbara Goosen, Antoinette Moltzan, Jack Pursel, Marilyn Rossner, and Alan Vaughan. What we would consider the highest quality of "channeled" material can be characterized as being beneficial to humanity rather than to one person, oriented toward service rather than toward fame and fortune, supportive of love and empowerment rather than fostering fear and negativity, allowing for choice rather than demanding obedience, cognizant of a higher power rather than claiming ultimate authority for itself, presenting knowledge creatively rather than rehashing old platitudes, is focused and intelligent rather than effusive and contradictory, and emphasizing the personal labor needed for personal growth rather than claiming that enlightenment can occur without work and effort.

In our study of spiritual healing, we have identified two major dimensions of the assistance attributed to mediumship. The *source* of spiritual healing is said to be the "other worlds"—those transcendent levels of reality not ordinarily available to most people. The other dimension of spiritual healing is its *content*—diagnostic information, treatment procedures, and prognosis for recovery. In regard to mediumship, the source of the information is said to be discarnate entities, but the nature of these spirits is a matter of conjecture. Indeed, they might be discarnate entities; but they could also be a subpersonality of the client, the result of role-playing while in an altered state of consciousness, or the result of some other psychological or physiological process. Yet even if we were to make allowances for those mediums, spiritists, and "channelers" who are fraudulent and disturbed, there still would be a body of interesting information that is worthy of study. Some of the advice, prescriptions, and procedures that are "channeled" are vague, incoherent, and worthless. But other material has been helpful, inspiring, and empowering to those who have sought assistance from the deities, spirits, and entities from the "other worlds."

Eight

Sorcerers And Witches

In his study of magical and religious practitioners, Winkelman identified an entire category of people who specialized in malevolent practices. These practitioners would use medicines, spells, and magical rites not to help people but to harm them, usually at the bidding of someone who had purchased the sorcerer's or witch's services. Some cultures sharply differentiated between witches and sorcerers while others did not. Among the Navaho Indians, malevolent witches supposedly learned their skills from relatives, were able to assume animal forms, and were motivated by envy, financial greed, or sexual desire. Malevolent sorcerers, according to the Navahos, were able to use power animals, spells and chants to cause illness or destroy crops (Kluckholm, 1944). However, Winkelman observed that a society would rarely have more than one type of malevolent practitioner and that the distinction between sorcerers and witches was continuous rather than discrete.

Winkelman also reported that a society needed to be organized politically beyond the local level in order for either the malevolent witch or sorcerer to emerge and take on a separate role from that of the shaman. Some American Indian tribes believed that both the shamanic healer and the sorcerer acquired their spirit guides through dreams. In other societies, the degree of training for both practitioners was equally rigorous, because the sorcerer was needed to work magic against tribal enemies in times of war. Winkelman also found that the shaman and the shamanic healer frequently were persecuted during the time that sorcerers were trying to usurp their power.

Winkelman's cross-cultural study of practitioners of religion and magic identified four groups: the shamanic practitioners (shamans, shamanic healers, shamanistic healers), priests and priestesses, mediums and spiritists, and malevolent practitioners (sorcerers and witches). These terms work quite well to describe spiritual healers in past eras, but today's sorcerers and witches are not always malevolent. Historically, the term "witch" has been used to describe both helpful as well as harmful practitioners. At the present time, Witchcraft exists as a religious movement, also referred to as the new paganism or goddess worship.

These practitioners resemble shamanic healers, priests, and priestesses, rather than the ancient dispensers of harmful hexes and spells. Further, malevolent practitioners violate the code of ethics once formulated as the "Wiccan Rede" but still held by contemporary Neo-Pagan Witchcraft: "And [if] it harm none, do what you will."

Sorcerers and Zombies in Haiti

Shortly after the slaves were brought to North America, they were enveloped by a feeling of total helplessness, knowing they would never see their homes again. The overwhelming aspect of the slave's experience in the New World was the brutal severing of every element basic to his or her personal identity. As a group, the French were the harshest slavemasters in America. Slaves in Haiti were often herded into a church with whips, ordered to kneel, baptized en masse, then sent back to work. The religious practitioners among the slaves maintained a modicum of their native beliefs by identifying deities in the West African pantheon which resembled Roman Catholic saints, and led ceremonies—when it was possible—in their worship. However, these practitioners' influence depended on kinship ties and on religious institutions that no longer existed.

African shamanic healers and sorcerers were also brought to Haiti as slaves; both were more successful in continuing the practice of their respective crafts than were the priests. The shamanic healers found tropical plants in their new surroundings whose properties were similar to those of the herbs from which they had formerly concocted medicines. The sorcerers were feared and often hated in Africa, but they became more acceptable and more powerful in the slave community due to the confusion and disorientation that existed.

Voodoo mediums in Haiti today have synthesized the functions of priests and shamanic healers, but the "bokor," or sorcerer, still exists as a separate practitioner in many parts of the country. During Krippner's 1980 visit to Haiti, he asked about zombies—those individuals who are held in servitude by bokors after being robbed of their souls. Krippner and his group were told that zombies do exist because bokors can administer drugs that induce a death-like coma; following the victim's burial, he or she is unearthed, revived, and instructed to follow the sorcerer's bidding.

Wade Davis (1985), an ethnobotanist, made a thorough investigation of these reports and identified the preparation used by the bokors, finding that the chief active ingredient was a paralytic nerve poison distilled from puffer fish. When Davis administered it to animals, he found that it produced anesthesia and paralysis with full mental alertness—the same symptoms reported by the zombies and ex-zombies he had interviewed. He also was able to identify the chemical composition of the salve used to awaken the zombie when he or she was removed from the grave, and to demonstrate the importance of the social context in convincing victims that they had become zombies. This study is controversial because an attempted replication with a different sample of animals did not immobilize them (Walsh, 1988). However, investigations of this nature are needed to determine the reality of anomalous phenomena, and to suggest an explanation.

From a sociological point of view, Haitian voodoo assumes importance. Sorcery often serves as a means of redirecting anxiety and stress. For Haitians and other oppressed people, hexes and spells serve as an attempt to exert a modicum of control over an existence which seems to be dictated by external forces. If the sorcerer's rites work only a small percentage of the time, they still provide hope and a vestige of power. Furthermore, downtrodden Haitians can always be grateful that they are not zombies—a fate even worse than being poor and hungry.

Dona Vielka and Don Juan

During Krippner's 1985 trip to Panama, he was introduced to Vielka Lee, a "hechicera" or witch who lived on the outskirts of Panama City. She demonstrated her procedures to him by shuffling a deck of Tarot cards, then rapidly laying them on the table while reciting a series of statements about Krippner. Some of dona Vielka's statements were very general and could have applied to virtually anyone, e.g., "You need to have time and space for deep concentration to do well." "You have had a difficult life with many setbacks." "You have many financial demands." "Many people around you have serious personal problems." However, others were quite specific, e.g., "You have two children, a boy and a girl. Your son is in the military." Krippner has a stepdaughter as well as a stepson who was, at that time, an officer in the U.S. Navy.

Most of dona Vielka's clients are executives and manag-'

ers who consult her about their business and financial decisions. Her reputation is splendid, especially regarding advice on investments. It can be seen that the witch is a perennial fixture in human cultures, but a witch's role is a flexible one, changing as society changes.

The most highly publicized alleged practitioner of sorcery in recent years is don Juan Matus, a purported Yaqui Indian hermit magician who is said to have taught Carlos Castaneda (1984) the sorcerer's world-view. Rather than emphasizing malevolent practices, don Juan instructed his students to retain awareness while dreaming, to "stalk" (or observe) nature in unusual ways, and to master their "will" and "intention" so as to acquire personal power. The anthropologist Richard deMille (1980) has amassed considerable data demonstrating that don Juan probably did not exist as a historical person. DeMille pointed out contradictions within Castaneda's alleged field reports, and between these reports and the physical and cultural environment in which they were supposedly collected. Thus, deMille concluded:

> Don Juan is not a sorcerer in any accepted anthropological sense. Sorcerers are feared and hated by other members of their community because they employ evil spirits or magical projectiles to make people sick; don Juan is a hermit who has no enemies and employs his plant allies to discover other worlds and ontological essences. Far from being a sorcerer, he is a rather benign, mystical magician.

Nevertheless, deMille gives Castaneda credit for creating a series of allegories that can stimulate readers to examine their own concepts of reality as well as their methods of evaluating personal experience. This may not have been Castaneda's goal, but it is not an insignificant accomplishment.

"Irregular" Healers and "Regular" Physicians

Some people accused of being witches in medieval Europe and colonial North America were emotionally disturbed and others were, indeed, intent on engaging in evil practices. However, most of them subscribed to the model of benevolent practice we have described when discussing other healers, serving as midwives, herbalists, and healing practitioners. Why were they persecuted by church authorities on both continents and severely punished? It is likely that witches were a convenient scapegoat to deflect people from the doctrinal disputes, wars, and plagues of the time. An additional motive has been identified by the psychiatrist Thomas Szasz (1971), who claims that when the Roman Catholic church, with the support of secular authorities, took control of medical education and practice, it decided to repudiate the skills of the non-professional healer. Because of witches' empirical, pragmatic attitude toward healing, surgery, and birthing babies, it was an easy matter to accuse them of deviating from religious dogma and of consorting with Satan. The Holy Inquisition's witch-hunts began in the 14th century and lasted well into the 17th century, having found their way into Protestant doctrine as well. Of the tens of thousands of people convicted and executed, some 85% were women. The 17th century witch trials in colonial America claimed a few hundred additional victims, most of them women.

In addition to being accused of religious heresy, sexual misbehavior, and political subversion, witches were often charged specifically with possessing medical and obstetrical skills, with giving contraceptive aid, and of performing abortions (Achterberg, 1990). The most authoritative book on witch-hunting, *The Hammer of Witches*, stated "No one does more harm to the Catholic Church than midwives." However, witches were often the only healing practitioners for people who had no access to physicians and hospitals. Many of the herbal remedies developed by witches still have their place in modern pharmacology as pain-killers, digestive aids, and anti-inflammatory agents. By contrast, medieval medical training was largely restricted to ancient philosophical texts and outdated practices. It is no wonder that European physicians arriving in the New World brought remedies with them that were generally inferior to the herbal preparations used by American Indian medicine men and medicine women.

Because of the lack of physicians who wanted to settle in the English colonies, medical practice was open to anyone who could demonstrate healing skills. Anne Hutchinson, the 17th century religious free-thinker, was a practitioner of general medicine. Many Protestant ministers and their wives practiced medicine; surgeons' wives often delivered babies and served as gynecologists. Some of their treatments seem naive by modern standards, but no more so than those taught in medical schools, e.g., "bleeding," in which a patient was "purged" of excessive fluids by opening a vein. Many physicians were not even trained in "bleeding," but sent patients to barbers for this form of treatment; nor were they trained in surgery, which was considered to be a misuse of their valuable time.

In the early 1800s, a movement was initiated by formally trained physicians to separate themselves from the large number of lay practitioners. By 1830, 13 states had passed medical licensing laws that outlawed "irregular" practice. This led to a reaction, the so-called Popular Health Movement of the 1830s and 1840s that emphasized preventive medicine and personal hygiene. "Regular" doctors of that time regarded frequent bathing as a vice; advocates of the Popular Health Movement endorsed bathing for sanitary purposes, but objected to the use of "bleeding." The Popular Health Movement organized its own medical schools, including those giving instruction in homeopathy, and by the late 1840s, medical licensing laws had been repealed in most states.

The livelihood of the "regular" physicians was threatened by the Popular Health Movement, so in 1848 they organized the American Medical Association. The AMA attacked lay practitioners on a number of grounds, one of them being the large number of women in the Popular Health Movement, another being the use of "occult" procedures and fraudulent practices. By the end of the 19th century, the AMA had adopted the "germ theory" as the basic cause of disease and had won the support of the new American industrial corporations that supported the construction of medical schools where allopathy, not homeopathy, would be taught.

The Carnegie Corporation sent a staff member on a tour of American medical schools to determine which ones were deserving of financial support. The Carnegie Report, published in 1910, established medicine as a branch of "higher learning," accessible only through lengthy and expensive university training. It condemned most small, poor medical schools; as a result they collapsed by the dozen. Six of America's eight medical schools for African-Americans closed, as well as most of the "irregular" medical schools that had been a haven for female students. The newly-founded Carnegie and Rockefeller Foundations gave financial support to the "regular" medical schools. Medicine in the United States had become a male, middle class profession in which any type of spiritual healing was eliminated from serious consideration.

The AMA's next targets were the midwives who were delivering about half of American babies in 1910. A study by a Johns Hopkins University professor in 1912 indicated that most "regular" physicians were *less* competent than midwives; they often were unsanitary and tended to utilize surgical techniques needlessly. This report was ignored as state after state passed laws outlawing midwifery, restricting the practice of obstetrics to physicians. Therefore, for poor and working class women, the one type of obstetrical care open to them was denied; a study conducted in the state of Washington revealed an increase in the rates of infant mortality following the passage of the anti-midwifery law (Ehrenreich and English, 1973).

The only remaining occupation for women interested in health care was nursing. At first the "regular" physicians underestimated the nurses' value, but they changed their opinion once they observed the nurses' devotion and obedience. Healing consists of both curing and caring, both doctoring and nursing. The spiritual healers of an earlier time had combined both functions, but with the development of the modern medical profession, the two functions were split. Curing became the exclusive province of the doctor; caring was relegated to the nurse.

The Model of Healing in Witchcraft

Despite the negative stereotyping and misconceptions stemming from the medieval "burning times," witches have often assumed a benevolent role in complex societies, functioning as practitioners of healing. Indeed, many witches had a well-articulated world-view that included a model of healing. In recent times, many people have reclaimed the use of the word "Witch" to refer to these healing practices as well as their religion (hence the capitalization of the term), a religion whose roots go back to pre-Christian Europe. One of us (Krippner) interviewed the late Sybil Leek in 1975. He met Selena Fox in 1976 and interviewed her in 1990. Both of us have found additional facets of the model in books by Leek (1971), Fox (1989), the American writer Erica Jong(1981), the American Witch Miriam Simos, better known as Starhawk (1979), and the book *Witches and Witchcraft* for which Fox was a consultant (Doyle, 1990).

Diagnosis, in Witchcraft, often utilizes such conventional procedures as gathering background data regarding problematic symptomatology through clinical interviews and dialogue counseling. Some Witches, such as Selena Fox, utilize a variety of divinatory techniques such as Tarot cards, the *I Ching*, runestones, dreams, and intuition to facilitate insights on the part of the client as well as the healer. In addition, diagnosis is often accomplished or enhanced by entering an altered state of consciousness and "reading" a client's "aura." According to Starhawk, there are three types of "subtle energy" reflected in the "aura": "elemental energy" or "ectoplasm" (the elemental vitality that sustains life), "astral energy" (as observed in thoughts, dreams, and fantasies), and "energy of the high self" (which links someone to the Divine). Jong points out that many Witches are aided in their work by a "familiar," a common domestic animal with special powers, among them the ability to enhance the Witch's "elemental energy." The "familiar" provides a link to Nature—and the honoring of Nature is the basis of contemporary Neo-Pagan Witchcraft.

Practitioners of Witchcraft commonly perceive unity between body and mind, as well as between the person and Nature. Thus, the most common *etiology* of disease is seen as an imbalance within a person's nature and/or an imbalance with Nature. Improper nourishment and one's abuse of his or her body are seen as common causal factors in illness by Sybil Leek. She remarked, "How well we know that the stresses and strains of modern life also cause an imbalance in the body....These tensions build up to produce their own body illnesses, and we get the phenomena of organic bodily diseases caused by psychological stresses or psychosomatic illnesses." According to Fox, physical, mental, and emotional disorders often are manifestations of a spiritual imbalance, or sometimes a process of change. For Starhawk, the most useful model is "not one of health and sickness, but one of personal power." The Witch's road to power-from-within can include knowledge of Nature, healing practices, the provision of food, divination, and the erotic.

When one's "elemental energy" is low, a person can become physically exhausted or emotionally depressed.

Harmful spiritual forces can enter through "astral energy"; they are not always external entities but may be elements in a person's unconscious. To Leek, Starhawk, and Fox, self-knowledge is important because it allows the illumination of what ordinarily would remain a "shadow" aspect of the self. The *subject's behavior* can reflect one's self-awareness. A person's "shadow" contains latent power; if not acknowledged, it can turn against a person and induce sickness. The "shadow" can also be projected outward, producing an "enemy" who embodies the denied aspects of the person doing the projecting. Harmful magical practices can also represent an etiological basis for illness; some Witches claim that they need to use their skills to fight hexes induced by malevolent magical practitioners against their clients.

Witchcraft and Healing

Treatment in Witchcraft occurs through magic-making, defined by Fox as "directing spiritual energy to bring about a change within oneself, within another, and/or in one's environment." A connection of some type needs to be developed between the healer and the client. For direct healing purposes, the individual requiring assistance should be physically present. For absent healing, an "object link" to the person will suffice, such as a strand of hair, a piece of clothing, or even a written signature. If nothing else is available, the practitioner can use the client's name. Any of these may serve as a focus for the Witch's attention, which can then be enhanced by chanting, dancing, or making rhythms, and can be directed through mental imagery. The Witch casts a "spell," a type of healing prayer, through connection with "Divine healing power" and then evoking a "healing image" of the treatment's desired goal. In the case of working with a child with a broken leg the image could depict the child running normally on a beach. At the end of the healing transmission, assimilation of the energy by the client occurs and "thanksgiving" is offered to those aspects of Divine healing with which the Witch has worked.

Due to the spiritual nature of treatment and healing in Witchcraft, practitioners work with various aspects of the Divine, both female and male, represented by their various gods and goddesses of various cultural pantheons. Neo-Pagan Witches conceptualize these deities in various ways. Similar to pre-Christian Pagans, some believe that their deities are actual entities who inhabit the spiritual realm. Others believe that their gods and goddesses represent "thought forms" built up over the centuries or "archetypes" that symbolize deep-seated aspects of the human psyche. Examples of gods and goddesses typically called up by many Neo-Pagan Witches include Isis, the Egyptian goddess of healing (Farrar and Farrar, 1987); Gaia, the Greek Earth goddess; Hygieia, the Greek goddess of health (Jayne 1962); Aesculapius, the Greek god of dream healing; Apollo, the Greek god of musical healing; Dionysus, the Thracian and Greek god of wine and vegetation (Farrar and Farrar, 1989); Yemanja (or Yemaya), the Yoruba goddess of the waters who assists in childbirth; Brigid, the Celtic goddess of fire and healing; and the Great Spirit, the Native American deity of all Nature (Steiger, 1984). Some practitioners worship female deities in a triple form, e.g., Maiden, Mother, and Crone, and associate them with the waxing, full, and waning phases of the moon. They may worship male deities in a dual form, and associate them with the waxing and waning of the solar year.

A variety of features characterizes the healing work of Witches. Above all, it is important to prepare a "sacred space" or to "cast a circle" within which the healing work is carried out. This healing space is marked by the four directions, North, East, South, and West, and in some paths the Heavens above, the Planet below, and the Center. While great variability exists regarding which attributes are assigned to these directions, the system utilized by Fox typifies that of many Witches and assigns North to the Earth Element and the realm of physical healing. East represents the Air Element and the realm of mental healing. South represents the Fire Element and the realm of energy healing. West represents the Water Element and the realm of emotional healing. The Center encompasses Spirit, Divine Unity, the connection with "All-that-is," and the realm of spiritual healing.

Within the sacred space one can find a central healing altar that contains objects representing the Elements of Nature, e.g., a platter of salt for Earth, incense and/or a blade (an "athame") for Air, a candle and/or magic wand for Fire, a chalice of water for Water, and crystals and/or images of the deities for Spirit. Sometimes the proverbial broom may be included, but in modern times it is typically used as a tool for purification (and for sweeping the floor of the healing center) rather than a vehicle for consciousness-alteration and travel. Ritual implements such as bells, drums, rattles, and feathers may be used as healing tools. Music and meditation often are included in the healing process; shamanic techniques such as working with power animals and plant allies may be incorporated as well.

While herbs may be used nutritionally and/or medicinally in rituals, they are more often used magically as the contents of an amulet or charm which is charged with "elementary energy" and given to the client to wear. Regardless of what objects and symbols may be utilized, Starhawk points out that the ritual itself creates a healing space. According to Fox, set and setting are important ingredients for healing rituals, just as they are with inner journeys and other magical work utilizing alterations in consciousness.

Prognosis depends on how diligent the client is in repairing the rupture with Nature. Witches believe that there is no rift between spirit and body when a person is in good health; illness represents an imbalance that needs to be corrected. Fox (1984) conceptualizes the issue of prognosis in this manner:

My clients do not have to be Pagan and they don't
have to adopt my beliefs or world view in order to
get better. This is not "faith healing" as most people
would define it. My clients don't even have to
accept psychic phenomena as real. My clients do
have to be open to exploring the spiritual dimensions of themselves to get new perspectives on their
lives, and they must be willing to help in the healing
process. I see myself as a catalyst to help my clients
connect more fully with their own Inner Selves and
make their own decisions from this dimension of
being that will help them achieve balance and
wellness in their lives.

As reflected in Fox's comments, prognosis depends
upon the readiness of her clients to take an active role in the
process and to allow healing and balance to be a part of their
lives. Other factors contributing to successful healing include
the skills and powers of the healer and the rapport which
develops between the healer and the client. On the part of the
healer as well as the client, the expectation that healing can
occur—without undue attachment to specific outcomes—is
important. Fox's experience has shown her that healing can
take place as a result of a single one-to-one or group ritual, or
that it might take several rituals over a period of time. Fox
stresses that it is extremely important to view spiritual healing
as a part of an entire spectrum of healing modalities, and that
spiritual healing can be used in connection with most other
approaches, including allopathic medicine. Just as traditional
healers in other parts of the world have carried out healing
rituals for clients in hospitals, Fox, as a legally recognized
minister, has done direct healing work for some clients in
emergency rooms and other hospital settings.

In cases of terminal illness, Witches help dying individuals arrive at an understanding and acceptance of death as part
of the cycle of Nature. When working with such clients, it is

important that an acceptance of all possible outcomes, including death, be reached in order for extraordinary healing to
remain a possibility. Regarding *death, dying, and suicide*,
Leek conceptualized a natural process of birth, death, and
rebirth both within an incarnation and during incarnations.
She believed that a person develops spiritually by being born
and reborn until he or she has acquired the wisdom that
elevates them to a level of consciousness where reincarnation
is no longer necessary. For Leek, suicide generally interferes
with the process and simply delays the natural cycle. Some
Neo-Pagan Witches modify this viewpoint in such cases as
prolonged suffering from terminal illnesses.

Functions, Rights, and Responsibilities

Some Witches, both male and female, work on their own
as solitary practitioners; others work together in groups called
"circles" or "covens." The *function of the institution*, in this
case, is to support and guide each member of the group. The
group may attempt to raise the "elemental energy" of its
members by forming a circle while meditating, chanting, or
dancing. The attention of the group members is directed to the
center of the circle to "raise the cone of power." Another
method is to confront each member of the group with
"shadow" elements of his or her psyche that are being projected rather than confronted and integrated. In fact, some
psychologists see contemporary Wiccan Witchcraft and other
types of Neo-Paganism as a form of "folk therapy." *Personnel*
in the group traditionally number 13 but now may consist of
any number; Leek described one coven that consisted of over
200 members. The 1990 edition of the *Circle Guide to Pagan
Groups* lists more than 200 covens, circles, and similar groups
in North America and other parts of the world. While these
groups differ according to focus, structure, symbols, tools,
and rituals, most include healing magic as part of their
practices (Circle Staff, 1990).

Rights and duties of the client need to be carefully determined when someone outside the coven or circle is the focus of attention. Fox emphasized the importance of clients giving consent to healing magic being worked on their behalf. Leek believed that sickness can be seductive in that it can absolve the individual from responsibility, allowing him or her to luxuriate in passivity. Thus one duty of the client would be to face the "shadows" of the unconscious. One "right" would be the knowledge of Divine Love; another would be the "right" for spiritual guidance. Starhawk (1987) believes that the human body is sacred and that sexuality is a sacred process;

> With the AIDS epidemic threatening so many lives, it is more important than ever to assert the sacred value of the erotic. Caution about transmitting AIDS may restrict some aspects of our erotic expression, but AIDS does not change the sacred nature of our sexuality any more than it invalidates the medical use of blood transfusions.

Rights and duties of the family would be similar; in addition, Witches would request that families of a client or of a coven member respect that person's right to worship as he or she chooses. *Rights and duties of society*, above all else, need to center around tolerance. Contemporary Witches express disdain when uninformed people equate their male deities (such as the Greek god Pan and the Celtic god Cernunnos) with Satan. They observe that Satan and the Antichrist are part of the Christian worldview, and not part of Paganism. Wiccan spirituality has its origins in pre-Christian Pagan cultures, and includes veneration of the Divine in goddess forms. It does not include worship of the embodiment of evil by any name or aspect.

Starhawk insists that the value of an individual can not be separated from a concern for social justice. She and her associates have engaged in civil disobedience actions at the

Diablo Nuclear Plant and the Livermore Weapons Laboratory in California, integrating magic and ritual into their fight against nuclear energy and weaponry. For Starhawk, "Value is embodied not just in the individual but in the greater earthbody, the complex organism in which all creatures are cells" (Jamal, 1987).

The *goal* of this model has been stated by Sybil Leek: "Many people are spiritually sick and in every case the solution lies in seeking means to restore a harmonious existence, a balance in life, so that these people can seek their own way toward ultimate good." Fox adds that "walking in balance through life" is a goal of Wiccan spiritual healing.

Witchcraft as a Spiritual Movement

As conceived by Leek, Starhawk, Fox, and their contemporaries in the United States, this form of Witchcraft can be an exemplary form of spiritual healing, one reflecting a venerable tradition. In fact, there has been a growing revival of interest in benevolent Witchcraft under the name of "Wicca," the "Old Religion," or simply the "Craft." One prominent member of this movement is Margot Adler (1986), granddaughter of the renowned psychotherapist Alfred Adler. Her book, *Drawing Down the Moon,* documents the diversity of the Neo-Pagan movement throughout North America.

One of the organizations that has played an important part in the development of contemporary Wiccan spirituality and other forms of Neo-Paganism is the Wisconsin-based Circle (Guiley, 1989). Founded in 1974 by Selena Fox and others, Circle has grown considerably in size and scope over the years and eventually has come to serve as a non-profit global resource center for "Nature Religions," as well as a legally recognized Wiccan church and multi-cultural Pagan temple. Circle is coordinated by Selena Fox and her husband, Dennis Carpenter, a former school psychologist. The various aspects of Circle's activities reflect its connections with

Native American and other native peoples' shamanic practices, as well as with Wiccan spirituality.

Circle has organized a network that attempts to assist those involved in Wicca, Neo-Paganism, goddess studies, shamanic practices, and related Nature Religions connect with each other as well as deepen their relationships with the spiritual dimensions of Nature. Circle carries out a variety of activities including publishing a quarterly newspaper, *Circle Network News*, sponsoring the Pagan Spirit Gathering each summer, and coordinating a number of seminars, festivals, and ritual events throughout North America. Circle sponsors training programs in the "Nature Mystic Path," which blend Wicca, shamanism, and spiritual psychology; it also sponsors a spiritual healing ministry.

In 1983, Circle began its purchase of a 200-acre nature preserve, referred to as Circle Sanctuary, located in southwestern Wisconsin. While left primarily as a wildlife sanctuary, a number of ritual areas have been developed, including a stone circle, a sweat lodge, outdoor shrines, and an indoor temple. These sacred places are used for worship, meditation, and spiritual healing. Several prehistoric Native American sites have been discovered on the land and are also utilized for ritual and meditative work.

Fox and Carpenter serve as the high priestess and high priest of Circle and, in these roles, coordinate Circle's activities. Spiritual healing represents a major emphasis in their ministry. Each month, near the time of the full moon, a healing ceremony is conducted at Circle Sanctuary. Throughout the month prior to this ritual, network members and other individuals send in written requests for healing. Upon receipt of these requests, they are placed in a healing basket in Circle's indoor temple. Each request is focused upon individually by one of the participants in the ritual. In addition, group efforts are enhanced through such means as chanting and the shaking of rattles. It is believed that a "cone of energy" is raised, sending healing to all those requesting it. This energy is also directed to the crystals and other objects in the healing basket so that they are "energized" to serve as healing catalysts throughout the coming month.

In addition to this absent healing work, individuals needing help are sometimes assisted within the context of a group ritual or in one-to-one therapeutic sessions. Fox and Carpenter see clients for spiritual counseling, offering dreamwork, "creative visualization," "past life regression," Tarot Card readings, meditative work, and other approaches to help clients develop a greater awareness of the factors operative in their lives, and the options available to them. The Circle's concept of health resembles the definition adopted by the United Nations—"a state of complete physical, mental, and social well-being and not merely the absence of disease and infirmity" (World Health Organization, 1974).

The Social Context of Witchcraft

Many solitary practitioners, as well as groups such as those affiliated with Circle, incorporate aspects of the feminist and ecological movements. The recognition of the female as well as the male aspects of Divinity has attracted many feminists to Neo-Pagan Witchcraft since the 1960s. A concern for the healing of Mother Earth evolved out of the ecological movement; in recent years, many individuals and groups have incorporated Planetary Healing work into their rituals in an attempt to counteract the devastating impact that industrial societies are having on the planet. Planetary Healing can take the form of rituals directed toward specific endangered species and their habitats or can be directed more generally to the well-being of the planet as a whole. To ecologically-oriented Witches, Mother Earth (or Gaia) is seen as a living organism with whom humans must live harmoniously in order to survive. Fox (1990) reflects this position:

> I am a Pagan. I am part of the whole of Nature. The
> Rocks, the Animals, the Plants, the Elements, and

the Stars are my relatives. Other humans are my
sisters and brothers, whatever their races, colors,
genders, ages, nationalities, religions, and
lifestyles. The Earth is my Mother and the Sun is my
Father. I am part of this large family of Nature, not
the master of it. I have my own special part to play
and I seek to play that part to the best of my ability.
I seek to live in harmony with others in the family
of Nature, treating others with respect, not abuse....

I hear the cries of Mother Earth who is upset with the
harm being done to the Planet's environment by
humankind. I am upset too by the pollution of the
air, the soil, and the waters, and by the domination
games being played by nations with the fire of
nuclear missiles and other weapons of mass destruction. I also am concerned about spiritual pollution on the Planet—selfishness, hatred, greed for
money and power, addiction, violence, despair.
Yet, as I perceive these problems, I also perceive a
cleansing and healing energy manifesting on Planet
Earth at this time. I know that I can help bring the
Planet into greater balance by seeking balance in
my own life. I know that my attitudes and my way
of living can make a difference. I endeavor to be a
channel for healing and balance. I make the practice
of environmental responsibility a personal part of
my daily life. I endeavor to live in harmony with the
other members of the family of Nature. This is the
essence of Paganism, and I am a Pagan.

Consistent with the theme of living in harmony with
Nature, individuals and groups celebrate lunar phases, in
particular the new moon and the full moon. Witches, both
female and male, may "draw down the moon" and "incarnate"
the various aspects of the Lunar Goddess. In addition, many

Witches celebrate the seasonal changes marked by the solstices, the equinoxes, and the "cross quarter" days in between. As described by Fox, this system creates eight solar holidays marking the turning of the Wheel of the Year including, for those in the northern hemisphere,

1. Samhain (or Hallowe'en), a time for gazing into the future and for paying homage to the ancestors and other loved ones in the spirit world.

2. Yule (the Winter Solstice), a festival of peace, light, and celebration of the new Sun Child, the Mother Goddess, and the Father God.

3. Candlemas (also known as Imbolc or Groundhog's Day), a festival of spiritual purification and preparation for spring.

4. Ostara (the Spring Equinox), a festival of renewal and welcoming spring.

5. Beltane, a festival of fertility, sensuality, and creativity.

6. Litha or Midsummer (the Summer Solstice), a grand gathering time with dancing and lighting sacred bonfires to the rhythms of drums.

7. Lammas (or Lughnassad), a festival of prosperity and giving thanks for the first fruits of the harvest.

8. Mabon (the Fall Equinox), a time of thanksgiving for all the harvests in life.

While practitioners of Wiccan Witchcraft and other forms of Neo-Paganism have viewed themselves as a harmonious movement, bringing healing to the planet, some groups in the United States have seen them as heretical and dangerous. In 1985, a political drive was launched to remove tax exempt status from Wiccan churches and to define, at the federal level, Witchcraft as satanic and illegal. The American Civil Liberties Union, in combination with the Circle network and several Christian and Jewish organizations concerned with preserving religious freedom, successfully defeated this proposed legislation. Shortly after this event, Circle was involved in another battle for religious freedom as its right to hold religious activities on its Nature preserve was challenged. In 1988, after nearly two years of legal struggles, and with the help of the American Civil Liberties Union, Circle won church zoning status and its right to hold religious activities on its land was upheld. The magazine *Shaman's Drum* reported that this was the first time since the Middle Ages that a Witchcraft group had been legally recognized and publicly sanctioned as a church by a unanimous vote of local government officials (Earth Circles, 1988).

Other Neo-Pagan groups and individuals, in response to harassment and discrimination, also have chosen to take legal action to uphold their religious freedom, and have won a variety of court battles. They have also attempted to disseminate information about Wiccan spirituality and the Neo-Pagan movement through the mass media in an effort to help gain recognition and legitimacy. Some organizations, such as Circle, have won public acceptance as well as legal recognition as churches; some are involved in interfaith networking with mainstream churches and councils, such as the World Council of Churches. Various universities offer courses examining the history of Neo-Paganism, and academic research on the movement has been initiated (Melton, 1978). In 1987, it was estimated that there were between 50,000 and 100,000 members of Wiccan and related Neo-Pagan movements in the United States (Roelofsma, 1987).

Satanism and Dissociative Disorders

North American Witches shifted their image and role in the late 20th century, becoming more a group of benign healers and Nature worshipers than isolated malevolent magic-religious practitioners. The image of sorcerers appears to have shifted as well; they are seen—at best—as self-serving operators and—at worst—as reprehensible agents of evil. Some operate within the framework of an organized religion, an example being the Temple of Set (or Seth) in St. Louis whose members worship the Egyptian god of darkness. While Witchcraft takes the attitude of "Do what you will, as long as it harms no other," present-day Sorcery appears to adopt the attitude, "I do what I want, as long as it furthers my ends."

However, the Temple of Set is fairly innocuous in comparison with the many alleged satanic groups that probably attain more publicity than their numbers and activities deserve. Indeed, believers in the "satanic conspiracy" are convinced that a network of Satan-worshiping cult members exists in North America. Entire families participate, raising their children to assist them in rituals involving animal and human sacrifice, mental and physical abuse, kidnapping and child pornography, "Black Masses" and drug-related magical ceremonies. They infiltrate child care centers, funeral parlors, and even the police force.

Individuals suffering from post-traumatic stress, multiple personality disorders, and other dissociative syndromes often appear to recall satanic activities under hypnosis or during psychotherapy. Dissociation involves a withdrawal from one's ordinary stream of consciousness when pain or fear becomes unbearable. Sometimes the terrifying experience is suppressed; at other times, the dissociation produces an alternate or "alter" personality. In either event, the psyche's integrative functions fail to function properly; in later years, the individual might suffer from nightmares, amnesia, blackouts, and other symptoms of dissociative disorders.

It is quite likely that patients suffering from dissociative disorders have suffered some form of abuse or life-threatening experience. But the proportion of them who have actually engaged in satanic sorcery is a matter of dispute. Satanic rituals may be metaphors for the actual sexual or physical abuse they experienced as children, metaphors reinforced by the media and by the network of "survivors" who organize support groups, conferences, and newsletters. Sometimes a well-meaning lawyer, police officer, or psychotherapist will use satanic terminology when describing shocking cases of reprehensible behavior outside of their own background and comprehension—but which have nothing to do with actual satanic groups.

A series of drug-related killings in northern Mexico were dubbed "satanic" by Texas law officials and the popular press even though there was no indication that the suspects worshiped Satan or were members of satanic cults (Hicks, 1990). Nevertheless, the sensational media reports were followed by rumors that children were to be ritually murdered in a nearby church named "The Church of Fire." The church was burned to the ground and several members were threatened (Carlson, 1989).

Richard Noll (1989), a clinical psychologist, has examined the data on the alleged satanic cults and their connection with victims of dissociative disorders. Noll has concluded that "some experiences are undoubtedly true. Most...are merely the screen memories of childhood abuse at the hands of adults (perhaps even parents) but which have taken on a mythic, almost archetypal form, in their representation of the essential evilness of the experience." As for the individuals that appear to actually have participated in satanic cult activity, a group of Canadian researchers has produced data indicating that they lack a sense of mastery over their environment, and that the cult confirms their marginality and negative self-perception. None of these findings support the purported benefits of membership put forward by cult advocates (Bourget, Gagnon, and Bradford, 1988).

One of us (Krippner) is a charter member of the International Society for the Study of Multiple Personality and Dissociation. In 1990, psychiatrist Frank W. Putnam, a member of that society, urged his fellow members to "proceed very slowly and very cautiously with regard to disseminating information on alleged ritual abuse and satanic activities....The credibility of [our society] depends on our taking a dispassionate, scientific view of the evidence for and against the allegations of a world-wide international satanic conspiracy that is committing large-scale ritual abuse." We are in agreement with this statement. At the same time, we take the position that even the small number of abuse cases definitely linked with satanic activities must not be tolerated. Child abuse is one of the most disgraceful phenomenon of human history; that it should be prevalent in societies that presume themselves "civilized" makes us wonder if that term, as well as the term "primitive," can still be considered descriptive or useful.

Nine

Investigating
Spiritual Healing

In addition to being the first health practitioners, shamans were the world's first scientists. They identified medicinal herbs on a trial-and-error basis, by observing the eating
habits of animals, and by trying out the remedies on themselves. They designed rituals to improve the skills of hunters
and gatherers so that they could more accurately locate and
obtain game and food. If the shaman's techniques helped sick
people get well or increased the tribe's food supply, the
shaman's social and political status improved. If the shaman's
attempts to placate spirits, predict the weather, and to keep the
tribe fed and healthy were not successful, he or she was
ridiculed, demoted, exiled, or even killed.

Humanity now lives in a scientific age; any new idea in
medicine must be subjected to rigorous testing to determine its
worth. Research data on the value of spiritual healing will
have a considerable impact on how quickly it will permeate
allopathically-oriented health services. In 1987 the National
Council Against Health Fraud issued a statement acknowledging "the potential value of faith healing rituals for allevi-

ating or curing psychological conditions, but also points out that the failure of such emotionally meaningful rituals to achieve subjective benefits could be harmful...by inducing feelings of guilt or rejection" (NCAHF, 1987).

The National Council Against Health Fraud also stated that beneficial outcomes may be regarded as fortuitous and most probably involving psychological mechanisms "unless such outcomes are clearly miraculous." For this reason, the Institute of Noetic Sciences in Sausalito, California, has initiated a project to catalog cases of unexplained remission from serious illness without allopathic intervention. In 1987, the Institute announced that they had assembled over 3,000 articles describing such cases from nearly 900 medical journals in more than 20 different languages (O'Regan, 1987). In our investigation of spiritual healing, we are interested in these cases because some of the remissions were said to have been evoked by practitioners who believe that there is a spiritual realm or dimension of reality that has not been identified by Western science (Kirkpatrick, 1981). But even if these cases are not substantiated, spiritual healing still raises important research issues. We have used the term "spiritual" to describe awareness of a broader life meaning and/or domain that transcends the immediacy of everyday encounter and expediency. Investigators have probed the efficacy of the herbal preparations that have been used over the years by spiritual practitioners. They have also looked into the psychotherapeutic effectiveness of the chemical analogues of various sacramental substances. Frequently used spiritual healing techniques have been studied, principally mental imagery and meditation.

In regard to the latter techniques, there is little consensus among qualified investigators regarding the effectiveness of any type of "mental" self-regulation and healing. Wallace Sampson, a Stanford University Medical School oncologist, discounts the data linking purported effects of the "mind" on disease by way of meditation, "positive thinking," and the like. He asks, "What brain function set up by meditation could cause the immune system to effectively attack a malignancy?" In the first place, according to Sampson, "boosting" the immune system is more often harmful than helpful; in some auto-immune disorders (such as multiple sclerosis and lupus) the system is "boosted" to the point that it attacks everything, including one's own body tissue. Secondly, cancerous tissue does not consist of "foreign" material; cancer is composed of one's own body cells gone haywire.

To Sampson, the idea that our immune system could conduct a selective siege on a certain number of its own cells because of "positive thinking" requires us to assume that specific instruction could be directed from a thought process to an immunological response. Sampson has reviewed medical articles in the authoritative *Journal of the American Medical Association*, noting that what he considers the "four best studies" find "no significant correlation between one's state of mind and the incidence of or cure of cancer" (Sampson, 1990).

Sampson has been especially critical of the physician Bernard Siegel (1986) who, Sampson asserts, "may have turned hundreds of thousands of cancer victims away from scientifically demonstrated life-saving therapies" with his stress on positive attitudes. He also attacks O. C. Simonton (1978), an oncologist who "does not give so much as a hint about a mechanism" to make his link between stress, depression, and cancer sensible. Sampson is bitter about Norman Cousins, a journalist who wrote several books about his own recovery from sickness through humor and positive thinking, because "he gave no credit...to his surgery and [post-operation] therapy."

Cousins (1990), whose books and articles on health won him a position on the medical faculty of the University of California at Los Angeles, took a very different position. He cited data from a UCLA study of 75 cancer patients demonstrating that "a direct connection exists between the mental state of the patient and the ability of the immune system to do its job." Specifically, "Liberation from depression and panic is frequently accompanied by an increase in the body's interleukins, vital substances in the immune system that help activate cancer-killing immune cells." Cousins concludes that "people need to be re-educated about their health....They need to understand the concept of a patient-physician partnership in which the best that medical science has to offer is combined with the magnificent resources of mind and body."

The Fetzer Institute and The Institute for the Advancement of Health describe their purpose as the improvement of health through behavioral and mind-body interactions. Their journal, *Advances*, records new studies on the topic, summarizing them for its readers. The Spring 1990 issue lists several such investigations that would support the position taken by Cousins and refute the assertion of Sampson that reliable data are absent linking attitudes and disease. The close link between the immune system, the endocrine system, and the brain was outlined by T.C. Theoharides (1990), who wrote that these interactions may play an important role in neuroinflammatory conditions. The link between depression and physical symptoms was reviewed by Z.J. Lipowski (1990). Reduced immune system functioning was found among depressed patients as well as among those with life threatening illnesses in a hospital study of 36 patients (compared with a control group) (Irwin et al., 1990). Psychosocial aspects of work demands apparently was related to cardiovascular risk factors in a survey of 12,555 men in five different investigations (Pieper, La Croix, and Karasek, 1989). A 12-year followup study of 610 people found psychological distress to be predictive of mortality rates (Somervell et al., 1989). The same issue of *Advances* reported "mental" and "attitudinal" treatments for medical disorders, e.g., hypnosis and cognitive therapy. This single issue of *Advances* is representative of the state of the art. Studies are published frequently, many with large numbers of subjects, supporting the premise that mind-body connections are reflected in immune system functioning. In addition, a very small number of studies, most of them with very few subjects, is reported that support the utilization of "mental" and "attitudinal" treatments for sickness and physical malfunction.

Eventually, this controversy may be resolved by advances in the field of psychoneuroimmunology which focuses on the interaction of the autonomic nervous system (both its neurological and its psychological aspects) and the body's immune system. Sometimes the endocrine system is included as well, giving the field the somewhat cumbersome name of psychoneuroendocrinoimmunology. A topic of consequential interest to psychoneuroendocrinimmunologists is the way that neuropeptides connect the nervous system, endocrine system, and immune system. The primary role of the immune system is to resist the onset of infection by bacteria, fungi, and viruses. As such, the immune system functions by using B cells to produce antibodies that combat infectious agents, T-helper cells to produce inflammatory reactions, T-killer cells to eliminate invasive organisms, memory cells (special T and B cells) that allow the system to "remember" how to fight viruses previously encountered, macrophages to consume invading microbes, and non-specific lymphoid cells to eliminate malignant cells. The interaction of the autonomic nervous sytstem, the endocrine system, the immune system, and the neuropeptide system has led the psychologist E.L. Rossi (1986) to view "all biological life as a system of information transduction."

The same neurological structures involved in the immune system are also implicated in emotional responses; physical stressors and emotional distress consistently influence the nervous system. The endocrine system produces hormones (gonadal steroids, thyroid hormones, adrenal hormones, etc.) that affect immune responses. In addition, brain neurotransmitters such as the endorphins and enkephalins can enhance the immune system's functioning (Locke, 1982). In our opinion, there is considerable evidence that emotions, attitudes, and negative stress can adversely affect the functioning of the immune system. There is far less evidence, however, concerning the effectiveness of psychological factors in fighting illness and enhancing immune functioning.

In 1990, Arnold S. Relman, editor of the prestigious *New England Journal of Medicine*, stated the position of mainstream science: "It's a well established fact that emotions can be reflected in pulse rate, respiration, skin temperature, [and] gastric secretion....As for whether mental states can influence the course of disease, there is simply no hard scientific evidence" (Stewart, 1990). Marcia Angell, executive editor of the journal, proclaimed, "It has not been shown unequivocally that someone's state of mind can cause or cure a specific disease" (Findlay and Brownlee, 1990). And at that point the issue has been joined, waiting for additional research data to help resolve the controversy.

Non-Sacramental Herbal Preparations

An extremely important line of research in spiritual healing concerns the effectiveness of herbal preparations used by North American healing practitioners. Sometimes the herb was magical, as when it was used to remove a hex or to cast a spell. At other times it was sacramental, as when it evoked a vision or message from the spirit world. Most often, however, the herb was felt to be medicinal in nature. A compilation of botanical preparations used by American Indians uncovered 1,305 species of plants used in the preparation of nearly 5,000 pharmaceutical remedies (Moerman, 1977).

Strips of willow bark and willow roots, often boiled, were used by the Alabama Indians to relieve fever, by the Chickasaws for headaches, and by the Klallams for sore throats. Later, these trees were discovered to be the source of salicylic acid, the raw material for aspirin. Women of the Shoshones and several other Native American tribes chewed stoneseed for birth control purposes. It now has been found to contain estrogen-like substances similar to those used in modern oral contraceptives.

Diarrhea often was treated by the root of a cherry tree, the leaves of the horsetail weed, and/or the root of the blackberry. Dried mulein leaves and mulein roots were smoked for respiratory ailments. The juice of the milkweed plant was utilized to stop bleeding. Wild licorice was chewed for footaches. Indians ate swamp root, manzanilla buds, or twigs from the juniper tree for upset stomachs. Some Indian tribes used the jimson weed to treat asthma, cholera, and epilepsy; today, chemicals from this plant are distilled for use in tranquilizers and eye dilation. In addition, Native American medicine men and medicine women made wide use of various anesthetics, cathartics, emetics, and febrifuges (Brown, 1975).

There is some evidence that American Indian herbal remedies were more effective, on balance, than the medicines brought to the New World by the European settlers. It has been estimated that 60% of the medicinal plants used by the Rappahannock tribe had unquestioned medicinal value (Stein, 1942). The European pharmacopoeia was far less efficient. In 1962, the U.S. National Academy of Science reviewed the effectiveness of all drugs marketed since 1938; out of the 4,300 substances tested, supportive evidence could be found for only 40%—and in just half of these cases could the therapeutic claims of their manufacturers be justified. This shocking discovery led to the stringent testing procedures now required by the U. S. Food and Drug Administration (Wade, 1973).

In 1987, the National Cancer Institute in Bethesda, Maryland, initiated an eight million dollar program to support collectors of natural substances that might have medicinal properties and to screen at least 10,000 of them each year against the AIDS virus and 100 different types of cancers. Already, a blue-green algae from Hawaii has been found to show promise as a treatment for leukemia, and the bark of the

Pacific Northwest yew tree has displayed anti-cancer activity. One investigator has returned from Belize with several herbal remedies obtained from a curandero, lamenting, "These people are encyclopedias of local flora, and they're not being replaced" (Booth, 1987). The United Nations World Health Organization has undertaken a similar project, using a computerized international database to study folk remedies for such diseases as arthritis, cancer, rheumatism, and nervous disorders (Land, 1986).

We would render a favorable judgment on the investigations of herbal remedies, even though no attempt has been made to compare and contrast the effects of magical plants against those considered to be only medicinal. There are obvious problems of dosage level and purity when herbs rather than drugs are prescribed. However, their benefits are apparent to the groups that are conducting research in a race against time. Tribal shamans are disappearing as are rain forests and the other natural sources of their medicines. A concerted effort should be made to protect both the jungles and the native healers against the ravages of pollution, erosion, acid rain, deforestation, slash-and-burn farming, and acculturation.

Psychotherapeutic Uses of Sacramental Plants

The Spanish conquerors of Mexico attempted to eliminate the use of the three major psychedelic plants used for sacramental purposes—teonanacatl (the "sacred mushrooms"), ololiuqui (morning glory seeds), and peyotl (peyote cactus buds). Teonanacatl use survived and has recently resurfaced among the Mazatecs and other tribes. The sacramental use of peyotl (or peyote) is incorporated in the rituals of the Native American Church, which numbers some quarter of a million members; it has been found to be both a preventive and therapeutic agent in alcoholism (Albaugh and Anderson, 1975). The psychoactive chemicals in ololiuqui are similar to those in LSD, a drug synthesized by the Swiss chemist Albert Hoffman in 1938, but whose mind-manifesting qualities were first discovered in 1943.

Because of the purported ability of LSD to evoke spiritual experiences, several researchers have attempted to use these experiences psychotherapeutically. For example, Charles Savage and O. L. McCabe (1973) treated 37 heroin addicts with a high dose of LSD during 6 weeks of residential therapy; they were compared with 37 matched subjects who were given weekly outpatient group therapy. One year later, a much higher proportion of the LSD group was totally abstinent from heroin—25% vs. 5%. Of the 13 subjects in the LSD group who had a perfect rating on a global adjustment test, 12 had reported a spiritual experience under the influence of LSD.

In their survey of the research literature, Lester Grinspoon and J. B. Bakalar (1979) concluded, "There is no doubt that LSD often produces powerful immediate effects on alcoholics; the question is whether they can be reliably translated into enduring change". The data indicate that the changes are more likely to be long-lasting if LSD ingestion is accompanied by a spiritual experience, e.g., an encounter with God, an image of Jesus, a sense of "oneness" with the cosmos. Albert Kurland and his associates (1967) reported a study involving 69 long-term alcoholics who were given three weeks of preparatory therapy followed by a high dose of LSD. Of this group, 75% reported a spiritual experience and there were immediate substantial improvements on psychological tests; after six months, 23 of the 69 had maintained abstinence. One of Kurland's patients was an illiterate, middle-aged, unskilled laborer who had been an alcoholic for four years. He later recalled an important part of his LSD experience:

I was afraid. I started to run, but something said "Stop!" When I stopped, everything broke into many pieces. Then I felt as if ten tons had fallen from my shoulders. I prayed to the Lord. Everything looked better all around me. The rose was beautiful....I changed my mind from alcohol toward Christ and the rose came back into my life. I pray that this rose will remain in my heart and my family forever (Kurland, 1967).

A week later his score on a test for neurotic traits had dropped from the 88th to the 10th percentile; six months later his psychological tests were within normal limits. After one year, in which he maintained the loyal support of his family, he was still sober.

One of us (Krippner) has observed Kurland's work as well as several psychotherapeutic sessions conducted by Salvador Roquet (1971), a Mexican psychiatrist, who adapted the ritual use of psychedelic plants by native practitioners for his own patients. Using mushrooms, peyote, and other psychedelic plants to trigger intense spiritual experiences, Roquet has reported long-lasting behavioral changes among his patients. The cessation of research into LSD's therapeutic effects suggests that psychedelics may have intruded prematurely into Western cultures; the illegal use and abuse of LSD indicates that most members of industrialized societies were not prepared for such an immediate and dramatic access to unconscious thoughts and images. Under the direction of their shamans, tribal people employed psychedelic plants fairly wisely, embedding their use in ritual and tradition. Psychiatric and psychological studies of psychedelic psychotherapy rarely discuss the spiritual aspect of these programs even though this may have been the crucial determinant of those benefits that were long-lasting.

Our judgment on psychedelic psychotherapy must remain skeptical. On the one hand, there is empirical evidence that the religious experiences evoked by the drug tended to strengthen and lengthen the therapeutic effect. However, LSD-type drugs must be utilized in the proper set and setting to have a maximum effect, and it is difficult to separate the drug's impact from that of the therapist. Nevertheless, it is clear that research into the psychedelics was aborted before the case for their usefulness was either demonstrated or negated. Furthermore, we regret the 1990 decision of the U.S. Supreme Court which gave state laws against the use of peyote primacy over the religious rights of the Native American Church, despite the church's apparent record of sacred use rather than hazardous abuse.

The Role of Mental Imagery

The ability to experience mental imagery in some form appears to be an innate human capacity (Rossman, 1987). The cultivation of one's imaginative powers was an important goal for shamans, as this enhanced capacity was needed to make contact with the "other world," to create myths, and to divine the future. Mental imagery can be defined as the schematic representation of objects and/or activities internally, in a manner resembling one or more sensory modalities. Mental images exist in the absence of those stimulus conditions that are known to produce their genuine sensory counterparts.

In 1987, we interviewed Jeanne Achterberg (1985), an American biofeedback specialist, who has described shamanism as "the medicine of the imagination" and speculates that shamans knew that mental images communicate with tissues and organs to effect a change. Achterberg differentiates between "preverbal imagery" in which one's imagination supposedly acts upon one's own physical being, altering cellular and biological activity, and "transpersonal imagery" which embodies the assumption that information from one person can be transmitted to others, affecting their physical condition. Her study of shamanism was an impetus for the development of the Imagery of Disease Test which asks patients to draw images of their disease, their immune system, and their current treatment. The images are given scores from 1 to 5 on 14 dimensions, e.g., activity level, symbolism, vividness, and frequency of positive images.

The total score on the Imagery of Disease Test was found to predict the degree of speech clarity among patients with laryngectomies as well as rehabilitation qualities in mastectomy patients. The Imagery of Disease Test predicted the status of cancer with 93% accuracy for those in total remission from cancer, and 100% accuracy for those who had died or who had rapid deterioration at a two-month follow-up. Patients who were to experience new tumor growth often drew their cancer cells as large, hard, impregnable objects (submarines, crabs, lobsters, scorpions, etc.); on the other hand, snails and slugs were related to a better prognosis. Negative symbols for the immune system's white blood cells were snowflakes, clouds, and similar weak and amorphous objects. Positive symbols for white blood cells were white knights, Vikings, and religious figures (Achterberg and Lawlis, 1979).

These findings are similar to clinical data obtained from a cancer treatment program originated by an American oncologist, O. C. Simonton. The program combines physical exercise, relaxation, and imagery training to supplement conventional medical treatment. In a psychological analysis of 70 patients who significantly outlived their predicted life expectancies, it was found that these patients were open to new ideas, would reject taking "no" for an answer, were feisty individuals who argued with their physicians, and sought the best treatment they could afford even if it was unconventional. In general, these traits are not considered desirable in social circles, particularly among women who are typically reinforced for humility, graciousness, and non-assertiveness (Achterberg et al., 1977).

In regard to the use of imagery, one of Simonton's

patients reported visualizing her white blood cells as vacuum cleaners that were sucking away the cancer cells. Another patient imagined that his cancer cells were being protected by thick walls that chemotherapy were breaking down with dynamite. A young boy reported visualizing cowboys using lassos made of white blood cells, capturing the bandit cancer cells, and destroying them. Simonton has also assisted patients to confront the possibility of death and to consider the meaning their lives have had for themselves and others. Imagery has played an important part in recognizing and clarifying these existential concerns.

Hypnosis, Meditation, and the Immune System

Mental imagery practice involves relaxation, an important healing agent in its own right, as do meditation and most forms of hypnosis (Porter and Norris, 1985). Considerable research has been carried out in these areas, but only a few studies have measured the impact of relaxation, meditation, or hypnosis on the immune system. In one well-known study, 45 elderly people were taught relaxation and guided imagery techniques three times a week for one month. By the end of the training, the relaxation-trained group showed a significant increase in immune system functioning in comparison to a group receiving no training and another group which substituted visits from outsiders for the relaxation (Kiecolt-Glaser et al., 1985).

Meditation is a form of self-regulation that, according to Joan Borysenko (1987), "keeps the attention pleasantly anchored in the present moment." One form of meditation, the "relaxation response," has been found to reduce the release of adrenaline and cortisol—two potent inhibitors of the immune system (p. 14). In other studies, meditation has been able to lower the body's metabolic rate, heart rate, and respiration rate, producing a sense of tranquility and calmness.

The practice of meditation also has been found to be associated with an increase in mental health, as measured by various tests. In one such study, William Seeman, Sanford Nidich, and Thomas Banta (1972) found that experimental subjects who practiced "transcendental meditation" (or TM) over a period of two months showed significant gains on half of the 12 scales of a measure of "self-actualization" when compared to a control group of nonmeditators. In a replication of this study, significant differences were found between meditators and nonmeditators on 10 of the 12 scales (Nidich, Seeman, and Dreskin, 1973). On the other hand, significant differences were not found in two studies using less highly motivated subjects, a shorter period of time, and somewhat different meditative techniques (Wulff, 1991).

After reviewing the research literature on meditation from 1931 to 1988, Michael Murphy and Steven Donovan (1988) reported no consensus on the question of whether meditation is a separate state of consciousness, or whether it is similar to any number of other conditions produced by muscle relaxation or sporadic sleep. Nevertheless, they found considerable evidence that meditation as a "spiritual practice reduces stress and anxiety."

Although there are several forms of meditation, there are four steps common to most of them:

1. The meditator finds a quiet place in which he or she will not be disturbed for about 20 minutes.

2. The meditator finds a comfortable body placement, usually a sitting position.

3. The meditator selects a word, an object, or his or her own breathing. The word is repeated, the object is focused on, or the breathing process is followed, breath by breath.

4. The meditator "lets go" of all extraneous thoughts and feelings. If his or her attention wanders away from the focal word, object, or breath, the meditator simply brings his or her attention back to it (Martin, 1990).

With regular practice, perhaps once a day, the meditative

process usually becomes easier. Distracting thoughts, emotions, and memories often come up. Rather than fighting to suppress them, these diversions can simply be acknowledged, then released.

Meditation is similiar to self-hypnosis in that a quiet environment is beneficial if both are to proceed well. In self-hypnosis, an individual proceeds to relax himself or herself, then gives specific suggestions. Most of the research in this field, however, has been conducted with hetero-hypnosis in which someone else assists the individual to relax, then gives the mutually agreed upon suggestions.

In one study, the psychologist Howard Hall (1983) gave 20 healthy people blood tests before they were hypnotized. The tests were given again one hour after hypnosis and one week later to measure the response of the immune system's lymphocytes to hypnosis. When hypnotized, the subjects were told to visualize their white blood cells as "sharks" swimming through the bloodstream attacking weak, confused germs. They practiced self-hypnosis twice a day for one week, retelling themselves the shark story. The results were positive; younger subjects and those people who were easily hypnotized showed the greatest increase in number of lymphocytes after the hypnosis sessions.

In their book *The Healing Brain*, Robert Ornstein and David Sobel (1987) review this study, noting that the changes in immune functioning were small. But they also note that the treatment was a minor intervention consisting of only one hypnosis session followed by a week of self-hypnosis. They ask, "If such a minor series of events can lead to real changes in immune functioning, what might be the possibilities of increasing our ability to control the immune system?"

After surveying a number of techniques that purport to enhance human performance, the U.S. National Research Council gave its highest marks to mental rehearsal, stating that "mental practice is effective in enhancing the performance of motor skills" (Druckman and Swets, 1988). It is our conclusion that almost as strong an endorsement could be made of mental imagery and associated techniques. Obviously, their effects are limited and they may not be useful to everyone. Nevertheless it is apparent that shamans exercised a wise directive when they stimulated the imaginative powers of their clients. Furthermore, their work anticipated what E.L. Rossi and David Cheek (1988) have described as the "information-substance receptor system," which appears to be the basis of mind-body communication and the frontier of research in psychoneuroendocrinoimmunology. Shamans utilized less technical terms, but their use of imagination empowered their clients and left a legacy of benefit and bounty.

Ten

Anomalies In Spiritual Healing Research

For as long as human beings have kept records of their experiences, they have described reveries that appeared to transmit thoughts of another person, dreams in which they seemed to become aware of faraway events, rituals in which future happenings supposedly were predicted, and mental procedures that were said to produce direct action on distant physical objects. These purported occurrences may have been instances of phenomena that parapsychologists now call telepathy, clairvoyance, precognition, and psychokinesis. Collectively they are referred to as "psi"—reported interactions between organisms and their environment (including other organisms) in which information or influence has taken place that can not be explained through mainstream science's understanding of sensory-motor channels. In other words, these reported activities are potentially *anomalous* because they appear to preclude the constraints of time, space, and force (Parapsychological Association, 1989).

Psychology is the scientific study of behavior and experience. Parapsychology studies those reported anomalies of behavior and experience that appear to stand outside of the currently recognized explanatory mechanisms that account for organism-environment and organism-organism information and influence flow. Most contemporary scientists are skeptical of these reports, or dismiss them as delusions, fraud, or coincidence. The National Research Council's 1988 investigation of techniques for the enhancement of human performance found "no justification...for the existence of parapsychological phenomena" (Druckman and Swets, 1988). However, the Parapsychological Association (an international society of researchers and theorists in this field) retorted by claiming that the Council's investigation was biased and flawed (Palmer, Honorton, and Utts, 1989).

Research on Anomalous Dreams

One of us (Krippner) was a member of a team of researchers who, for over a decade, investigated anomalous dreams at the Maimonides Medical Center in Brooklyn. Although the results were not conclusive, enough statistically significant data were collected to challenge the notion of some psychotherapists that clients who report dreaming about the future or about distant events must be hallucinating or lying. The Maimonides team used volunteer dreamers who spent one or more nights in a sleep laboratory, and who were awakened whenever their brain waves and eye movements indicated that they were dreaming. In some experiments they attempted to dream about a picture postcard that would be randomly selected the next day. In other experiments, they tried to dream about a picture that had been chosen randomly once they went to bed and that was being focused upon by an experimenter in a distant room.

One night Henri Rousseau's painting "Repast of the Lion" was on the postcard selected as the dream target. It portrays a lion biting into the body of a smaller animal. The dreamer had several dreams about violence and animals; in one dream about dogs, "the two of them had been sort of fighting before. You could kind of see their jaws were open and you could see their teeth....They would continue to try and go on with this playing biting....It's almost as though blood could be dripping from their teeth." A team of judges attempted to match dreams and target pictures without knowing the actual order; in the case of this particular dreamer, they matched five of the eight correctly; one correct match would have been expected by chance—the odds against chance of five correct were over one thousand to one (Ullman and Krippner, 1989).

These results were criticized by one psychologist for lack of a control group, in other words nights during which no picture would be sent to the dreamer (Alcock, 1981). However, the critic overlooked the fact that in the experiment using "Repast of the Lion," target pictures from another study were matched against the typed dream reports from that study. The results were exactly at chance level. This procedure achieved the same goals as those the critic requested and the results supported the original above-chance results. Again, a practical application on these data would be to caution psychotherapists against denigrating anomalous dream reports from their clients; these dreams might be due to coincidence, they might be due to the unconscious processing of information already known, or they might—indeed—be anomalous. They might sometimes be the results of lies or delusions, but the Maimonides studies should cause a responsible, thoughtful therapist or counselor to consider the alternatives.

It appears that the controversy over parapsychology will continue into the indefinite future. In the meantime, there are a small number of parapsychological research studies that are relevant to spiritual dimensions of healing. In presenting them, we have attempted to take a balanced point of view; they are compelling but not conclusive, provocative but not persuasive. One can accept the importance of spiritual healing without accepting the research data produced by parapsychologists. "Psi" ability, if it exists, is not necessarily tantamount to someone's spiritual status. There are many renowned spiritual leaders who have made no claim of telepathic or psychokinetic skills—and many individuals who supposedly demonstrated clairvoyance, precognition, and the like have been strikingly lacking in any type of spiritual development.

Nevertheless, parapsychological data are important to consider for the implications they have for spiritual healing. If valid, they suggest a connecting thread between human beings and other living organisms that exists at a profound level. If valid, they indicate that the claims of many native healers regarding anomalous talents may have some basis in fact. If valid, they point to ways in which the Western worldview is incomplete, ways in which shamanic and religious worldviews could have something of value to consider. And, if valid, they could be used for negative as well as for positive purposes but, valid or not, "psi" abilities could be demonstrated by charlatans, leading to financial and emotional misfortune on the part of gullible people.

"Laying-On" of Hands

The human significance of touching is considerably more profound than most people realize. The anthropologist Ashley Montagu (1978) insists that "the raw sensation of touch as stimulus is vitally necessary for the physical survival of the organism." Touching may take the form of caressing, cuddling, holding, stroking, or patting. Although many psychotherapists reject the practice of touching their clients, Montagu feels that it can assist the healing process if carefully and judiciously employed.

The "laying-on" of hands was practiced by kings who claimed that their "Royal Touch" had divinely-granted power. More recently, it has been used by gypsy "gyaja" (female shamanistic healers) and Touch-for-Health practitioners. It has been studied by various investigators, among them Bernard Grad (1970), a Canadian biologist. Grad worked with a well-known shamanistic healer, Oskar Estebany, who was asked to "heal" mice fed an iodine-deprived diet to induce goiter. The mice, housed in cages of 10, received either a treatment in which Estebany held the cage between his hands, a heat tape placed around the cage (to control for the warmth of Estebany's hands), or no treatment at all. Of these three conditions, Estebany's group showed significantly slower development of goiter than the other two groups. Grad extended his work by studying Estebany's effects on wounded mice. Over a two-week period, the measurements showed clearly that the healer-treated group was healing more rapidly than the heat tape group and the no treatment group.

After studying the "laying-on" of hands approach to healing, Dolores Krieger (1984), a professor of nursing, derived a healing method she called "therapeutic touch." Krieger reasoned that touch is a basic sensation because touch and nerve tracts are the earliest to develop a protective myelin sheath. She conceptualized the therapeutic touch as involving the channeling of an "energy flow" by the healer to supplement the deficient energy level of the "healee." On a material level, she suspected that this might occur by electron transfer resonance and that alterations in this resonance would be reflected in changes in the client's hemoglobin. Simply put, Krieger has stated, "We simply try to actualize the healee's own recuperative powers. It's a process of transferring energy."

Krieger was assisted by the Canadian healer Oskar Estebany for her initial studies, obtaining significant rises in hemoglobin values for those healees treated with therapeutic touch. Krieger began to teach the technique to nurses, having them first "listen" to their hands as they scanned the bodies of the healees. She then taught them to place their hands on the areas where she sensed that the healee needed "energy," trying to redirect their own "energies" and positive thoughts to their healees. When she conducted a formal study of her nurses' effects on healees, Krieger again observed a significant rise in hemoglobin values. Krieger's students have conducted additional investigations, finding that therapeutic touch significantly lowered anxiety levels and raised the pain threshold, even when the nurse's hands were held slightly above the healee's skin (Heidt, 1981).

A critical evaluation of Krieger's studies recommended the use of additional controls (Clark and Clark, 1984). And, in 1991, Arnold S. Relman stated that "When there is objective evidence that...laying-on of hands or thinking good thoughts or any other so-called alternative approach to the treatment of disease works, we'll publish it." Relman, editor of the *New England Journal of Medicine*, went on to say, "Our assumption...is that there is some mechanistic explanation. We assume that all phenomena occur in the world of space, time, and physical reality, and that these phenomena can be measured by physical and chemical means. In principle, we don't have any problem with publishing reports of objectively documented phenomena for which there is presently no physical explanation. But we're not going to publish hearsay, anecdotes, testimonials, or undocumented, unmeasured, uncontrolled observations" (Stewart, 1990).

Researching Therapeutic Touch

Another nurse, Janet Quinn (1984), has conducted research with therapeutic touch, focusing not so much on measurable results but on the means by which the effects are obtained. Quinn accepted the notion that humans have an "energy field" that interacts with environmental "energies"; hence, in therapeutic touch, there is an interaction of "energy" fields that takes place whether or not actual physical contact is made. In her experiment, the nurse administering therapeutic touch moved the hands over the healee's body from head to feet for five minutes, keeping the hands four to six inches distant from the healee's body. A control group of healees was given a "placebo" treatment in which a nurse moved the hands over the healee's body but without the intent to heal that characterized healers in the experimental group.

The healees were 37 men and 23 women hospitalized in a cardiovascular unit of a medical center in New York City; the experimental and control groups were similar regarding age, gender, ethnic background, religion, medical diagnosis, and number of days after surgery. A test of anxiety was administered to both groups before and after treatment. Members of the experimental group (i.e., those receiving therapeutic touch) showed a significantly greater decline in anxiety than members of the control group (i.e., those receiving placebo treatment). A slight decline in anxiety was noted among members of the control group but far less than the 17% drop noted among healees who had received therapeutic touch. Quinn's study underlined the importance of intent and focus on the part of the healee, and suggests that therapeutic touch cannot be administered mechanically and casually if it is to be effective.

An innovative study that met many of Clark and Clark's recommendations was designed by Daniel Wirth (1989), whose 44 subjects (all male college students) permitted themselves to receive minor, intentionally inflicted wounds on their shoulders. The students were asked to extend their affected arms into a room in which a female therapeutic touch practitioner was located; she "treated" 23 of them without making physical contact with the arm. The healer was not in the room when the other 21 subjects extended their arms. The physician who had administered the wounding of the students was unaware of the study's purpose and made the measurements at the end of 8 and 16 days. After 8 days, the "treated" group's wounds had shrunk an average of 93% compared to 67% for the group that received no "treatment." The wounds of 13 of the subjects who had been "treated" had disappeared after 16 days; none of the wounds of the "untreated" subjects had completely healed. Their wounds had shrunk by 91% compared to "treated" groups' average of 99% at the end of 16 days. When the students were told the results, none of the "treated" group recalled feeling physical contact during "treatment," and none in either group said that they had doubted the story they were told—that Wirth was studying the body's electrical conductivity. Wirth claimed that this study had "eliminated the influence of suggestion and the expectation of healing, as well as the placebo effect, by utilizing a double blind design."

We have observed therapeutic touch several times and one of us (Krippner) has discussed the research studies with Krieger and her students. This is a difficult topic to study because a great many variables need to be controlled if living animals (including humans) are going to serve as subjects. Furthermore, the proponents of therapeutic touch have never made it clear what type of "energy" is being "transferred." We are unconvinced that any "energy transfer" occurs, but would agree with an evaluation of therapeutic touch offered by the psychologist Jerry Solfvin (1984): "While these experiments lack the rigor of tight controls, they clearly suggest practical utility." Furthermore, when rigorous controls are introduced, as was the case in the Wirth study, the "treated" group may still demonstrate more significant gains than the "untreated" group.

Healing at a Distance

Lawrence LeShan, a psychologist, has developed a training program emphasizing meditation and mental imagery that purportedly facilitates "distant healing." To examine this approach, Joyce Goodrich (1974) randomly assigned a number of "healees" to several healers trained by LeShan. (Both LeShan and Krieger prefer the term "healee.") An initial meeting took place between the practitioner and the healee and a healing was attempted at that time. Future sessions were conducted at a distance, supposedly at times when the healer and healee were focusing on each other. In reality, Goodrich had arranged it so that only half the sessions would be synchronous; for the other sessions, healers and healees were given different times. Neither partner knew which sessions were synchronous and which were non-synchronous. Healees were given notebooks to record their mood, feelings, sensations, and emotions. The notebooks were given to a team of judges to determine if they would be able to identify the synchronous sessions; the judges accomplished this more often than would be expected by chance.

Shirley Winston (1975) extended Goodrich's work by examining the relationship between healer and client. Winston assigned healers and clients to four levels of face-to-face contact (from "low" to "high"). There were few differences between levels, but healing at a distance appeared to be more effective when the degree of contact was "low." Winston proposed that direct contact between healer and client may involve the erection of psychological defenses and inhibit the later effectiveness of healing at a distance. A related study of the effects of "intercessory prayer to the Judeo-Christian God" on coronary care patients was conducted by R.C. Byrd (1988). When the 192 patients who were prayed for (at a distance) were compared with 201 patients who were not prayed for, the former had a significantly lower severity score after 10 months. Both groups knew that prayer was involved but did not know whether or not they would be the recipients of the prayer. LeShan (1974) has explained these effects by conceptualizing a "clairvoyant reality" in which healer-client contact may occur during distant healing sessions.

Some studies of healing at a distance lend support to LeShan's model of reality but others do not. C. R. B. Joyce and R. M. C. Weldon (1965) studied 19 matched pairs of patients over 18 months with a crossover between the control group and the prayer group at 6 months. During the first half of the study the prayer group did better, but in the second half the control group did better. The final results showed no significant differences as a result of prayer. P.J. Collipp (1969) conducted an experiment in which 10 out of 18 leukemic children received distant prayer healing without the knowledge that they were part of a research project. Using months of survival after diagnosis as the criterion, the results demonstrated a trend in favor of the "healed" children, but the data were not statistically significant. R.N. Miller conducted a test of distant healing with 96 hypertensive clients and eight healers. He reported a significant improvement in systolic blood pressure for the "healed" versus the "control" clients, while the diastolic pressure and heart rate showed no effects (Benor, 1982).

From a critical view we would conclude that the research data are promising, but too sparse to allow any firm conclusion to be drawn. Not all of the research studies cited were published in scientific journals that subjected their manuscripts to rigorous review. Further, if the effect is a strong one, it should be replicable by other investigators, but to date, research data on distant healing have not yielded a pattern of replicability. Nor is there an obvious mechanism for distant interactions. As a result, investigators need to be circumspect as their results might be marred by individual differences among clients and healers, faulty research designs, or fraud on the part of either the client or the healer. Nevertheless, it is encouraging to observe that a beginning has been made to explore these types of reported effects as the implications for healing are profound.

Explanations of Distant Healing

"Laying-on" of hands, if verified by further research, could be explained—at least in part—by the expectation of the healees, by the personality characteristics of the healer, or by some type of energetic interaction (such as heat, static electricity, or a yet-to-be-defined "healing energy") between healer and healee. But what of distant healing? If further experiments verify the existence of this phenomenon, explanations become more difficult to propose because conventional notions of space and force would seem to be circumvented.

LeShan (1990) has noted that the healers he has studied propose four possible explanations, either alone or in combination with each other. The first is divine intervention; God is seen as the causative agent. LeShan describes the case of a middle aged man who had suffered from intractable psoriasis (a skin disease) for one and one half years. A healer, Edgar Jackson, was about 50 miles away when he prayed that God would do whatever was best for his healee. The healee, who knew that Jackson generally worked in the evenings, reported feeling a great deal of peace at about 9:30 PM. The next morning his skin condition was greatly improved and it disappeared within a few days. It had not returned when the case was followed up two years later.

Other healers LeShan has studied mention spirit intervention as the causal agent. He cites the case of a healer who was convinced that his spirit guides helped his healees. Indeed, the healer said that he refrained from working directly with healees, fearing his guides would become jealous! This healer also worked in the same room with healees; LeShan described one case where the healee's broken bone showed repair at what the attending physician described as "three-to-five times the normal rate" following a session with the healer and his purported spirit guides.

A third explanation proposed by some of LeShan's healers is some type of "energy." One group of "energy" healers claims they are generating the "energy" themselves while another group feels that they align themselves with the "energy" that is available in the cosmos. Sometimes healers refer to these groups as the "God within" and the "God without" healers, noting that the first group tires more easily than the second group because of the effort needed to generate "energy" internally.

The fourth explanation is termed "self-repair" by LeShan's healers. These healers believe that they evoke an internal healing response on the part of the healee, a response that is a basic human capacity, albeit one that is rarely utilized because of patients' tendencies to rely on outside intervention. These healers generally "unite" with the healee, altering their consciousness to achieve a sense of "oneness."

LeShan finds no major differences among these explanations in terms of their effectiveness, suggesting that it is the particular combination of healer and healee that is most important. Furthermore, some healers use a combination of two or more systems; for example, God may send "energy" to effect self-repair, or an angel may appeal to God for "healing energy." However, LeShan has observed that the explanations generally agree on the healing process as involving a change toward the direction of greater harmony—harmony between the parts of the healee, or between the healee and the environment. Healers regard their work as restoring a natural but broken integration; they generally feel that illness and disease indicate disharmony among the parts of oneself, between oneself and other people, or between oneself and God or Nature.

The Inner World of Healers

Janet Quinn's research study is one of the few that explored the inner world of healers engaging in therapeutic touch, revealing the potential importance of intent and focus. At the Mind Science Foundation in San Antonio, Texas, William Braud and his colleagues have conducted a series of experiments that have explored similar dimensions of healing. Five of the first nine experiments obtained statistically significant results, suggesting that healers were able to affect bodily processes of healees at a distance—in most cases the electrical properties of the healees' skin (Braud and Schlitz, 1983; Braud and Schlitz, 1989).

The healees in these experiments know what is going on because they have been told that someone at a distance will try to influence their bodily responses. However, they do not know when the attempts at influence will occur or what form they will take. The healees need do nothing special; they simply sit in a room that has been shielded against ordinary influence from the environment. When Braud interviewed the healers in the experiments in which distant influence appeared to have taken place, he found that they had tried one of four strategies. Some healers focused on the pen that had been connected to the electrical device that measured the healees' skin activity, "willing" the pen to move in the desired direction. Another strategy was for the healers to imagine the desired result in themselves, then make an attempt to transfer that change to the healee. For example, a healer might recall being in an exciting situation, then would try to imagine the healee being aroused in a similar manner. Third, some healers would simply imagine that the healee was having an experience that would produce the desired skin response, bypassing their own experiences and reactions. A fourth group of healers focused on the success of the experiment in general, ignoring the pen, the healee, and their own past experiences. There was no clear-cut superiority of one approach over the other; however, each strategy involved volition, imagination, and focus.

At Saybrook Institute Graduate School in San Francisco, M. Allan Cooperstein (1990) read 10 books written by healers and interviewed an additional 10 healers who had obtained striking results in laboratory experiments (such as those conducted by Quinn and Braud). An analysis of their written or spoken comments revealed that alterations in the healers' sense of self, their mode of attention, and their way of thinking were important elements in virtually all 20 of the individuals studied.

There was a general tendency among the 20 healers for their attention to be diffuse—neither exclusively focused externally nor internally, but simultaneously encompassing both the internal and external environment, with an emphasis on the former. There were many individual differences. One healer stated, "The attention would be stronger and much fuller. What I attempt to do is fill myself as fully as possible with the goal that I'm trying to produce." Another said, "On a case-by-case basis, I may focus more on the person or the situation than I would at other instances." But a different healer purported to be at two levels—"Internally, I can be in complete meditation or prayer and at the same time talking about everyday matters."

Some healers said that they became more active in their thoughts and attention, others claimed to become more passive, and still others alternated between activity and passivity. No matter how active the process, most healers went out of their way to point out that there was a transcendence of their ordinary ego concerns, expectations, and desires. Volition or "will" appeared to be useful up to a point, but personal, ego-centered "will" was eventually superseded by a "surrender" of the ego that allowed the healer to focus on the healing process itself rather than on any preconceived notions about the end result. There was a general tendency for healers to use mental imagery and to become absorbed in the process, often to the point of "merging" with the healee, or with their image of the healee. The types of imagery reported included mythic images that supported the healer's beliefs about the "healing state," images concerning diagnostic information, and imagery appropriate to the healing process and goal.

It can be seen that a variety of strategies were reported by the 20 healers in Cooperstein's study. A common thread running through the healers' accounts was a shift in their consciousness that enabled them to transcend their ordinary view of reality, their physical environment, and their personal concerns. Attention was withdrawn from the outer environment and focused upon inner experiences. A type of awareness emerged involving decreased "effort," enhanced sensitivity toward inner events, and an absorption that allowed a "surrender" to the healing process or to the healee. Such terms as "empathy," "selfless love," "sympathy," and "compassion" were used to describe the way in which the healers related to the healee. Emotional feelings were generally heightened during the healing process, especially feelings of interpersonal warmth, inner harmony, and joy.

The transcendence of dualities was common among the healers, many of whom reported being aware of both inner and outer events, combining "will" and "surrender," and shifting between activity and passivity. This transcendence also characterized the healers' thought processes; in general, they claimed that both rational and non-rational cognition was at work. One healer told Cooperstein, "I think that it's both rational and ordinary, and non-rational and non-ordinary....So it's probably a combination, switching back and forth."

Despite the similarities noted in the healers' reported experiences, the belief systems of the healers varied considerably. There was a general agreement that individual consciousness is connected with that of other living organisms as well as that of a higher source, but 10 of the 20 healers proposed that "spiritual laws" interacted with the laws of "objective reality," while 6 believed that "spiritual laws" superseded ordinary cause-and-effect. There was less disagreement on attitudinal issues; the qualities of spontaneity, love, and empathy were valued as well as the need to give unselfishly of one's self in order to be receptive to the needs of the healee.

Cooperstein's research demonstrates the complexity of the inner world of spiritual healers. Whether or not psychologists accept the possibility of a healer's distant effects on a healee, their reported experiences are valuable material for a more complete understanding of an alleged human capacity that has been virtually ignored by mainstream science.

Investigations of Faith Healers

There are two major models for healing prayers: the prayer of intercessory petition in which God is asked to heal someone, often in the name of Jesus or a saint; the prayer of intention in which a "faith healer" is convinced that he or she is aligned with the will of God and can command a sick person to recover. The latter type of prayer characterized the healing services of the late Kathryn Kuhlman, a controversial American faith healer and two physicians who investigated her produced diametrically opposing conclusions. H. R. Casdorph (1976) documented eight recoveries from serious illness purportedly associated with Kuhlman's healing services.

W.A. Nolen (1974), on the other hand, attended one of Kuhlman's services and interviewed several people who claimed to have been healed; he found no significant change in any of them. It must also be recalled that most illnesses are self-limiting; the human body is capable of handling them without external intervention. If a healer's ministrations happen to coincide with the body's successful attempts at self-healing, it is the healer rather than the body's healing mechanisms that is likely to receive the credit.

The placebo effect may also play a role in alleged "cures" brought about by faith healers. In 1955, a physician observed the progress of three hospitalized patients; one had chronic gall bladder disease, one had severe pancreatitis accompanied by weight loss, and the third had inoperable cancer of the uterus accompanied by weakness and anemia. The physician asked a local faith healer to attempt to treat the three patients without their knowing about it. During a dozen sessions in the next few weeks, the faith healer attempted to project a "healing force" to the patients, none of whom had been informed about the healer's efforts. There was no change in their condition.

After the faith healer had stopped working on the cases,

the patients were told that a powerful healer was prepared to project his "energy" onto them. A few days after the supposed "healing," the patient with gall bladder disease became free of pain and was symptom free for about a year. The patient with pancreatitis had a restoration of normal bowel function, was able to leave her bed, and gained 30 pounds. The patient with cancer experienced an increase in appetite, an improvement of her anemia, and was able to leave the hospital and return to her home. Although she died some three months later, she was able to live an active life up to the end and remained in good spirits. Although it could be argued that the benefits were due to the delayed benefits of the faith healer's efforts, patient expectancy is a more likely cause for the dramatic results (Rheder, 1955).

James Randi is an American conjurer who headed the Faith Healing Investigation Project for the Committee for a Scientific Examination of Religion. One of the faith healers whose claims he studied was the Reverend Walter Vinson Grant, minister of the Eagle's Nest Cathedral in Dallas, Texas, whose radio and television shows bring in financial contributions from various parts of the country. Randi and his associates attended one of Grant's religious healing meetings, as did many people who were physically disabled. However, Randi observed that Grant's staff members supplied wheelchairs to several members of the audience who did not seem to need them. One man was interviewed by Randi and recalled that a pastor told him to sit in a wheelchair even though he could move around without it. In another instance, a man with deteriorating vision, carrying a white cane, was declared "healed." Grant threw the man's cane onto the stage—but at the close of the meeting the man had to ask that the cane be returned so that he could make his way out of the auditorium. Nevertheless, Grant's magazine, *New Day*, declared that the man had been "blind all of his life" and that after Grant's prayer "he saw for the first time."

Randi's associates observed that one of Grant's staff

members was standing at the back of the auditorium using hand signals to point to the part of the body where a person being interviewed by Grant was afflicted. This information could have been obtained by pre-program interviewing, from letters accompanying requests for tickets, or from notes enclosed in the donations brought to the meeting by most of the members of the audience. Randi and his team found the discarded letters in Grant's garbage; the details in those letters matched the statements made by Grant on stage, suggesting that Grant may have read some of the letters himself. Indeed, much of the vital information had been summarized on sheets of paper also found in Grant's garbage. Randi concluded:

> W. V. Grant is, to put it bluntly, doing a magic act disguised as healing miracles....If he was pretending to heal headaches, backaches, depression, or other psychosomatic ailments, he could to a considerable extent escape condemnation for interfering with the well-being of his victims. But he goes all the way, claiming to treat such problems as cancer, bacterial infections, physical imperfections, bone fractures, organic defects, circulatory disease, and internal disorders simply by praying them away. Grant is literally practicing medicine without any qualifications whatever (Randi, 1986).

Randi (1987) has also investigated Peter Popoff, a minister whose headquarters are in Upland, California. One night, Randi and his colleagues arrived early at an auditorium where Popoff was scheduled to appear; they were approached by Popoff's wife and interviewed extensively, noticing that Mrs. Popoff repeated each detail slowly and loudly. Randi discovered that an electronic transmitter was concealed in her handbag and that every word was being transmitted to her husband's upstairs office. When Popoff made his entrance, he was wearing a small device in his ear, enabling his wife to continue transmitting information during the healing service. For example, Randi's team heard Mrs. Popoff describe one woman who was about to make a request: "She lives at 4267 Masterson, and she's praying for her daughter Joy who's allergic to certain foods." The woman was amazed at Popoff's accuracy; he claimed that he had received the information from God. At one point in the meeting, Popoff asked the sick people in the audience to "break free of the Devil" by throwing their medications onto the stage. Dozens of people came forward and tossed bottles on the platform—digitalis, nitro-glycerin tablets, diabetes medication, and various pills and tablets. Popoff responded to Randi's exposure by explaining that he was merely following the suggestions of the Holy Spirit; however, most of his followers thought differently and the self-styled faith healer pleaded bankruptcy within a year.

Randi is a controversial figure in parapsychological research but we would agree with the observations made in the July, 1986 *Newsletter of the American Society for Psychical Research*: "We are united on this front and should work together to help protect the desperate and the credulous against those who would exploit their deepest needs" (McCormick, 1986). The sexual and financial scandals of such celebrated American faith healers as Jimmy Swaggart, and Jim and Tammy Bakker do not lend encouragement to the purity of intention that they claim must precede their healing prayers. On the other hand, there is some evidence that people with a stable network of friends and family supporting them are likely to live longer and that individuals who belong to a church or temple have lower mortality rates than those who do not (Berkman and Syme, 1979). We propose that the faith that is embedded in a network of love and friendship will prove to be more conducive to health than a faith that can be manipu-lated by a high-powered preacher.

Eleven

Integrating Spiritual Healing Into Counseling And Psychotherapy

According to the United Nations World Health Organization (WHO), over 70% of the world's population relies on non-allopathic systems of healing. Determined to insure that medical care was available to all the people of the earth by the year 2000, WHO realized that this goal was beyond the scope of personnel trained in Western medicine. As a result, WHO initiated a program that is preparing native healing practitioners to serve as health auxiliaries. Halfdan Mahler (1977), when he was the Director-General of WHO, pointed out:

> WHO has proposed that the great numbers of traditional healers who practice today in virtually every country of the world should not be overlooked....Such traditional healers and local midwives can, at a very moderate expense, be

trained to the level where they can provide adequate
and acceptable health care under suitable
supervision....The age-old arts of the herbalists too
must be tapped. Many of the plants familiar to the
"wise-woman" or the "witch-doctor" really do have
the healing powers that tradition attaches to
them....Let us not be in any doubt: modern medicine
has a great deal still to learn from the collector of
herbs.

Mahler concluded that the utilization of native health
care providers "may seem very disagreeable to some policy
makers, but if the solution is the right one to help people, we
should have the courage to insist that this is the best policy in
the long run."

In 1972, WHO held a conference to stimulate the training
and employment of native birth attendants and, in 1977,
adopted a resolution urging governments to give adequate
importance to the utilization of their traditional systems of
medicine. Perhaps as a result of WHO's increasing support for
native health practitioners, as well as the extraordinary cost of
health care in the United States, the American Medical Association, in 1980, revised its code of ethics and gave physicians
permission to consult with, take referrals from, and make
referrals to practitioners without orthodox medical training.
This move opened the way for physicians to cooperate with
shamans, herbalists, spiritists, homeopaths, chiropractors,
and other non-allopathic physicians. Also in 1980, *Lancet*, the
world's most influential medical journal, stated, in an edito-
rial:

Even where modern medical care is available the
people may still prefer to consult their traditional
practitioners for certain troubles. This decision may
be quite reasonable, because systems of traditional
medicine have a holistic approach to illness, in

which the patient is seen in relation to the environment, ecological and social (Pros and Cons, 1980).

Many Native American healing practitioners had integrated the discoveries of allopathic medicine into their approaches long before the American Medical Association took its position. The Navaho Indians, for example, divide illnesses into categories that require treatment from different specialists. "Lightning sickness" and "lizard sickness" are considered best treated by Navaho practitioners; tuberculosis and appendicitis are best treated by allopathic physicians. Snakebites can be treated by either type of professional. Pima Indians regard snakebites as untreatable, but refer many types of "wandering sickness" to Western-trained physicians.

Spiritual Crises

The influence of Native American healers can be seen in some of the practices of the Spiritual Emergence Network (Chamberlin, 1986). Stanislav and Christina Grof organized the network with the assistance of several therapists who had special understanding of such phenomena as supposed spirit communication, unusual mental imagery (visions, voices, etc.), shifts in body sensations (out-of-body experiences, stigmata, etc.), religious experience (encounters with Jesus Christ, the Buddha, etc.), and mystical experience ("dissolving" into the cosmos or into "ineffable love"). Originally set up as a telephone service to deal with people undergoing spiritual crises, the group organized a residential treatment center in 1986. Located in the Bay area of California, its purpose is to offer a retreat facility where persons undergoing spiritual transformation can find support and guidance to enable them to work through and then integrate their experiences. The Grofs have organized a three-year training program for practitioners who want to become competent in assisting persons move through spiritual crises.

The Grofs (1989) have cited ten varieties of spiritual crises that conventional psychotherapists could easily diagnose as psychosis, prescribing isolation and medication instead of the counseling and networking provided by the Spiritual Emergence Network.

1. The shamanistic crisis. In these instances, individuals experience episodes that closely resemble shamanic "calls" and "initiations," e.g., images of physical and emotional torture, death and dismemberment, resurrection and rebirth; feelings of being "connected" with animals, plants, and elemental forms of nature; attempts to create rituals that resemble tribal ceremonies.

2. The "kundalini" awakening. In these cases, individuals experience intense sensations of "energy" and "heat" streaming up the spinal column. This is usually associated with violent shaking, twisting, and spasmodic movements. There may be images of brilliant light, of spiritual entities, and/or internally perceived sounds.

3. Episodes of "unitive consciousness." These experiences often have a sacred quality. People report "merging with Cosmic Energy," with "universal consciousness," or with God.

4. Episodes of "cosmic combat." Individuals who report these experiences often speak of feeling like a "battlefield" where a war is transpiring between good and evil, light and darkness, life and death. They may be preoccupied with death themes (ritual killing, sacrifice, martyrdom), the afterlife, or the problem of opposites (male and female, passivity and action).

5. The crises of "psychic opening." These reports may contain dramatic references to out-of-body experiences, telepathy, clairvoyance, precognition, psychokinesis, or to uncanny coincidences. The latter, often called "synchronicity," may link inner and outer reality—dreams to waking life events, visions to everyday life.

6. "Past life" experiences. These reports usually take the form of detailed life events taking place in other historical periods and/or other countries. They are typically accompanied by powerful emotions and physical sensations, and are recalled as "memories." There is a convincing sense of personally remembering and reliving something that one had personally experienced.

7. Communication with "spirit guides." These reports concern entities who seem to show interest in the person who has had the experience, assuming the position of a teacher, counselor, protector, or giver of information. Sometimes this information is "channeled" and an individual "transmits" messages from a purported external source, either by involuntarily speaking or writing them. Often an individual sees or hears (or even feels or smells) the alleged spirits, but sometimes they simply manifest themselves through the "channeling" process.

8. Experiences of being "possessed" by negative entities. This is one of the most serious "spiritual emergencies," because the behavior of the individual may alter radically to reflect the character of the "low spirit," "demon," or "intruder" who has purportedly taken over the individual's psyche and/or body.

9. Experiences of "aliens" or "unidentified flying objects." These reports describe moving lights that have an uncanny quality, sometimes in the form of aircraft. There may be reported abductions by the "aliens" who command these aircraft, usually with claims of physical examinations, sexual interactions, or scientific experiments carried out by the "aliens."

10. "Near-death" experiences. People reporting near-death experiences often witness a review of their entire life in a short period of time. They may find themselves moving through a "tunnel" toward a transcendental realm, sometimes being welcomed by deceased friends and relatives. Occasionally they report traveling toward a fearful, "hellish" domain. Near-death experiences frequently lead to spiritual emergencies because they challenge the belief system of the person experiencing them. On the other hand, a "heavenly" near-death experience might result in peace of mind, personal growth, and enhanced spirituality (Grof and Grof, 1990).

These ten spiritual crises have been conceptualized much differently in the past. The Roman Catholic Church's manual on exorcism lists many of them as signs that a person has been possessed by demonic forces, for example "the facility of divulging future and hidden events" (Karpel, 1975). More recently, a patient's claims of such abilities have been labelled "magical thinking," and considered to be symptoms of emotional disturbance by conventional psychiatrists (American Psychiatric Association, 1987). Neither of these stances recognizes the potential for growth inherent in a spiritual crisis, if it is treated with understanding, patience, and compassion rather than with an exorcism, a drug, or well-meaning dismissal.

Treating Spiritual Crises

It must be realized that some spiritual experiences have psychotic features. We would agree with the psychotherapist David Lukoff (1985) that "differentiating psychotic from spiritual experience is not easy. The task requires familiarity with the psychiatric perspective as well as the religous and philosophical content of the perennial philosophy." In treating these individuals, Lukoff (1988) has used creative writing and painting, as well as other therapeutic modalities. In working with a client (diagnosed as suffering from "manic psychosis") who claimed that he had been abducted by space aliens, Lukoff tried to understand the client's underlying personal mythology and its accompanying metaphors. Eventually, the client was able to understand his myths as well, and eventually communicated them in art and writing that he displayed and published. Even though he kept insisting that he actually had been abducted, he lost his preoccupation with the alleged incident and was able to get on with his life.

A psychiatrist, Rima E. Laibow (1990), has called upon psychotherapists and counselors to begin treating individuals reporting phenomena referred to by the acronym "EAT"— Experienced Anomalous Trauma. She has found resemblances between EAT sufferers and those diagnosed as having post-traumatic stress disorder. In the latter cases, the trauma was war combat, rape, physical abuse, or some other recognized assault. In the former cases, however, the trauma is considered anomalous because it is described as an abduction by alients, an attack by demonic forces, or some other incident *not* recognized by mainstream psychiatry or psychology. Laibow finds that EAT incidents tend to occur repeatedly, that they lend themselves to a variety of explanations, and respond to a number of different psychotherapeutic approaches.

In our opinion, psychotherapists and counselors dealing with spiritual crises have several critical decisions to make. They need to determine whether the experience has psychotic components. They need to decide whether the crisis is basically an *emergency* which has little growth potential, a spiritual *emergence* in which the client stands to gain something of value if the crisis is well handled, or whether it is an emergency that can lead to spiritual emergence. An obvious issue is whether the reported experiences (e.g., abduction by aliens, possession by a demonic entity, recalling episodes from a past life) are metaphors for an internal process, a non-anomalous trauma, or whether they should be taken literally. Sometimes a therapist can be non-judgmental about the issue; we have interviewed therapists who claim the successful use of hypnotically-elicited past-life reports in the treatment of phobias (unreasonable fears such as an anxiety about heights or a dread of spiders) Some of them frankly tell their clients that they take a neutral position on the "reality" of these reports, but that they find them effective in reducing or eliminating the phobic problem.

In addition, we have discussed these issues with several practitioners working with individuals who have reported abduction by aliens or satanic ritual abuse. Many of them told us that they believe these claims are metaphors for their clients' physical or sexual abuse by family members. The actual event is too threatening to be accepted. A disguised account of the abuse, however, may be unconsciously perceived as less harmful to the individual than would be other responses, e.g., a serious personality dissociation (which often leads to multiple personality disorder) or a repression of the incident (which often leads to severe psychosomatic problems).

The establishment of the Spiritual Emergence Network reflects the fact that a number of contemporary approaches to psychotherapy believe that clients' spiritual concerns are vital for behavioral and attitudinal change. These approaches include pastoral counseling (Jackson, 1974), shamanic counseling (Harner, 1986), Jungian analysis (Stein, 1982), Christian psychotherapy (Wilson, 1980), moral psychotherapy (Peck,

1978), "past-life" therapy (Woolger, 1987), personal mythology dreamworking (Feinstein and Krippner, 1988), guided fantasy encounter (Rochkind and Conn, 1973), attitudinal healing (Jampolsky, 1979), logotherapy (Frankl 1965), existential psychotherapy (Yalom, 1980), humanistic psychotherapy (Maher, 1978), and transpersonal psychotherapy (Kunz, 1985; Walsh and Vaughan, 1980).

Alcoholics Anonymous

One of the best-known therapeutic programs that emphasizes a spiritual dimension is Alcoholics Anonymous (AA). The psychiatrist Ruth Fox (1958) once declared, "The best therapy of all in alcoholism I believe to be Alcoholics Anonymous, and every patient is urged to associate himself with this group." In 1968, AA released the first broad-based survey ever done on its membership, randomly selecting meetings in all 50 states and each Canadian province where members were asked to fill out unsigned questionnaires. Of those responding, 41% had not imbibed alcohol since their first AA meeting, 23% stopped within a year, and 18% quit between two and five years after their first meeting (Twaddel, 1968). Twenty years later, the U.S. membership was estimated to be 750,000, with a success rate similar to the earlier figures.

Founded in 1935 by two alcoholics, a stockbroker and a surgeon, AA relies on a spiritual approach, calling upon a "Higher Power greater than ourselves." The chief ingredients of AA's "Twelve Steps" to recovery are moral and spiritual, progressing from "admission" that one is an alcoholic, to "submission" to the Higher Power, to "restitution" and reciprocal forgiveness, to "construction" which includes maintaining a spiritual approach to life and assisting others who are still suffering. AA's suggested prayer is, "God, I offer myself to Thee to build with me and to do with me as Thou wilt." To make the prayer meaningful to her purposes, a Buddhist revised it to read, "Force of rhythm and meaning moving

through all things including me...,I offer myself to you"
(Collett, 1988).

The Twelve Steps are worked through by each alcoholic
in consultation with a sponsor (typically a recovering alcoholic who has spent considerable time in the program). They
are also the centerpiece of each AA group meeting. Participants state that:

1. We admit we were powerless over alcohol and
    that our lives had become unmanageable.
2. We came to believe that a power greater than
    ourselves could restore us.
3. We made a decision to turn our will and our
    lives over to the care of God (as we understand
    God).
4. We made a searching and fearless inventory of
    ourselves.
5. We admitted to God, to ourselves, and to
    another human being the nature of our prob-
    lem.
6. We were entirely ready to have God remove
    these defects of character.
7. We humbly asked God to remove our short-
    comings.
8. We made a list of all people we had harmed
    and were willing to make amends to them all.
9. We made direct amends to these people when-
    ever possible except when to do so would
    injure them or others.
10. We continued to take a personal inventory and
    when we were wrong we promptly admitted it.
11. We sought through prayer and meditation to
    improve our own contact with God (as we
    understood God), praying only for knowledge
    of God's will for us and the power to carry it
    out.

12. Having had a spiritual awakening as the result
of these steps, we tried to carry this message to
alcoholics and to practice these principles in
our daily activities (Elliot, 1987).

Applying the Twelve Step Program

This Twelve Step program has been followed by groups
who feel that they are addicted to narcotics, sexual indul-
gence, food, and a variety of other substances and behaviors.
It is not without its critics; the use of the Twelve Step program
for individuals displaying promiscuous sexual behavior has
been called into question. Critics have charged that using the
addiction model in hypersexuality simplifies a complex issue,
focuses on symptoms rather than causes, and reinforces re-
pressive ideas of human sexual behavior (Avasthi, 1990).

Working in another area of human distress, a team of
therapists has applied it to Vietnam veterans suffering from
post-traumatic stress disorder. These psychotherapists asked
68 combat veterans to complete a questionnaire and rank 78
different disturbing experiences on a 10-point scale. The most
disturbing experiences were accidentally killing other Americans, seeing close friends killed, seeing Americans killed,
placing Americans in body bags, seeing atrocities committed
against Americans, and holding friends as they were dying
(Brende and McDonald, 1989).

These experiences produced feelings of guilt among
many veterans, for example, guilt about having taken a human
life, guilt about being part of a morally corrupt society, guilt
about having lost prior moral values as they began to freely kill
and commit atrocities, and guilt about discovering that killing
people was often thrilling and empowering. This unresolved
guilt was found to be a source of self-destructive attitudes and
behavior, a guilt perpetuated by the veterans' inability to
control violent thoughts and urges. Some even felt guilty that
they had become the instrument of evil forces, bargaining with

demonic forces to gain feelings of omnipotence over death. One veteran recalled, "I laid out in a field with 12 bullet holes in me for four hours and I have the feeling that I made a pledge to some spiritual power that I would do anything if he kept me alive. Ever since then, I have had a feeling of dread that I 'sold out' to the devil."

The team of psychotherapists, working at a Veterans Administration medical center, adapted AA's Twelve Step program, integrating such AA principles as interdependency of group members, conceptualizing recovery as a process rather than a cure, educating veterans to lead a meaningful life, and depending on a Higher Power to assist their recovery. The discussion and sharing of traumatic emotions and memories was encouraged to help the veterans work through their post-traumatic stress symptoms. The Twelve Steps were rephrased to deal directly with the veterans' stress, guilt, and alienation:

1. We acknowledge that we have become essentially powerless to live meaningful lives. Hence we hope to discover the presence of a "Good Higher Power" who can help.

2. We recognized that our lives have little or no meaning, hence we seek a purpose in having survived and open our minds to a "Good Higher Power" to show us that purpose.

3. We seek the capacity to trust not only friends and professionals who wish to help us, but God (as individually understood) who seeks our well-being.

4. We make a searching self-inventory of both negative and positive traits, acknowledging both those traits to someone we trust and to God (as individually interpreted), accepting those that are positive and asking for help to change those that are negative.

5.   We acknowledge our rage toward God and those we believe abandoned or betrayed us, and hope to understand the other sources of our continuing anger. We seek, with the help of those we trust and a "Good Higher Power," to control destructive rage and channel anger constructively.

6.   We seek to relinquish the "wall" around our feelings and with help from those we trust, and from God. With their help, we face the fear and withstand the terrifying moments we feel during day and night.

7.   We face our guilty secrets, revealing them to someone we trust and to God from whom we seek and accept forgiveness and help to forgive ourselves.

8.   We seek to grieve friends and loved ones who died and the death of parts of ourselves—our youth and innocence. We face these painful memories with the comfort of those we trust and our "Good Higher Power," and are thankful that our tears can heal our sorrows.

9.   We reveal to someone we trust and a "Good Higher Power" all suicidal plans and wishes and seek, with help, to replace them with a commitment to life.

10.   We acknowledge to a "Good Higher Power," to another person, and to ourselves all those whom we continue to hate. We seek to relinquish our revengeful wishes and seek to be a channel for forgiveness that flows from a "Good Higher Power" to those we have hated.

11.   We seek to discover who we are and why we are here, not only from those who wish to help us, but from a "Good Higher Power," so that we may find a personal relationship with God and seek God's direction for our lives.

12. We commit ourselves to those whose love we
     have taken for granted, help those who have
     suffered as we have suffered, and seek God's
     strength to love those we have not been able to
     love.

The psychotherapeutic team reported that only about
10% of the veterans rejected the program, usually because
they did not want "God forced upon them." Those who
participated were able to reduce their violent urges, their self-
destructive behaviors, and their guilt, while enhancing the
positive aspects of their self-identities. However, "the Veterans Administration was cautious—even hostile—towards
any [spiritual] program....But we found that these men were
more likely to sustain their recovery when involved in a
spiritual group similar to that found in Alcoholics Anonymous" (p. 339). One of us (Krippner) was told that the
psychotherapeutic team was terminated from this Veterans
Administration hospital because of their incorporation of
spiritual counseling into their work, despite the positive and
long-lasting results they obtained.

Like the small number of veterans in this study, not every
recovering alcoholic is comfortable with AA's appeal to a
Higher Power. Some of these people have founded the Secular
Organization for Sobriety (SOS) which appeals to atheists and
agnostics who believe they gain self-esteem by crediting
themselves rather than God (Christopher, 1988). SOS and AA
share a reliance on group processes to encourage sobriety, and
one AA member stated, "SOS has made the group their
'higher power.' I don't have a problem with that, if it works"
(Robertson, 1988). In the United States there are at least 10
million problem drinkers or alcoholics; AA reaches no more
than two million of them, indicating that there is room for
alternate approaches.

Curanderismo and Espiritismo

Curanderos and curanderas are the best-known folk healers and therapists among Mexican-Americans living in the United States. There are many varieties of these practitioners; some specialize in diagnosis, some in herbal treatments, and others combine magical spells with their herbal treatments. In addition, mediums are frequently found in Mexican-American communities. Both groups provide a health resource in their communities, and both have incorporated allopathic data about bacteria and viruses into their list of causative agents. Although they are rarely consulted by hospitals, physicians, or psychotherapists in the United States, in Cuba many curanderas have been given a two-month training course, then awarded positions as educators and assistants to personnel working in the health centers (Navarro, 1972). Two curanderos were placed on the staff of a California mental health center as "consultants," but there was so much opposition their title was changed to "religious specialist" (Torrey, 1986).

In the meantime, individual instances of cooperation have been reported. Jerold Kreisman (1975) has described two cases involving Mexican-American schizophrenic patients in which conventional psychotherapy was seriously stalled until treatment was adopted to conform appropriately to the curanderismo model. In one case, the patient was told she might have been "bewitched." She responded with great relief, discussed pertinent portions of her life that she previously had kept secret, and improved to the extent that she was released from the hospital as an out-patient. In the other case, the patient felt she had been "hexed"; when the hospital began to treat her within the parameters of this belief system, she responded well and returned to work. Richard Warner (1977) used the case of a Mexican-American woman who believed in witchcraft and "soul loss" to illustrate the value of operating within the belief system of the patient. When treated by a combination of home visits, family therapy, and medication, within the curanderismo framework, her delusions ceased and she regained her usual mood, working ability, sexual activity, and sleep patterns. She was still happy and active a year later.

Spiritism has been used as a supplementary healing system in New York City community mental health centers for several years. Alan Harwood (1977), an anthropologist, found both African and European spiritist influences among New York Puerto Ricans, the former more apparent in Santeria, the latter in espiritismo or Mesa Blanca ("White Table"). Mesa Blanca mediums tend to communicate with "intranquil" and "protector" spirits as they sit around a table covered with a white cloth, while Santeria mediums are able to contact more exalted levels of the spirit world. Some mediums combine the traditions as contact with both the "lower" and the "higher" spirits are needed for different aspects of healing (Murphy, 1988). Harwood instituted a collaborative program at a neighborhood health center in the Bronx, New York, where he educated health practitioners on how to work most effectively with Puerto Rican patients.

Another program in the Bronx was instituted, in the early 1970s, by Pedro Ruiz, who facilitated informal collaboration with spiritist practitioners. Mental health professionals were encouraged to visit the "centros" where espiritistas worked. espiritistas were invited to the Lincoln Community Mental Health Center so that professionals could observe their work. From this beginning, exchanges developed that often involved cooperation in working with the same patient, giving new status to these practitioners (Ruiz and Langrod, 1976).

In both the Harwood and the Ruiz programs, those ailments attributed to spiritual causes by the local Puerto Rican community were typically referred to spiritists, e.g., insomnia, nightmares, suicidal urges, loss of memory, and bizarre mood changes. Other problems, such as insanity and seizures, were held to be due to both spiritual and physical causes. Harwood found that the use of spiritists as a mental health resource tended to allow clients to conceptualize their illness as a rite of passage, moving them from one level of social status to another. Allopathic medicine and Western-oriented psychotherapy neglect these issues of transition, despite their potential creativity and therapeutic usefulness.

Collaboration in Puerto Rico

A successful project designed to facilitate collaboration between Western psychotherapy and spiritism has been initiated in several Puerto Rican community mental health centers. In 1979, one of us (Krippner) visited a center in Cayey, Puerto Rico, observing that spiritist healers and health professionals had been meeting twice a week over a 3-year period. The first week had been devoted to lectures by representatives from both groups. The second week focused on case conferences where both groups gave their input in regard to clients seen at the center. From this point on, the spiritist practitioners were accepted as members of a team that typically included a physician, a psychologist, and a social worker. Sometimes a psychiatrist was available for consultation as well. Krippner asked about the use of dreams in psychotherapy and was told that spiritists would use them to identify the client's helping spirits while the Western-oriented therapists would use them to understand the client's conflicts and problems. These two purposes are not contradictory, and both practitioners were able to use dream recall advantageously.

A research report by Joan Koss (1979) observed that the spiritists were highly motivated and committed to their work. It was also noted that spiritist therapy was more emotionally charged than Western psychotherapy and that spiritism utilized rituals and herbal remedies. Clients were urged to develop themselves spiritually; sessions often focused on the meaning of life and the individual's connection to God and to the cosmos. The clients' family often was called in, and advice was freely given. The Western-trained psychotherapists also gave advice but it pertained to the practical aspects of the case rather than to the spiritual dimensions of a client's life.

Koss described a client who was seen by both psychiatric and spiritist practitioners. When brought to the center she was given medication for her depression and visual hallucinations. The spiritist brought in four colleagues who allegedly exorcised eight malevolent spirits. Despite the seriousness of the case at the outset, the client was discharged a week later and resumed her classes at secretarial school. The two types of practitioners had worked cooperatively, addressing themselves to various aspects of the client's belief system.

Koss was surprised to discover that the mental health professionals frequently sought out spiritist counseling themselves. One psychologist consulted with a spiritist during his divorce proceedings and was given instructions on how to contact his spirit guides to help him win his court battles. With the help of spiritist practices, the psychologist worked through his problems in forming close relationships and eventually married again. He reported that spiritism had been far more effective in his case than any psychotherapy he had previously received.

Koss later followed up clients who had received Western psychotherapeutic treatment in Puerto Rico and compared them with the clients of spiritist healers, finding that the latter group reported greater improvement. Clients who visited spiritists (some 60% of all Puerto Ricans she questioned) also had higher expectations; this factor might have influenced the outcome. Koss noted that spiritist healers did somewhat better than psychotherapists on mood and behavioral complaints, while psychotherapists were deemed more successful with clients complaining of disordered thinking.

Native American Medical Practices

In the southwest United States, Navaho practitioners are often allowed to enter hospitals to work with Native American patients, where they frequently rely on the use of herbs and healing chants. This collaboration has proceeded well, with remarkable cooperation and open-mindedness, especially on the part of the Navaho shamanic healers. In 1969, a U. S. National Institute of Mental Health grant was awarded to finance the training of Navaho shamanic healers at Rough Rock, Arizona, so that the tradition would not be lost. The purpose of the training program was to teach apprentice medicine men and women the intricate Navaho healing ceremonies and techniques in order to preserve and propagate these procedures for the well-being of the Navaho people (Topper, 1987). These rituals are based on a worldview that sees personality as a totality, as a part of a family, and as inseparable from the tribe. Navaho medicine is not only dedicated to restore the health and harmony of the individual, but to restore family ecology, and any aspects of the tribe that have become disharmonious with nature.

The Navaho apprenticeship is complex and lengthy. For example, there are ten ceremonial chants that are frequently used and it might take years to learn just one of them. A chant consists of hundreds of songs; some chants are preceded by various purification rites, others are accompanied by the construction of a sand painting, and a few extend over several nights. The client is placed upon the sand painting; the shaman uses the sand to touch the parts of the client's body that are in need of healing. Upon completion of the ritual, the sand painting is destroyed and the client, if healed, is returned to the community (Sandner, 1979).

Several other tribes have moved toward making their mental health services more relevant to their cultural needs. In the early 1970s, several Papago Indians were recruited and trained as mental health workers by the University of Arizona department of psychology in Tucson. The Papago Indian client expects his or her therapist or healer to be very active in the healing session and to make suggestions freely (Torrey, 1986).

In 1987, an Arizona rancher was paid $4,140 by the

Crime Victim Foundation to reimburse him for 69 sheep that he gave a Navaho medicine man as payment for his services; the Foundation stated that "culturally speaking, a traditional medicine ceremony is just as valid as going to your local physician." In Ontario, Canada, the provincial government approved the hiring of an Ojibwa medicine man for a rural mental health program for American Indians. In Alaska, mental health services are trying to revive the traditional role of the shaman to assist with such problems as alcoholism, alienation, and chronic depression. One team of observers described what they had learned from their interface with Native Americans:

> If an Indian is told to take digitalis every day he will probably munch a few tablets and then forget about them. If he is told that the green medicine comes from the leaves of the foxglove, that his body must never be without it any more than his mind without a good song, and that he must take it every morning of his life when the first brightness of the day is in the east, one stands a much better chance of having the instructions carried out (Leighton and Leighton, 1941).

Standards for the Practitioner

It is apparent that psychotherapists and counselors need to be aware of the cultural and spiritual background of their clients. But many hesitate to discuss spiritual issues with their clients, even when it may seem appropriate. A survey of clinical psychologists, marriage and family counselors, psychiatrists, and clinical social workers found that 97 endorsed competent perception and expression of feelings as important for a psychologically healthy lifestyle. Examples were assuming responsibility for one's actions, being able to express and receive love, and taking care of one's health. However, there was less agreement on issues involving spirituality and sexuality. The clinical psychologists were the "least religious" of the four practitioners; even so, one third claimed to attend church regularly and another third considered themselves "spiritual" but not necessarily "religious" (in the sense of belonging to an institutionalized group and accepting its creed) (Bergin, 1990).

There is ample evidence that, in general, individuals with internalized spiritual and religious values score higher on measures of mental health than those who consider themselves non-religious, those who only give lip service to religious values, or those whose religious commitment takes the form of adherence to fanatical cults or uncompromising belief systems. A great deal of this value appears to emanate from the social support and community activites generated by fellow believers and participants (Justice, 1987). Other research data indicate that spiritual conviction and self-empowerment are positively related to physical health (Janis and Rodin, 1979), and that religiously-oriented people have higher scores on tests of mental health than do atheists (Wulff, 1991). These studies refute those critics who claim that religious beliefs, spiritual practices, and transcendent experiences are a danger to one's mental health (Ellis and Yaeger, 1989).

Given these findings, what position should psychotherapists and counselors take in regard to spiritual issues with their clients? It is our opinion that mental health practitioners need to have well thought-through opinions of their own, and to inform clients of those opinions if the therapeutic situation requires it. Therapists need to collaborate with clients in considering alternative actions on spiritual issues, and help them to realize the likely consequences of their actions. The final decision, however, is the responsibility of the client. The expertise of the therapist needs to shape the course of counseling, and this includes helping clients formulate a set of values, morals, and ethics that will guide them through life (Bergin, 1990). Such critical life issues as abortion and sexual practices are some on which therapists and clients might disagree, or which might cause the therapist to bring in a member of the clergy as a co-counselor. In any event, it is the client's growth toward autonomy and mature functioning that is the goal of therapy, not the conversion of the client to the therapist's worldview or religious orientation.

One prominent psychologist, Frank Barron (1963), has concluded that religion, at its best, "is not a dogma, not a set of forever-prescribed particularities, not static abstraction at all, but a formative process with faith as its foundation and vision as its goal—faith in the intelligibility and order of the universe, leading through necessary difficulties of interpretation and changing meanings to moments of spiritual integration which are themselves transient."

Twelve

Integrating Spiritual Healing Into Nursing And Medicine

The psychiatrist Thomas Szasz (1990) comments wryly that humankind is plagued by the fear of diversity, a fear that expresses itself in an insistence on monotheism, monogamy, and monomedicine. No one culture has a right to impose its concepts of disease, etiology, or treatment upon another culture. The only exception would be if a scientifically validated discovery is made in one society that could be beneficial in another society. In the early 20th century, the mental hospitals in the southern part of the United States were filled with pellagra victims. They suffered from diarrhea, skin inflammations, and—as the disease progressed—psychotic episodes. Eventually it was discovered that the disease resulted from poor nutrition and that vitamin C was an effective treatment. Thousands of inmates who had shown severe emotional disturbances were given vitamin C, and improved to the degree that they could be released. Western cultures are justified in sharing these kinds of data with other cultures and encouraging them to take appropriate action.

Imposing Cultural Standards

In contemporary North America, many people believe that Western cultures do not have the right to impose their standards indiscriminately. However, the European conquerors of the New World ridiculed and persecuted American Indians displaying divergent sexual behavior. Of the 99 tribes who kept written records, 88 made references to homosexuality, with 20 containing specific references to lesbianism. All of the 11 tribes who told anthropologists and other writers that their tribes never engaged in any type of homosexual interaction were located on the Eastern U.S. coast, in those areas of the longest contact with the Caucasian Christian culture that severely punished people who admitted to homosexuality (Grahn, 1986; Jacobs, 1968).

In the Crow tribe, the "berdache" (a French term applied to Native American men who did not fulfill the standard gender role in their society) was given the responsibility for cutting down the tree used in the Sun Dance ceremony. Among the Cheyenne, Dakota, and Illinois tribes, the berdache also played important roles in spiritual ceremonies. In several tribes, berdaches were shamans; in responding to their shamanic call in a dream or vision, the berdache would adopt the social role and accoutrements of the opposite sex, even to the extent of taking a husband. Even today, shamans and mediums may wear clothes of the opposite sex or incorporate spirits of that sex during rituals. In such a manner, they attempt to use the power of the opposite sex to supplement their own power, emerging the stronger as a result.

Transsexuals are not necessarily homosexuals, and vice versa. However, the European soldiers, explorers, trappers, and traders were contemptuous of both transvestites and homosexuals in their own cultures, and the worst persecution of homosexuals under the Inquisition and other agencies coincided with the heaviest periods of colonization. It is no wonder that homosexuals were often the first Indians killed.

Even when the tribes were tolerated by the settlers, their transvestites and homosexuals were mocked and punished; many of them changed their behavior for the sake of their people's safety. The Europeans' cultural dogmatism ended the tradition of peaceful integration of homosexuals into American Indian tribes and the regard in which lesbian warriors, homosexual artists, and shamanic transvestites were held (Williams, 1986).

Echoes of these past conflicts were heard in 1987 following the ousting from Haiti of "President-for-Life" Jean Claude Duvalier, who had purportedly engaged in voodoo sorcery. Some observers observed that voodoo practitioners "turned on Baby Doc in his final days and ensured his ouster" (Brock, 1987-1988). Nevertheless, according to *The New York Times*, dozens of voodoo mediums were put to death by fundamentalist Protestants (who called voodoo a "curse") and charismatic Roman Catholics (who branded it the "work of the devil"). Other voodoo practitioners were forced to convert to Christianity to save their lives (Simmons, 1986).

Frank Etienne, a Haitian writer, commented, "It is like the Inquisition, with people dragged off to church or lynched." One parish priest personally burned a collection of ceremonial voodoo drums, statues, and crosses. Frank Gentil, a 76-year-old voodoo medium, recalled that his father and grandfather had been killed in the last anti-voodoo campaign in 1942. Nevertheless, Gentile stated, "Voodoo went on and it will. This is the Haitian religion. No one can change that. We came from Africa with it." Indeed, in March 1987, Haitians voted to support a new constitution that eliminated the curb on voodoo, and the eight-month campaign of terror came to an end.

Dogmatic positions often block further interface between allopathic treatment and that of traditional healers. In the Lincoln Community Health Center program originated by Pedro Luiz, formal cooperation with the spiritists was blocked.

One strong reason was the opposition of the Catholic Church, which believes that *espiritismo* is the work of the devil; collaboration would thus have engendered strong opposition. Mental health professionals, with a few exceptions, have also not been enthusiastic (Torrey, 1986).

However, more Puerto Rican mental health professionals have been trained in recent years, making practitioners available to clients who speak Spanish and who are familiar with their worldview.

We have defined the spiritual dimension of life as that which deals with transcendent experiences. "Transcendent" refers to events, realms and processes that reach beyond ordinary limits, e.g., those evaluated as life's "highest" or "deepest" experiences, those marked by human nobility and magnificence, those associated with self-actualization and altruism, those representing purported communication with spirits or deities, and/or those in which someone claims to encounter or merge with God, with the "ultimate organizing principle of existence," with the "pattern that connects," or with the "ground of all being." However, a person does not have to believe in God in order to acknowledge the importance of transcendent experiences; the psychologist Andrew Neher, (1990) a skeptic concerning purported "occult" or "paranormal" phenomena, acknowledges the utility of transcendent experiences in coping with stress-reduction, maintaining health, and reinforcing positive patient attitudes and practices.

There are also indications that initiation into spiritual practice can change the lives of the practitioner. Professional nurses who study therapeutic touch often stop thinking of themselves as agents of a pharmaceutical technology and, instead, began to understand themselves as transmitters of "healing energy." One nurse remarked, "I see myself as...a vehicle through which energy can go to the patient in whatever way he or she can use it" (Fuller, 1989). This new philosophy can redefine the nurses' concepts of human health and their role in restoring it.

The ways in which spirituality manifests itself will differ from culture to culture. At its best, spiritual experience can be an impetus for growth, development, and the expression of a person's or a group's full capacity for love and service. In one survey, the individuals who reported having had deep "mystical" experiences scored higher than any other group on a standard test of psychological well-being (Greeley, 1975). At its worst, however, spiritual experience can lead to rigid, self-righteous attitudes and the persecution of those whose beliefs and behaviors deviate from a particular dogma or creed.

Similar distinctions can be made in conventional health care. Sidney Wolfe, a physician who heads the Public Citizen Health Research Group, estimates that between 5 and 15% of U.S. doctors are incompetent, poorly trained, or addicted to drugs or alcohol. It takes over two years for a state medical board to revoke an incompetent physician's license once action is taken, and the chances of them being disciplined is extremely small (Walls, 1986). Even competent practitioners tend to ignore spiritual and moral issues; Norman Cousins, the distinguished journalist who was selected to teach a course on medical humanities at the UCLA School of Medicine, found that his students seemed reluctant to attach importance to a physician's communication skills, to medical ethics, or to the circumstances of a patient's life when making a diagnosis or conducting treatment.

An Imaginary Letter

As an exercise in cross-cultural understanding, let us imagine a letter written by a tribal shamanic-healer to her peers in Central America after spending some time visiting American hospitals and clinics:

In the United States, I found that sick people must leave their villages and go to the house of the doctor just to get a naming of the sickness. After a long wait, the sick people don't learn much about their own illness from the doctor, but they do learn a great deal about other diseases from the people with whom they sit in the waiting room.

The American doctor looks inside the body with special lights and rays, but the rays that doctors use can't detect the colored auras around the patients' heads. Nor are these lights of any use in discerning the benevolent spirits of the dead ancestors who might be in the room.

As for the evil spirits, I saw them laughing when the American doctors appeared with their costumes. In their ears, the American doctors wear black ropes that are supposed to look like snakes. They also wear a round disc on their foreheads that looks like a shiny eye. Well, this costume didn't scare the evil spirits away; it just made them laugh.

American doctors are still using the cutting medicine that we save for emergencies. In fact, only the sick person's will to live allows some of them to survive this barbaric practice. In our country, over-population is controlled by famine, which is not such a good idea. But in America, population growth appears to be controlled by the cutting medicine.

There is also the poisoning medicine. This has almost replaced the roots, herbs, and flowers of the past. Entire villages are supported by the money that is made by the poisoning medicine. These medicines are called "drugs" and are sometimes used to drive sick people's spirits out of their bodies.

Often, sick people do not have enough ancestral spirits to save them from both the poisoning medicine and the cutting medicine. If fact, I must send the American doctors our books on herbal medicines because their poisons often do more harm to the body than the sickness itself.

Some of the equipment is very poor in the United States. I have seen many ancestral spirits fall asleep with boredom because the American doctors don't use masks and costumes that are colorful or imaginative. Their masks only go from the nose down to the mouth, and their costumes are all white instead of colored.

Furthermore, I didn't see one drum or one rattle. But I did see an epidemic of money sickness, even among the doctors. Many Americans get sick by chasing after money. Our tribe knows about this sickness and how to cure it by special prayers, music, and community service.

In the locked houses for people with the crazy sickness, I saw terrible things. Not only did I see poisoning and cutting—in this case cutting of the brain—but I saw machines that make a sick person tremble like a leaf in a hurricane. And when people with the crazy sickness were not put on these trembling machines, I saw and heard a lot of talking. The doctors and their patients do so much talking! The doctors don't seem to realize that evil spirits can control their patients' minds. So the doctors keep talking to the patients, not realizing that the voice they hear might be that of an evil spirit.

Some of our people want to offer foreign aid to the United States. If they want money, we will send them the precious stones and metals that we do not need. In exchange, we want the American doctors to send us their people with the crazy sickness. The possessed among them will be exorcised and re-

turned home. Others will be given herbal treatments, and their energy will be balanced. But those
with the spirit vision, whom we don't consider
crazy at all, will be kept and trained in our medical
ways.

We will teach them exorcism. We will teach
them aura reading. We will teach them how to
balance energy. We will teach them the use of
natural substances. We will teach them how to
make masks and costumes. We will teach them the
healing prayers and music.

Our gift of these medical ways will cement our
friendship with the United States as no other gift
can. I am going to support this proposal when I
return to my tribe—if only I can survive the food
available here (LaPatra, 1978).

In this fictitious letter, the tribal model of healing is
contrasted with the allopathic model. Procedures used by
American physicians and psychiatrists are seen to be foolish—and sometimes even harmful—from another perspective. European physicians took the same point of view toward
indigenous healers when they arrived in North America, not
realizing that many of their own medical practices were based
on false assumptions and superstitious beliefs.

A few of the early physicians established an interface
between the two healing models, especially insofar as herbal
treatments were concerned. The "channeled" readings of the
American sensitive Edgar Cayce enunciated the philosophy
of what is now called holistic medicine and this enterprise
attracted a few adventurous physicians, nurses, and psychotherapists. Gladys McGarey is one physician who has found
innovative ways to integrate the Cayce viewpoint into her
medical practice; for example, she helps women contemplating an abortion to consider their decision at a deep spiritual
level. If they decide to abort the fetus, McGarey has them write

the fetus a letter explaining their decision. Despite the efforts of McGarey and others, a full-scale assimilation of spiritual concerns into allopathy never took place, and Western medicine has been the poorer for this neglect.

Based on an interview study with U.S. physicians, D.R. Slavitt (1987) discovered that "those students who enter medical school with some kind of religious orientation very often lose it, either in the first year when they confront...their cadavers, or, later on, by the third year when they go into the wards to see...brave and good people and innocent children going down in pain without any kind of chance." In our opinion, religious convictions of this type are better off lost because they are naive and superficial, having their roots in the notion that "bad things don't happen to good people." This worldview is remarkably similar to the belief system of some native tribes who attributed all disease to the breaking of taboos, misdeeds by one's ancestors, sorcery, or magic. We take the position that neither worldview is congruent with scientific findings. But we also hold that scientific data and spiritual perspectives can be quite compatible when one's convictions about the "highest" and "deepest" human potentials and values are based on both reason and intuition, both intellect and feeling, both personal observation and the accumulated wisdom of one's medical, nursing, or therapeutic discipline.

Spiritual Healing and Medicine

Between 1984 and 1986, we interviewed four allopathic medical practitioners who have been pioneers in integrating the spiritual dimension with their work. They included Dolores Krieger (1979; 1984), Professor of Nursing at New York University and the developer of therapeutic touch; Larry Dossey (1982, 1984, 1989), a specialist in internal medicine once affiliated with the Dallas Diagnostic Association, Dallas, Texas and now practicing in Santa Fe, New Mexico;

Rachel Naomi Remen (1980), a psychotherapist and Clinical Director of Commonweal in Bolinas, California; and Lewis E. Mehl (1986) (a clinical psychologist as well as a physician), once Medical Director of the Center for Recovery from Illness, Berkeley, California, and now practicing in Tucson, Arizona. Their comments have helped us to conceptualize a model of medicine that interfaces with humankind's spiritual needs.

When Krieger uses therapeutic touch for *diagnosis* she first makes an "assessment" by entering a state of "relaxed concentration." Then she moves her hands up and down the patient's body (but rarely touching it), searching for places where the "energy field" is blocked. Maintaining that people's "energy fields" extend a considerable distance beyond the boundaries of their skins, Krieger sometimes diagnoses at a distance, using "vivid visualization," which she describes as a type of mental imagery.

Dossey conducts physical examinations and talks with his patients to obtain a personal history. He proceeds according to the medical model but incorporates the spiritual aspects of the person's situation into his diagnosis, attempting to understand their purpose in life and their sources of inner strength. Many physicians view health as an "object" but Dossey (1985) views health as an "experience" and his diagnostic procedures reflect this position. He attempts to discover how patients interpret their illnesses and how they relate to the body, its functions, and its dysfunctions.

Remen feels that proper diagnosis includes the patient's body, thoughts, feelings, and spirit. Limiting diagnosis to the physical plane can ignore the most important issues in a person's illness. She also points out that diagnostic terminology often inclines patients to think of themselves not as *having* a disease but as if they *are* a disease. People are labelled "epileptics" and "diabetics" as if this term encompasses their total being. She often encourages a patient to say, "I have epilepsy but I am not an epileptic," as a step toward a positive self-concept.

Mehl attempts to discover a patient's belief systems by means of "exploratory visualization" which involves mental imagery techniques, progressive relaxation, and story-telling. A holistic approach is needed, even in cases of physical ailments, to uncover all possibilities. Mehl observes that when an individual's sensations and experiences are given a name (i.e., a diagnosis), a pattern is set in motion by which the client is locked into the attributes of that name. Clients often return home and read all about their "condition," now given a name. Physicians believe they can predict what will happen to the patient for the next 10 years on the basis of the diagnosis.

For Remen, *etiology* must be considered on various levels. At the purely physical level, there is typically a disease "agent" such as a bacteria, virus, or genetic factor. However, she sees agents as the *means* of the disease rather than the *cause* of the disease. Krieger conceptualizes two different causal agents: the "congestion of energy" and the "imbalance of energy." Each can involve neurophysiological and endrocrinological factors, as well as the patient's early life experiences.

Mehl sees a number of possible causes as affecting the patient, e.g., diet, heredity, environment, stress, emotions, attitudes, beliefs, acculturation, family systems, community systems, religion. Etiology, for Mehl, needs to be considered at three levels: *originating factors* (e.g., genetic causes), *maintaining factors* (e.g., environmental causes), and, once treatment is instigated, *resolving factors* (e.g., medicine, diet, exercise). Dossey believes that there are many causative agents, e.g., viruses, germs, bacteria, genetic factors, environmental effects, and one's personal belief systems about the body and the self.

Behavior of the Patient

The *patient's behavior* is of great importance to Krieger, who listens for nuances in his or her voice, tense breathing patterns, and the use of unusual metaphors in the description of one's symptoms. Krieger also observes the patient's posture, bodily movement, and balance. Remen told us that she has developed a sensitivity to "body language" that can convey important information about the patient.

Patients' behavior provides important clues to Dossey. He is especially attentive to how they treat their bodies (e.g., exercise, diet, other health habits), the image they have of the body, and the manner in which they move various parts of the body. A patient's bodily movement can be a metaphor as to whether he or she is moving toward health, or remaining passive and becoming a victim of the disease. Dossey views the patient holistically, paying special attention to attitudes and to mind-body relationships.

Mehl uses a technique he calls "exploratory visualization" to understand what he has observed. Drawing upon his Cherokee Indian heritage, Mehl has combined story-telling techniques, mental imagery, and progressive relaxation to enable patients to describe their inner world. He also observes behavioral patterns; he recalls how one patient's diabetes became worse during times when she would visit her parents. Mehl believes that the body is the most intimate way people have to express themselves, hence bodily reactions can provide important therapeutic clues.

It can be observed that the models of healing held by these practitioners include all of the diagnostic procedures utilized by other allopathic physicians and nurses. In addition, however, Krieger, Dossey, Remen, and Mehl attempt to learn about a patient's spiritual problems, concerns, and beliefs, attempting to understand how one's spiritual status may have contributed to the illness as well as how it could be used therapeutically. They also appear to deliberately utilize their own intuitive skills in making judgments about patients.

These models of healing are congruent with the emergence of "third line" medicine—a partnership between patient and physician that sometimes provides an opening to unconventional treatment procedures. The "first line" of treatment is basic health care; the "second line" is specialized medicine. According to Melvyn Werbach (1986), a physician and medical school professor, the opposition to "third line" medicine comes from entrenched specialists and an insurance industry bias against psychological care that encourages physicians to "cut" instead of "talk."

"Third line" medicine encourages options that inspire patient confidence, that attempt to strengthen the patient's natural adaptive and self-healing mechanisms, and that examine the patient's spiritual issues. An example would be the work of the National Jewish Center for Immunology and Respiratory Medicine in Denver, Colorado; in treating asthma, patients are taught how to understand the condition and manage it themselves. The Jewish Center teaches asthmatic patients to measure their flow of breath with a special meter, allowing them to predict when they might become subject to attacks. In a three-year study with 34 patients, it was found that their admittance to hospitals dropped 44%, their emergency room visits fell 31%, and their total hospitalization costs were cut in half (Holzman, 1987). At other clinics, asthmatics have been taught to control their attacks through hypnosis. Further, hypnosis and self-hypnosis have helped some patients to eliminate warts and hemophiliacs to control bleeding. Researchers at Beth Israel Hospital in Boston have produced data indicating that hypnosis may help people control their immune responses (Spiegel, 1987).

Spiritual Treatment in Medicine and Nursing

Mehl's *treatment* procedures include many modalities, including acupuncture, homeopathy, massage, natural substances, hypnosis, mental imagery, nutrition, and "Touch-for-Health." Drawing upon his Native American background,

Mehl may even help patients find their power animals! Mehl states that underlying each procedure is the spiritual relationship between himself and his patient. Depending on the need of his patient, Dossey may prescribe surgery, chemotherapy, medicine, psychotherapy, mental imagery, meditation, color therapy, and/or involvement in creative activities. He also will make referrals to specialists when it is advisable.

Remen's treatment is psychotherapeutic in nature, focusing on the attitudes patients have towards themselves and towards life. She helps her patients work toward achieving their potentials of paying special attention to their capacities to organize their activities, to take a positive perspective on their illness, and to function adequately in society. To Remen, truly healthy people are evolving and growing people; treatment should facilitate this dynamic movement in a meaningful way.

Krieger's primary mode of treatment involves sending "energy" to "activate the patient's own recuperative powers" and to "unify the patient's field," reducing the asymmetries and uneven heat patterns detected during the "assessment." Krieger says that she has no difficulty interfacing her treatment with any applicable traditional or alternative therapy. Her background in yoga enables her to use the so-called "chakras" (or "energy centers") in treatment, whether they be hers or those of her patients.

Remen sees the *prognosis* as favorable if patients use their capacities to transform the experience of being sick to attitudes that will improve the quality of their lives. For her, there is a "healthy" way to be ill or to face a crisis if a person thinks of the experience as an opportunity to learn and to grow. This procedure resembles that used by the "wounded healers" so frequently found in shamanism; for example, Jose Rios and Leslie Gray were involved in serious accidents yet, upon recovering, used those events as opportunities to develop their own healing abilities.

For Mehl, there is a close connection between the prognosis and the patient's belief system; positive attitudes and constructive activities make it more likely the patient will recover. Krieger's attempt to "unify the patient's field" often provides prognostic information about the rapidity with which self-healing will occur. Dossey finds that patients' commitment to themselves and to their treatment are associated with a positive prognosis.

According to Dossey, *death* only produces anxiety if the concept is based upon the notion of linear time; death need not be "final" if people modify their belief that everything must have a past, present, and future. Cultures that think of time as cyclical and non-linear often have a less threatening view of death than do Western cultures which emphasize linearity. When Mehl works with clients who are seriously ill, he invites them to make a commitment to the process of working together regardless of the outcome. On his part, Mehl promises these clients to support them and to be with them in death or in life.

Krieger has used therapeutic touch to ease the pain of her terminally ill patients. Remen states that the *dying* process provides an opportunity for self-confrontation. Some people undergo a type of healing as they die because they learn a great deal about life in the process. Remen tells her patients, "Without acceptance you just react out of fear. If you can accept even the fact of death, then you can use it to tell you what's important." One of Remen's young patients at Commonweal, a treatment center for people suffering from cancer, told the group, "You think I'm dying but I'm really teaching you all how to live."

Suicide, for Remen, can be a response to suffering; nevertheless, one's cosmic task remains, even if it manifests itself in a future lifetime. Dossey views suicide attempts as evidence that the relationship between one's spirit and the rest of the psyche is disparate and divided. Neither Krieger nor Remen feel that death is inevitably the patient's enemy; sometimes it may be welcomed. Further, the process of dying can enhance learning and spiritual development. Dossey conceptualizes death as a transforming experience; life would lack meaning without death, as there would be no contrast.

As we examine the attitudes of these four practitioners regarding treatment, prognosis, death, and suicide, we can see the importance that spirituality plays in their work. One's spiritual capacities play an important part in recovery from illness and disease; the spiritual connection between the practitioner and the patient becomes an integral part of treatment. Death, dying, and suicide are issues to be discussed intensively, rather than to be mentioned superficially or avoided completely.

Institutional and Social Functions

For Remen, the *function of the institution* is to provide a place where she, or others, can see their patients and conduct their therapeutic work. Remen conceptualizes medical practice as a social institution in that it is currently in an historic crisis, but one that affords an opportunity for constructive change. Krieger also takes the position that the role of the hospital is in transition, offering patients more options for support, acceptance, and recovery than it has in the past.

Dossey holds that the function of the institution is to provide medical services so that human suffering can be alleviated. Mehl believes that the institution needs to give accurate feedback to patients, and to insure that adequate time is given to them by health professionals. All of these practitioners have met with resistance from some medical institutions because of their beliefs, yet each has been able to find (or found) an institution that supported them and their work.

Dossey would include nurses and various aides along with physicians as important *personnel* in the health care system. Remen feels that many physicians can also be healers, at least for some patients. Healing is holistic, and a physician might be able to engage a particular patient on several levels (e.g., spiritual, emotional, intellectual) yet be able to reach a different patient only on the physical level. Remen believes that a physician "cures" and "fixes" people while a healer "teaches" and "heals" them. She believes that health care workers sometimes may need to step beyond their professional image to mobilize the self-healing ability of their patients, e.g., expressing positive regard and feeling to demonstrate concern for someone who is ill, listening carefully to patients' descriptions of their illnesses, and providing information about treatment when it is requested.

For Krieger, therapeutic touch is an accessory to medical treatment; personnel would consist primarily of nurses and other health professionals. Allopathic, osteopathic, and homeopathic physicians have all incorporated therapeutic touch into their practice. However, some lay people have been taught the technique to assist their family members and friends. Krieger often refers patients to physicians for medicine or surgery, but she may also send them to homeopaths, herbalists, nutritionists, or other practitioners. As of 1988, Krieger had trained over 12,000 people (most of them health professionals) to administer therapeutic touch and her students have taught at least again as many.

Mehl utilizes a wide variety of health care providers in his practice, observing that there is "a direct benefit from a warm and caring provider-client interaction" and that "a negative client-provider relationship can detract from the efficacy of any therapies being applied." Mehl's reputation for being able to integrate a variety of modalities into his treatment has brought a steady stream of curious physicians to observe his procedures.

Rights and Duties

Rights and duties of the patient, for Remen, include taking responsibility for his or her "thread in the tapestry of consciousness." She asks her patients to question their lifestyles, and shows them how illness can be a spiritual path if it results in attitudinal shifts. In addition, patients have the right to be listened to, and to feel cared for and appreciated by health professionals. Dossey believes that patients have the right to receive health care from competent professionals and the duty to cooperate with those health care workers.

Krieger sees the patient's major right as the expectation of generalized relief from therapeutic touch. His or her duty is to acknowledge the illness, to cooperate with the practitioner, and to take a conscious and responsible role in bringing about the recovery. Mehl holds that patients have the right to a healing relationship when they contact a practitioner; they have the duty to promote their own well-being, both during and following the treatment.

Rights and duties of the family are important to Mehl, who believes that family counseling often can be more therapeutic than medication. For Krieger, the family needs to maintain intimacy with the patient and must express love and caring during the treatment period. Family members have the right to use therapeutic touch on each other if they apply it under the guidelines Krieger has established.

Remen uses her background as a pediatrician to help families explore the meaning of a family member's illness and both its consequences and opportunities for all the people involved. Remen cites the case of a mother who saw her son fall off his tricycle, hit his head on the cement, and roll into the swimming pool. His mother phoned for help, jumped into the pool, pulled the boy out, and administered mouth-to-mouth resuscitation. Remen examined the boy and found him in good condition, yet sensed that her work with the family was not complete. She told the boy's parents that the mother's quick action had saved the child's life. The woman responded, "Doctor, I'm afraid of the water. I don't even know how to swim." The incident was the beginning of many changes for the woman. She had always been timid, shy, and fearful, but through this experience she came to know a more courageous side of herself. She organized a support group for parents whose children had had similar accidents to enable them to examine both their feelings of guilt and the strengths. In addition, the woman learned how to swim!

Mehl has observed instances in which a person's illness is an attempt to solve problems existing in the family system. Therefore, it is the patient's right not to become the focus for a family's dysfunctional behavior. Some patients do well in a hospital but relapse on return to their families. Family members did not realize that they were subtly encouraging the patients to get worse. However, this was the outcome of the family's attempt to maintain the previous pattern of relationships—those that were a cause of the disease. Thus, treatment is facilitated if patients are conceptualized as part of their family and community systems.

Dossey observes that the death rate in surviving spouses (widows and widowers) is twice as high as the average for others of their ages. This finding supports Dossey's view that consciousness not only operates within a person (such as when people's cholesterol levels drop following a series of visualization or meditation sessions) but may operate between individuals. Widowers and widows have the right to receive the support they need during their periods of grief and stress.

Rights and duties of society, for Krieger, include the right to take an interest in its citizens' well-being and the duty to protect them from disease. Society also has the duty to permit the dissemination of training in therapeutic touch. According to Mehl, society has the duty to direct resources toward the treatment of those in need. Dossey points out that there is only one human family and, "although we may be indifferent to starvation or suffering somewhere on the globe, if we were sensitive enough to the reality of our interconnectedness we would know we're losing a member of our family when someone dies."

Remen would encourage society to facilitate the choice-making capacities of its citizens. She believes that the very nature of contemporary life has made individual choice the single most important factor in maintaining health because one can *choose* to avoid such potential lethal activities as over-eating, drug and tobacco addiction, alcoholism, drunken driving, and stressful lifestyles. She, like the other three prac-titioners we interviewed, remains aware of the patient's family, friends, and society during treatment. From the position of spiritual healing, the social context of the patient must be an integral part of treatment.

The *goal of the model*, for Mehl, is the patient's growth in wisdom with respect to his body; healing is a synergistic result of treating the patient within the context of a spiritual relationship. Dossey's goal is to relieve human misery, keep-ing in mind that "the state of highest health is beyond harm, beyond the touch of the ephemerality of the body. It is the goal of all enlightened therapies." As a Buddhist, Krieger sees life as a meaningful continuum; she acknowledges that she feels a sense of personal responsibility that evokes a compassionate support of persons in need. The goal of her treatment is to bring about a profound "relaxation response" that will allevi-ate patients' pain and accelerate their self-healing capacities.

Remen conceptualizes health as a balance in a person's life; disease is a disruption of this equilibrium. The goal of medicine and psychotherapy is to provide this balance, bring-ing about an "open energy system" where energy is readily available for a person's activities. For example, in a healthy person, energy is available for pursuing spiritual growth as a way of healing. Remen holds that universal service is a person's major task, one that is carried between lifetimes, just as a thread carries each bead in a necklace. Illness is a spiritual challenge as are many other life events; one needs to use these incidents as opportunities for spiritual growth.

All four practitioners have deeply-felt spiritual attitudes and beliefs that affect their work with patients. They do not isolate their spiritual life from their professional life; instead, spirituality permeates everything they do and serves as the focus for their work with patients. Although their backgrounds and beliefs differ, ranging from Native American to Buddhist, the practical outcome of their spirituality is remarkably similar in its concern for assisting patients to find meaning in their lives, to draw upon their deepest resources and highest goals, and in forging bonds of affiliation and love with those people and groups around them that can help them cope with illness and disease.

Conclusion

After investigating these various models of healing, it is obvious to us that it would be foolish to abandon the best of allopathic medicine and Western-oriented psychotherapeutic practices. There is abundant evidence that these procedures can be practical and powerful, especially as carried out by competent, caring practitioners. However, we have also observed an emergence of support for the position that Western medicine and therapy has neglected the spiritual aspects of healing to their peril. Allopathic practitioners and conventional psychotherapists need to integrate a concern for the spiritual aspects of life into their practice, and/or consider using spiritual healers in a supplementary way.

The four health care professionals we interviewed had no difficulty integrating spirituality in their practice. They have found ways in which spiritually-oriented procedures (e.g., meditation, mental imagery, attunement, positive thinking) could be therapeutic for both physical and mental illnesses. They agreed that health as well as disease take on different meanings when viewed within a spiritual context. They observed ways in which a spiritual orientation could provide direction and motivation for themselves as well as for their patients.

In this book, we have focused on spiritual healing in North America (including Central America and the Caribbean), as that has been the geographical focus of our investigations. North America contains a wide variety of healers and practices that allows us to compare and contrast several different approaches. We have observed how the models of health and healing adhered to by traditional healers pay special attention to transcendent realms and the experience of transcendence. For us spirituality implies awareness of broader life meanings that transcend the immediacy of everyday life. If allopathic medicine and conventional psychotherapy could participate in this awareness, health care in North America would more closely reflect the wholeness and integrity of individuals as well as the meaningfulness of interactions with their families and their societies.

There are some encouraging signs. The lead article of the August 1987 issue of the American Association for Counseling and Development's newsletter was titled, "Counselors Address Spiritual Needs of Clients." The article noted that "spirituality is recognized as an essential part of wholeness" and that "spiritual issues are no longer sidestepped." In two separate surveys, about eight out of ten of potential clients said they would prefer counselors with a spiritual orientation and a majority of clinical psychologists stated that spirituality was relevant in their lives and their work. In other words, there is more interest in spiritual issues than the official statements of mainstream therapy groups admit (Cohen, 1986). In 1990, a national poll of psychotherapists was published in which 68% of those surveyed agreed with the statement, "I seek a spiritual understanding of the universe and one's place in it." By contrast, only 44% endorsed having a "religious affiliation in which one actively participates" (Bergin and Jensen, 1990).

A 1987 survey of 118 licensed California psychologists, psychiatrists, and social workers revealed that 83% usually consider a minority client's cultural background during evaluation and treatment and that two-thirds believe that the interpretation of symptoms must be considered within the context of the client's ethnic group (Chance, 1987). In 1984, the prestigious Institute for the Advancement of Health sent its members—for their examination—a statement (from another group) in which the term "complementary" was used to describe such therapies as acupuncture, biofeedback, chiropractic, dietary programs, homeopathy, herbalism, naturopathy, osteopathy, and relaxation techniques that, rather than replacing medicine, can "work alongside it" as the situation demands.

A major obstacle to the acknowledgement of spirituality by health care specialists is the animosity that various religious groups have held toward each other. To avoid entanglement in doctrinal disputes over such topics as abortion, euthanasia, and genetic engineering, physicians, nurses, and psychotherapists have found it expedient to avoid the mention of spirituality altogether. However, spiritual concerns can overshadow (or undercut) religious dogma; a respect for denominational beliefs does not imply agreement. The spiritual dimensions of human beings are too important to be ignored by secular practitioners. Instead, with a modicum of ingenuity, imagination, and insight, the health of the spirit could become an integral part of medical and therapeutic concern and treatment.

References

References for Chapter One

Grossinger, Richard. *Planet Medicine: From Stone Age Shamanism to Post-Industrial Healing* (rev. ed.). Boulder, CO: Shambhala, 1982, pp. 105-106.

Halifax, Joan. Profile 1. In Michele Jamal, *Shape Shifters: Shaman Women in Contemporary Society*, pp. 15-19. New York: Arkana/Simon and Schuster, 1987, p. 19.

Heinze, Ruth-Inge. *Shamans of the 20th Century*. New York: Irvington, 1990.

Shafranske, E.P. Factors associated with the perception of spirituality in psychotherapy. *Journal of Transpersonal Psychology*, 1984, *16*, 231-241.

Wildschut, William. *Crow Indian Medicine Bundles*. New York: Heye Foundation, 1975.

Winkelman, Michael. *A Cross-Cultural Study of Magico-Religious Practitioners*. Unpublished doctoral dissertation, University of California, Irvine, 1984.

References for Chapter Two

Bahr, D.M., Gregorio, J., Lopez, D.I., and Alvarez, A. *Piman Shamanism and Staying Sickness*. Tucson: University of Arizona Press, 1974.

Cassell, E.J. *The Healer's Art*. Middlesex, England: Penguin Books, 1979, p. 18.

Eliade, Mircea. *Shamanism: Archaic Techniques of Ecstasy*. Princeton, NJ: Princeton University Press, 1964.

Fontana, B.L. Foreword. In D.M. Bahr, Juan Gregorio, D.I. Lopez, and Albert Alvarez. *Piman Shamanism and Staying Sickness* (pp. ix-xi). Tucson: University of Arizona Press, 1974.

Frank, Jerome D. *Persuasion and Healing,* revised edition. New York: Schocken Books, 1973.

Kiev, Ari. *Curanderismo: Mexican American Folk Psychiatry*. New York: Free Press, 1968.

Levi-Strauss, Claude. The structural study of myth. *Journal of American Folklore*, 1955, *78*, 428-444.

Siegler, Miriam, and Osmond, Humphry. *Models of Madness, Models of Medicine*. New York: Macmillan, 1974.

Trotter, R.T., III, and Chavira, J.A. *Curanderismo: Mexican American Folk Healing*. Athens: University of Georgia Press, 1981, pp. 144-145.

References for Chapter Three

Bourguignon, Erika. World distribution and patterns of possession states. In Raymond Prince (Ed.), *Trance and Possession States* (pp. 3-34). Montreal: R.M. Bucke Memorial Society, 1968.

Boyer, L.B., Boyer, R.M., and De Vos, G.A. An Apache woman's account of her recent acquisition of the shamanic status. *Journal of Psychoanalytic Anthropology*, 1982, *5*, 299-331.

Boyer, L.B., Klopfer, B., Brawer, F.B., and Kawai, H. Comparisons of the shamans and pseudoshamans of the Apaches of the Mescalero Indian reservation: A Rorschach study. *Journal of Projective Techniques*, 1964, 28, 173-180, p.179.

de Rios, Marlene Dobkin. *Hallucinogens: Cross-Cultural Perspectives.* Albuquerque: University of New Mexico Press, 1984, p. 57.

Devereux, George. Shamans and neurotics. *American Anthropologist,* 1961, *63,* 1088-1090.

Dow, James. *The Shaman's Touch: Otomi Indian Symbolic Healing.* Salt Lake City: University of Utah Press, 1986.

Grim, J.A. *The Shaman: Patterns of Siberian and Ojibway Healing.* Norman: University of Oklahoma Press, 1983, pp. 144-145.

Hultkrantz, Ake. Ecological and phenomenological aspects of shamanism. In V. Dioszegi and Mihaly Hoppal (Eds.), *Shamanism in Siberia* (pp. 27-58). Budapest: Akademiai Kiado, 1978.

Kaweit, Holger. *Dreamtime and Inner Space: The World of the Shaman.* Boston: Shambhala, 1988, pp. 99-100.

Krippner, Stanley. Shamans: The first healers. In Gary Doore (Ed.), *Shaman's Path* (pp. 101-114). Boston: Shambhala, 1988.

Lynn, S.J., and Rhue, J.W. The fantasy-prone person: Hypnosis, imagination, and creativity. *Journal of Personality and Social Psychology,* 1986, *51,* 404-408.

Neher, Andrew. Auditory driving observed with scale electrodes in normal subjects. *Electroencephalographic and Clinical Neurophysiology,* 1961, *13,* 449-451.

Noll, Richard. Mental imagery cultivation as a cultural phenomenon: The role of visions in shamanism. *Current Anthropology,* 1985, *26,* 443-452.

Oswalt, W.H. *Alaskan Eskimos.* San Francisco: Chandler, p. 222.

Peters, L.G., and Price-Williams, Douglass. Towards an experiential analysis of shamanism. *American Ethnologist,* 1980, *7,* 397-418.

Rogers, S.L. *The Shaman: His Symbols and His Healing Power.* Springfield, IL: Charles Thomas, 1982, p. 21.

Silverman, Julian. Shamans and acute schizophrenia. American *Anthropologist*, 1969, *69*, 21-31, p. 22.

Topper, M.D. The traditional Navajo medicine man: Therapist, counselor, and community leader. *Journal of Psychoanalytic Anthropology*, 1987, *10*, 217-249.

Wilson, S.C., and Barber, T.X. The fantasy-prone personality: Implications for understanding imagery, hypnosis, and parapsychological phenomena. In A.A. Sheik (Ed.), *Imagery: Current Theory, Research, and Application* (pp. 340-387). New York: John Wiley and Sons, 1983.

References for Chapter Four

Black Elk, Wallace, & Lyon, W. S. *Black Elk: The Sacred Ways of a Lakota*. San Francisco: Harper and Row, 1990.

Boyd, Doug. *Rolling Thunder*. New York: Random House, 1974, p.21.

Dubin-Vaughn, Sarah. Elizabeth Cogburn: A Caucasian shaman. In Ruth-Inge Heinze, *Shamans of the 20th Century* (pp.70-85). New York: Irvington, 1991.

Gerber, Richard. *Vibrational Medicine*. Sante Fe, NM: Bear, 1988, p.419.

Estrada, Alvaro. *Maria Sabina: Her Life and Chants*. Santa Barbara, CA: Ross-Erickson, 1981, pp. 153-154.

Halifax, Joan. *Shaman: The Wounded Healer*. New York: Crossroad, 1979, p. 251.

Harner, Michael. *The Way of the Shaman*. San Francisco: Harper and Row, 1980, pp. xi-xii.

Harner, Michael. Shamanic counseling. In Gary Doore (Ed.), *Shaman's Path* (pp. 179-187). Boston: Shambhala, 1988, p. 186.

Krippner, Stanley. Shamans: The First Healers. In Gary Doore (Ed.), *Shaman's Path* (pp.179-187). Boston: Shambhala, 1988, pp.105-107.

Krippner, Stanley, & Villoldo, Alberto. *The Realms of Healing* (third edition). Berkeley, CA: Celestial Arts, 1987, pp.5-6, 11.

Lyon, William. Black Elk's view of American culture. *AASC Newsletter: Association for the Anthropological Study of Consciousness*, December, 1987, pp. 1-2, 7-8.

Neihardt, J.G. *Black Elk Speaks: Being the Life Story of a Holy Man of the Ogala Sioux*. New York: Washingtion Square Press, 1972. Original work published 1932.

Nitsch, Twyla. *Wisdom of the Seneca*. Albany, NY: University of the State of New York, 1979, p.41.

Orellana, S.L. *Indian Medicine In Highland Guatemala*. Albuquerque: University of New Mexico Press, 1987.

Shaffer, C. R. Dr. Leslie Gray, bridge between two realities. *Shaman's Drum*, Fall, 1987, pp. 21-28, p. 23.

Steward, J.H. *Native People of South America*. New York: McGraw Hill, 1959.

Van de Castle, R.L. The Psychology of Dreaming. Morristown, NJ: General Learning Press, 1971.

Villoldo, Alberto, & Krippner, Stanley. *Healing States*. New York: Fireside/Simon and Schuster, 1987.

Wasson, R. G. *Maria Sabina and her Mazatec Velada*. New York: Harcourt Brace Jovanovich, 1974.

Weil, Andrew. *Health and Healing*. New York: E.P. Dutton, 1983, p. 163.

References for Chapter Five

Anonymous. *A Course in Miracles: Text*. Huntington Station, NY: Huntington Graphics, 1975, p. 227.

Cannon, W.B. Voodoo death. *American Anthropologist*, 1942, *4*, 169-181.

Frank, Jerome D. and Frank, Julia B. *Persuasion and Healing*, third edition. Baltimore: Johns Hopkins University Press, 1991, p. 108.

Freud, Sigmund. *Collected Papers*, Vol. 1, 2nd ed. London: Hogarth Press, 1940, p. 249.

Fuller, R.C. *Alternative Medicine and American Religious Life*. New York: Oxford University Press, 1989, p. 122.

Gibson, R.G., Gibson, L.M., & MacNeill, A.D. Homeopathic therapy in rheumatoid arthritis: Evaluation by double-blind clinical therapeutic trial. *British Journal of Clinical Pharmacology*, 1980, *61*, 453-459.

Josephy, A.M., Jr. (Ed.). *The American Heritage Book of Indians*. New York: American Heritage, 1961.

Levi-Strauss, Claude. *Structural Anthropology*. New York: Basic Books, 1963.

Levy, R.I. Tahitian folk psychotherapy. *International Public Health Research Newsletter*, 1967, *9*(4), 12-15.

McGuire, Meredith, and Kantor, Debra. *Ritual Healing in Suburban America*. New Brunswick, NJ: Rutgers University Press, 1988.

Morowitz, Harold J. Much ado about nothing. *Hospital Practice*, July, 1982, pp. 215-216.

Otto, Herbert, and Knight, James (Eds.). *Dimensions in Wholistic Healing*. Chicago: Nelson-Hall, 1979, p. 13.

Rogers, Carl R. The necessary and sufficient conditions of therapeutic personality change. *Journal of Consulting Psychology*, 1957, *21*, 95-103.

Sacks, Adam D. Nuclear magnetic resonance spectocscopy of homeopathic remedies. *Journal of Holistic Medicine*, *5*(2), 172-176.

Summer Catalog, The Center of the Light, P.O. Box 540, Great Barrington, MA 10230, 1988, p. 4.

Torrey, E. F. *The Mind Game*, New York: Bantam Books, 1973, p. 10.

Torrey, E.F. *Witchdoctors and Psychiatrists*, New York: Harper and Row, 1986, pp. 16-17.

References for Chapter Six

A matter of faith. *Time*, September 10, 1973, p. 76.

Elkins, D.N. On being spiritual without necessarily being religious. *Association for Humanistic Psychology Perspective*, June, 1990, pp. 4-5.

English-Lueck, J.A. *Health in the New Age: A Study in California Holistic Practices.* Albuquerque, NM: University of New Mexico Press, 1990.

Frank, J.D. *Persuasion and Healing*, revised edition. Baltimore: Johns Hopkins University Press, 1973, p. 72.

Geddes, Frances. *Healing Training in the Church.* Unpublished doctoral dissertation, San Francisco Theological Seminary, 1981.

Halstuk, Martin. Religious freedom collides with medical care. *San Francisco Chronicle*, April 25, 1988, p. A4.

Kitman, Marvin. Double trouble at CBS. *New Leader*, June 25, 1984, pp. 21-22.

Krieger, Dolores. *The Therapeutic Touch.* Englewood Cliffs, NJ: Prentice-Hall, 1979.

LeShan, Lawrence. *The medium, the mystic and the physicist.* New York: Viking Press, 1974.

MacNutt, Francis. *The power to heal.* New York: Bantam Books, 1977.

Numbers, R.L., and Amundsen, D.W. (Eds.), *Caring and Curing.* New York: Macmillan, 1986.

Peck, M. Scott. *People of the Lie.* New York: Simon and Schuster, 1983, p. 190.

Randi, James. *The Faith-Healers.* Buffalo, NY: Prometheus Books, 1987, p. 208.

Reed, H. Defining spirituality. *Venture Inward*, May/June, 1990. p. 7.

Sandford, John, and Sandford, Paula. *Healing the Wounded Spirit.* South Plainfield, NJ: Bridge, 1985.

Sanford, Agnes. *The Healing Light.* New York: Ballantine Books, 1972.

St. Clair, David. *Psychic Healers.* Garden City, NY: Doubleday, 1974, pp. 147-173.

Ward, Colleen. Therapeutic aspects of ritual trance: The Shango cult in Trinidad. *Journal of Altered States of Consciousness*, 1979-1980, 5, 19-29.

References for Chapter Seven

Beyerstein, B.L. Neuropathology and the legacy of spiritual possession. *Skeptical Inquirer*, Spring, 1988, pp. 248-262.

Bourguignon, Erika. *Possession*. San Francisco, Chandler and Sharp, 1976.

Bro, H.H. *A Seer out of Season: The Life of Edgar Cayce*. New York: New American Library, 1989.

Daniels, Pat, and Horan, Ann (Eds.). *Psychic Powers*. Alexandria, VA: Time-Life Books, 1987, p. 94.

Deren, Maya. *Divine Horsemen: The Voodoo Gods of Haiti*. New York: Dell, 1970.

Doyle, R.A. *Magical Arts*. Richmond, VA: Time-Life Books, 1990. pp. 80-81.

Hammond, Sally. *We Are All Healers*. New York: Harper and Row, 1973.

Hanly, Elizabeth. With the saints. *Mother Jones*, September/October, 1990, pp. 85-85.

Haskins, Jim. *Voodoo and Hoodoo*. New York: Stein and Day, 1978.

Haynes, Renee. Faith healing and psychic healing: Are they the same? *Parapsychology Review*, July-August, 1977, pp. 10-13.

Hunt, Dave. *The Cult Explosion*. Eugene, OR: Harvest House, 1980.

Michaelsen, Johanna. *The Beautiful Side of Evil*. Eugene, OR: Harvest House, 1982.

Ness, R.C., and Wintrob, R.M. Folk healing: A description and synthesis. *American Journal of Psychiatry*, 1981, *138*, 1477-1481.

Rodriguez, Felix. *Luz de la Verdad Espiritual*. Buenos Aires: Kier, 1973.

Rogler, L.H., and Hollingshead, A.B. The Puerto Rican spiritualist as a psychiatrist. *American Journal of Sociology*, 1961, *67*, 17-21.

Sandoval, M.C. Santeria as a mental health care system: A historical overview. *Social Science and Medicine*, 1979, *13*(3), 137-157.

Sugrue, Thomas. *There Is a River*. New York: Dell, 1970.

Weldon, John, and Levitt, Zola. *Psychic Healing: An Expose of an Occult Phenomenon*. Chicago: Moody Press, 1982.

References for Chapter Eight

Achterberg, Jeanne. *Women as Healers*. Boston: Shambhala, 1990.

Adler, Margot. *Drawing Down the Moon*. Boston: Beacon Press, 1986.

Bourget, Dominique, Gagnon, Andre, and Bradford, J.M.W. Satanism in a psychiatric adolescent population. *Canadian Journal of Psychiatry*, 1988, *33*, 197-202.

Carlson, Shawn. CSER reports on satanism. *Bay Area Skeptics Information Sheet*, December, 1989, pp. 6-7.

Castaneda, Carlos. *The Fire from Within*. New York: Simon and Schuster, 1984.

Circle Staff (Ed.). *Circle Guide to Pagan Groups*. Mt. Horeb, WI: Circle Sanctuary, 1990.

Davis, Wade. *The Serpent and the Rainbow*. New York: Simon and Schuster, 1985.

DeMille, Richard (Ed.). *The Don Juan Papers*. Santa Barbara, CA: Ross-Erickson, 1980, p. 57.

Doyle, R.A. (Ed.). *Witches and Witchcraft*. Alexandria, VA: Time-Life Books, 1990.

Earth circles. *Shaman's Drum*, Spring, 1988, p. 14.

Ehrenreich, Barbara, and English, Deirdre. *Witches, Midwives, and Nurses: A History of Women Healers*. Old Westbury, NY: Feminist Press, 1973.

Farrar, Janet, and Farrar, Stewart. *The Witches' God*. Custer, WA: Phoenix Publishing, 1989.

Farrar, Janet, and Farrar, Stewart. *The Witches' Goddess*. Custer, WA: Phoenix Publishing, 1987.

Fox, Selena. Circle's center for shamanic psychotherapy. *Circle Network News*, Winter, 1984, p. 11.

Fox, Selena. *Goddess Communion Rituals and Meditations*. Mt. Horeb, WI: Circle Sanctuary, 1989, p. 11.

Fox, Selena. I am a Pagan. In Circle Staff (Ed.). *Circle Guide to Pagan Groups* (pp. 48-50). Mt. Horeb, WI: Circle Sanctuary, 1990.

Guiley, R.E. *The Encyclopedia of Witches and Witchcraft*. New York: Facts on File, 1989.

Hicks, R.D. Police pursuit of satanic crime. *Skeptical Inquirer*, Summer, 1990, pp. 378-389.

Jamal, Michele. *Shape Shifters: Shaman Women in Contemporary Society*. New York: Arkana/Routledge and Kegan Paul, 1987, p.125.

Jayne, W.A. *The Healing Gods of Ancient Civilizations*. New Hyde Park, NY: University Books, 1962.

Jong, Erica. *Witches*. New York: Harry N. Abrams, 1981.

Kluckholm, Claude K. *Navaho Witchcraft*. Cambridge, MA: Harvard University Press, 1944.

Leek, Sybil. *The Complete Art of Witchcraft*. New York: World, 1971.

Melton, J.G. *The Encyclopedia of American Religions*. Wilmington, NC: McGrath, 1978.

Noll, Richard. Satanism, UFO abductions, historians and clinicians: Those who do not remember the past. *Dissociation*, 1989, *2*, 251-253.

Putnam, F.W. The role of the ISSMP&D with respect to allegations of ritual abuse. Letter submitted to the Executive Committee Meeting of the International Society for the Study of Multiple Personality and Dissociation, 1990.

Roelofsma, D.R. Inside the circle of witches. *Insight*, June 8, 1987, pp. 59-61.

Starhawk. *The Spiral Dance: A Rebirth of the Ancient Religion of the Great Goddess*. San Francisco: Harper and Row, 1979.

Starhawk. *Truth or Dare*. San Francisco: Harper and Row, 1987, p. 22.

Steiger, Brad. *Indian Medicine Power*. Gloucester, MA: Para Research, 1984.

Szasz, Thomas. *The Manufacture of Madness*. New York: Delta Books, 1971.

Walsh, John. Voodoo science. *Science*, 1988, *240*, 274-277.

World Health Organization. *Basic Documents*. Geneva: United Nations, 1974.

References for Chapter Nine

Achterberg, Jeanne. *Imagery and Healing: Shamanism and Modern Medicine*. Boulder, CO: Shambhala, 1985, pp. 5-6.

Achterberg, Jeanne, and Lawlis, G.F. *Imagery of Disease: A Diagnostic Tool for Behavioral Medicine*. Champaign, IL: Institute for Personality and Ability Testing, 1979.

Achterberg, Jeanne; Lawlis, G. F.; Simonton, O.C.; and Matthews-Simonton, Stephanie. Psychological factors and blood chemistries as disease outcome predictors for cancer patients. *Multivariate Clinical Research*, 1977, *3*, 107-102.

Albaugh, B.J., and Anderson, P.O. Peyote in the treatment of alcoholism among American Indians. *American Journal of Psychiatry*, 1975, *131*, 1247-1249.

Booth, William. Combing the earth for cures to cancer, AIDS. *Science*, 1987, *237*, 969-970.

Borysenko, Joan. *Minding the Body, Mending the Mind*. Reading, MA: Addison-Wesley, 1987, p. 36.

Brown, J.W. Native American contributions to science, engineering, and medicine. *Science*, 1975, *189*, 38-40.

Cousins, Norman. A nation of hypochondriacs. *Time*, June 18, 1990, p. 88.

Druckman, Daniel, and Swets, John A. (Eds.), *Enhancing Human Performance*. Washington, DC: National Academy Press, 1988, p. 20.

Findlay, Steven, and Brownlee, Shannon. The delicate dance of body and mind. *U.S. News & World Report*, July 2, 1990, p. 54.

Grinspoon, Lester, and Bakular, J.B. *Psychedelic Drugs Reconsidered.* New York: Basic Books, 1979, p. 215.

Hall, Howard. Hypnosis and the immune system: A review with implications for cancer and the psychology of healing. *American Journal of Clinical Hypnosis*, 1983, *25*, 92-103.

Irwin, M., Patterson, T., Smith, T.L., Caldwell, C., Brown, S.A., Gillin J.C., and Grant, I. Reduction of immune function in life stress and depression. *Biological Psychiatry*, 1990, *27*, 22-30.

Kiecolt-Glaser, Janice K., and associates. Psychosocial enhancement of immunocompetence in a geriatric population. *Health Psychology*, 1985, *4*, 25-41.

Kirkpatrick, R.A. Witchcraft and lupus erythematosus. *Journal of the American Medical Association*, 1981, *245*, 1937.

Kurland, A.A. The therapeutic potential of LSD in medicine. In R. DeBold and R. Leaf (Eds.), *LSD, Man, and Society* (pp. 20-35). Middletown, CT: Wesleyan University Press, 1967, p. 23.

Kurland, A.A., Unger, Sanford, Shaffer, J.W., and Savage, Charles. Psychedelic therapy utilizing LSD in the treatment of the alcoholic patient: A preliminary report. *American Journal of Psychiatry*, 1967, *123*, 1202-1209.

Land, Thomas. Herbal healing. *New Leader*, November 17, 1986, p. 3.

Lipowski, Z.L. Somatization and depression. *Psychosomatics*, 1990, *31*, 13-21.

Locke, S.E. Stress, adaptation, and immunity: Studies in humans. *General Hospital Psychiatry*, 1982, *4*, 49-58.

Martin, Marlene. Healing from within. *USAir Magazine*, August, 1990, pp. 80-84.

Moerman, D.E. *American Indian Ethnobotany*. New York: Garland, 1977.

Murphy, Michael, and Donovan, Steven. *The Physical and Psychological Effects of Meditation*. San Rafael, CA: Esalen Institute, 1988, pp. 18-19.

NCAHF Statement on Faith Healing, *NCAHF Newsletter*, July/August, 1987, pp. 1-2.

Nidich, Sanford, Seeman, William, and Dreskin, Thomas. Influence of transcendental meditation: A replication. *Journal of Counseling Psychology*, 1973, *20*, 565-566.

O'Regan, Brendan. Healing, remission and miracle cures. *Institute of Noetic Sciences Special Report*, May, 1987, p. 5.

Ornstein, Robert, and Sobel, David. *The Healing Brain*. New York: Simon and Schuster, 1987, p. 154.

Pieper, C., LaCroix, A.Z., and Karasek, R.A. The relation of psychosocial dimensions of work with coronary heart disease risk factors: A meta-analysis of five United States data bases. *American Journal of Epidemiology*, 1989, *129*, 483-494.

Porter, Garrett, and Norris, P.A. *Why Me? Harnassing the Healing Power of the Human Spirit*. Walpole, NH: Stillpoint, 1985.

Roquet, Salvador. *Operation Mazteca: A Study of Mushrooms and Other Mexican Hallucinogenic Plants*. Mexico City: Albert Schweitzer Association, 1971.

Rossi, E.L. *The Psychobiology of Mind-Body Healing: New Concepts of Therapeutic Hypnosis*. New York: W.W. Norton, 1986, p. 21.

Rossi, E.L., and Cheek, David. *Mind-Body Therapy*. New York: W.W. Norton, 1988, pp. 50-68.

Rossman, M.L. *Healing Yourself: A Step-By-Step Program for Better Health through Imagery*. New York: Walker, 1987.

Sampson and delightful thoughts. *Bay Area Skeptics Information Sheet*, June, 1990, pp. 1-2.

Savage, Charles, and McCabe, O. L. Residential psychedelic (LSD) therapy for the narcotic addict: A controlled study. *Archives of General Psychiatry*, 1973, *28*, 808-814.

Seeman, William, Nidich, Sanford, and Banta, Thomas. Influence of transcendental meditation on a measure of self-actualization. *Journal of Counseling Psychology*, 1972, *19*, 184-187.

Siegel, Bernard. *Love, Medicine and Miracles*. San Francisco: Harper & Row, 1986.

Simonton, O.C., et al. *Getting Well Again*. Los Angeles: J.P. Tarcher, 1978.

Somervell, P.D., Kaplan, B.H., Heiss, G., Tyroler, H.A., Kleinbaum, D.G., and Obrist, P.A. Psychologic distress as a predictor of mortality. *American Journal of Epidemiology*, 1989, *130*, 1013-1023.

Stein, P. A. Summary of probable values of Rappahannock herbal cures based upon their known medicinal properties. *Proceedings, Delaware County Institute of Science*, 1942, *10*, 49-59.

Stewart, Doug. Interview with Arnold S. Relman. *Omni*, May, 1990, pp. 78, 80, 82, 84-87, 117; p. 82.

Theoharides, T.C. Mast cells: The immune gate to the brain. *Life Sciences*, 1990, *46*, 607-617.

Wade, Nicholas. Drug regulation: F.D.A. replies to charges by economists and industry. *Science*, 1973, *179*, 775-777.

Wulff, D.M. *Psychology of Religion*. New York: John Wiley & Sons, 1991, p. 611.

References for Chapter Ten

Alcock, James. *Parapsychology, Science or magic? A Psychological Perspective*. New York: Pergamon Press, 1981.

Benor, D.J. *An Annotated Bibliography of Psychic Healing*. Unpublished manuscript, Albert Einstein Medical Center, 1982.

Berkman, L.F., and Syme, S.L. Social networks, host resistance, and mortality: A nine-year follow-up study of Alameda County residents. *American Journal of Epidemiology*, 1979, *109*, 186-204.

Braud, W.G., and Schlitz, Marilyn. A methodology for the objective study of transpersonal imagery. *Journal of Scientific Exploration*, 1989, *3*, 43-63.

Braud, W.G., and Schlitz, Marilyn. Psychokinetic influence on electrodermal activity. *Journal of Parapsychology*, 1983, 47, 95-119.

Byrd, R.C. Positive therapeutic effects of intercessory prayer in a coronary care unit population. *Southern Medical Journal*, 1988, *81*, 826-829.

Casdorph W.R. *The Miracles*. Plainfield, NJ: Logos International, 1976.

Clark, P.B., and Clark. M.J. Therapeutic touch: Is there a scientific basis for the practice? *Nursing Research*, 1984, *33*, 37-41.

Collipp, P.J. The efficacy of prayer: A triple-blind study. *Medical Times*, 1969, *97*, 201-204.

Cooperstein, M. Allan. *The Myths of Healing: A Descriptive Analysis and Taxonomy of Transpersonal Healing Experience*. Unpublished doctoral dissertation, Saybrook Institute Graduate School, 1990.

Druckman, Daniel, and Swets, J.A. (Eds.). *Enhancing Human Performance*. Washington, DC: National Academy Press, 1988. p. 22).

Goodrich, Joyce. *Psychic Healing—A Pilot Study*. Unpublished doctoral dissertation, Union Institute, 1974.

Grad, Bernard. Healing by the "laying on of hands": Review of experiments and implications. *Pastoral Psychology*, 1970, *21*, 19-26.

Heidt, P. Effect of therapeutic touch on anxiety level of hospitalized patients. *Nursing Research*, 1981, *30*, 32-37.

Joyce, C.R.B., and Weldon, R.M.C. The efficacy of prayer: A double-blind clinical trial. *Journal of Chronic Disease*, 1965, *18*, 367-377.

Krieger, Delores. Therapeutic touch and the metaphysics of nursing. In J. S. Gordon, D. T. Jaffe, and D. E. Bresler (Eds.), *Mind, Body and Health: Toward an Integral Medicine* (pp. 107-116). New York: Human Science Press, 1984.

LeShan, Lawrence. Explanations of psychic healing. *American Society for Psychical Research Newsletter*, Winter, 1990, pp. 1-3.

LeShan, Lawrence. *The Medium, the Mystic and the Physicist*. New York: Viking Press, 1974.

McCormick, Donna. Faith healer exposed. *Newsletter of the American Society for Psychical Research*, July, 1986, p. 23.

Montagu, Ashley. *Touching: The Human Significance of the Skin,* second edition. New York: Harper and Row, 1978, p. 317.

Nolen, W.A. *Healing: A Doctor in Search of a Miracle*. New York: Random House, 1974.

Palmer, J.A.; Honorton, C.; and Utts, J. Reply to the National Research Council study on parapsychology. *Journal of the American Society for Psychical Research*, 1989, *83*, 31-49.

Parapsychological Association. Terms and methods in parapsychological research. *Journal of Humanistic Psychology*, 1989, *29*, 394-399.

Quinn, J.F. Therapeutic touch as energy exchange: Testing the theory. *Advances in Nursing Science*, January, 1984, pp. 42-49.

Randi, James. "Be healed in the name of God!" An expose of the Reverend W.V. Grant. *Free Inquiry*, Spring, 1986, pp. 8-19.

Randi, James. *The Faith-Healers*. Buffalo, NY: Prometheus Books, 1987.

Rheder, Hans. An experiment in faith healing. *Hippokrates*, 1955, *26*, 577-580.

Solfvin, Jerry. Mental healing. In Stanley Krippner (Ed.), *Advances in parapsychological research* (Vol. 4) (pp. 31-82). Jefferson, NC: McFarland Publishers, 1984.

Stewart, Doug. Interview with Arnold S. Relman. *Omni*, May, 1990, pp. 78, 80, 82, 84-87, 117; p. 82

Ullman, Montague, and Krippner, Stanley; with Vaughan, Alan. *Dream Telepathy: Experiments in Nocturnal ESP*, second edition. Jefferson, NC: McFarland, 1989, pp. 111-112.

Winston, Shirley. *Research in Psychic Healing: A Multivariate Experiment*. Unpublished doctoral dissertation, Union Institute, 1975.

Wirth, D.P. Unorthodox healing: The effect of noncontact therapeutic touch on the healing rate of full thickness dermal wounds. *Proceedings of Presented Papers; the Parapsychological Association 32nd Annual Convention* (pp. 251-268). Durham, NC: Parapsychological Association, 1989.

References for Chapter Eleven

American Psychiatric Association, Task Force on Nomenclature and Statistics. *Diagnostic and Statistical Manual of Mental Disorders,* (revised edition) *(DSM-III-R)*. Washington, DC: American Psychiatric Association, 1987.

Avasthi, Surabhi. Sex addiction: Pros and cons of 12 Step treatment fuel controversy. *Guidepost*, September 1, 1990, pp. 1, 20-21.

Barron, Frank. *Creativity and Psychological Health: Origins of Personal Vitality and Creative Freedom*. Princeton, NJ: D. Van Nostrand, 1963, p. 169.

Bergin, A.E. Values and Religious Issues in Psychotherapy and Mental Health. Invited Address, Annual Convention, American Psychological Association, Boston, August 1990.

Brende, Joel, and McDonald, Elmer. Post-traumatic spiritual alienation and recovery in Vietnam combat veterans. *Spirituality Today*, 1989, *41*, 319-340.

Chamberlin, C.R. Supporting spiritual emergence. *Spiritual Emergence Network Newsletter*, Spring, 1986, pp. 1-3.

Christopher, Jim. *How to Stay Sober without Religion*. Buffalo, NY: Prometheus Books, 1988.

Collett, Lily. "Step by Step." *Mother Jones*, July/August, 1988, pp. 42-46, 48.

Elliot, Karen. (1987). *The Twelve Steps of Alcoholics Anonymous*. New York: Harper and Row/Hazelden Foundation.

Ellis, Albert, and Yeager, R. J. *Why Some Therapies Don't Work—The Dangers of Transpersonal Psychology*. Buffalo, NY: Prometheus Books, 1989.

Feinstein, David, and Krippner, Stanley. *Personal Mythology*. Los Angeles: J. P. Tarcher, 1988.

Fox, Ruth. Antabuse as an adjunct to psychotherapy in alcoholism. *New York State Journal of Medicine*, 1958, *58*, 2-9.

Frankl, V.E. *The Doctor and the Soul: From Psychotherapy to Logotherapy*. New York: Vintage Books, 1965.

Grof, Stanislav, and Grof, Christina. Spiritual emergency: The understanding and treatment of transpersonal crises. *ReVision*, 1986, *8*(2), 7-20.

Grof, Stanislav, and Grof, Christina. Spiritual emergency: Understanding evolutionary crisis. In Stanislav Grof and Christina Grof (Eds.), *Spiritual Emergency: When Personal Transformation Becomes a Crisis* (pp. 1-26). Los Angeles: J.P. Tarcher, 1989.

Grof, Christina, and Grof, Stanislav. *The Stormy Search for the Self*. Los Angeles: J.P. Tarcher, 1990.

Harner, Michael. The Harner method of shamanic counseling. *Center for Shamanic Studies Newsletter*, Summer, 1986, pp. 3-5.

Harwood, Alan. *RX: Spiritist as Needed: A Study of a Puerto Rican Community Mental Health Resource*. New York: John Wiley and Sons, 1977.

Jackson, E.N. *The Pastor and His People*. New York: Hawthorne Books, 1974.

Jampolsky, G.G. *Love is Letting Go of Fear*. Millbrae, CA: Celestial Arts, 1979.

Janis, I.L., and Rodin, Judith. Attribution, control and decision making: Social psychology and health care. In G.C. Stone, Frances Cohen, and N.E. Adler (Eds.), *Health Psychology* (pp. 487-521). San Francisco: Jossey-Bass, 1979.

Justice, Blair. *Who Gets Sick: Thinking and Health*. Houston, TX: Peak Press, 1987, pp. 130-131.

Karpel, Charles. *The Rite of Exorcism*. New York: Berkley, 1975.

Koss, Joan D. The therapist-spiritist training project in Puerto Rico: An experiment to relate the traditional healing system to the public health system. *Social Science and Medicine*, 1979, *14*, 255-266.

Kreisman, Jerold J. The *curandero's* apprentice: A therapeutic integration of folk and medical healing. *American Journal of Psychiatry*, 1975, *132*, 81-83.

Kunz, Dora (Ed.). *Spiritual Aspects of the Healing Arts*. Wheaton, IL: Theosophical Publishing House, 1985.

Laibow, Rima. Workshop presentation, Annual Convention, Parapsychological Association, Chevy Chase, MD, August, 1990.

Leighton, A.H., and Leighton, D.C. Elements of psychotherapy in Navaho religion. *Psychiatry*, 1941, *4*, 515-523.

Lukoff, David. Diagnosis of mystical experiences with psychotic features. *Journal of Transpersonal Psychology*, 1985, *17*, 155-181, p. 155.

Lukoff, David. Transpersonal perspectives on manic psychosis, creative, visionary, and mystical states. *Journal of Transpersonal Psychology*, 1988, *20*, 111-139.

Maher, A.R. *Experiencing: A Humanistic Theory of Psychology and Psychiatry.* New York: Brunner/Mazel, 1978.

Mahler, Halfdan. The staff of Aesculapius. *World Health*, November, 1977, p. 3.

Murphy, J.M. *Santeria: An African Religion in America.* Boston: Beacon Press, 1988.

Navarro, V. Health, health services and health planning in Cuba. *International Journal of Health Services*, 1972, *2*, 397-431.

Peck, M.S. *The Road Less Travelled: A New Psychology of Love, Traditional Values and Spiritual Growth.* New York: Touchstone, 1978.

Pros and Cons. *Lancet*, May 3, 1980, pp. 963-964.

Robertson, Michael. Sobriety without the hand of God. *San Francisco Chronicle*, May 25, 1988, pp. B3, B5.

Rochkind, Milton, and Conn, J.H. Guided fantasy encounter. *American Journal of Psychotherapy*, 1973, *27*, 516-528.

Ruiz, Pedro, and Langrod, J. The role of folk healers in community mental health. *Community Mental Health Journal*, 1976, *12*, 392-398.

Sandner, Donald. *Navajo Symbols of Healing.* New York: Harcourt, Brace, Jovanovich, 1979.

Stein, Murray (Ed.). *Jungian Analysis.* LaSalle, IL: Open Court, 1982.

Topper, Martin D. The traditional Navajo medicine man: Therapist, counselor, and community leader. *Journal of Psychoanalytic Anthropology*, 1987, *10*, 217-249.

Torrey, E.F. *Witchdoctors and Psychiatrists*, New York: Harper and Row, 1986, p. 153, 177-178.

Twaddel, William. Survey shows AA a success. *New York Daily News*, September 20, 1968, p. 9.

Walsh, R.N., and Vaughan, Frances (Eds.). *Beyond Ego: Transpersonal Dimensions in Psychology.* Los Angeles: J.P. Tarcher, 1980.

Warner, Richard. Witchcraft and soul loss. *Hospital and Community Psychiatry*, 1977, *28*, 686-690.

Wilson, W.P. Christian psychotherapy. In Richie Herink (Ed.), *The Psychotherapy Handbook* (pp. 86-89). New York: New American Library, 1980.

Woolger, R.J. *Other Lives, Other Selves.* Garden City, NY: Doubleday, 1987.

Wulff, D.M. *Psychology of Religion: Classic and Contemporary Views.* New York: John Wiley and Sons, 1991, pp. 504-505, 635.

Yalom, I.D. *Existential Psychotherapy.* New York: Basic Books, 1980.

References for Chapter Twelve

Bergin, A.E., and Jensen, J.P. Religiosity of psychotherapists: A national survey. *Psychotherapy*, 1990, *37*, 3-7.

Brock, David. Democracy's difficult birth in Haiti and the Philippines. *Insight*, December 28, 1987-January 4, 1988, pp. 26-28.

Chance, Paul. Therapists: A cultural bias? *Psychology Today*, September, 1987, pp. 16-17.

Cohen, Daniel. Spirituality and psychotherapy. *Omni*, January, 1986, p. 85.

Dossey, Larry. *Beyond Illness.* Boulder, CO; Shambhala, 1984.

Dossey, Larry. *Recovering the Soul.* New York: Bantam Books, 1989.

Dossey, Larry. *Space, Time and Medicine.* Boulder, CO: Shambhala, 1982.

Dossey, Larry. The future of medicine. In Dora Kuntz (Ed.), *Spiritual Aspects of the Healing Arts* (pp. 3-13). Wheaton, IL: Theosophical Publishing, 1985.

Fuller, R.C. *Alternative Medicine and American Religious Life.* New York: Oxford University Press, 1989, p. 122.

Grahn, Judy. Strange country this: Lesbianism and North American Indian tribes. *Journal of Homosexuality*, 1986, *12*, 43-57.

Greeley, A.M. *The Sociology of the Paranormal: A Reconnaissance*. Beverly Hills: Sage Publications, 1975.

Holzman, David. Unmasking the agents of asthma. *Insight*, June 15, 1987, pp. 50-51.

Jacobs, Sue-Ellen. Berdache: A brief review of the literature. *Colorado Anthropologist*, 1968, *1*, 25-40.

Krieger, Dolores. *The Therapeutic Touch*. Englewood Cliffs, NJ: Prentice Hall, 1979.

Krieger, Dolores. Therapeutic touch and the metaphysics of nursing. In J.S. Gordon, D.T. Jaffe, and D. E. Bresler (Eds.), *Mind, Body and Health: Toward an Integral Medicine* (pp. 107-116). New York: Human Science Press, 1984.

LaPatra, Jack. *Healing: The Coming Revolution in Holistic Medicine*. New York: McGraw Hill, 1978, pp. 52-53.

Mehl, L.E. *Mind and Matter: A Healing Approach to Organic Illness*. Berkeley, CA: Mindbody Press, 1986.

Neher, Andrew. *The Psychology of Transcendence*. New York: Dover, 1990.

Remen, Naomi. *The Human Patient*. Garden City, NY: Anchor Books, 1980.

Simons, Marie. Religious vigilantes fighting voodoo in Haiti. *The New York Times*, May 15., 1986. pp. 1,6.

Slavitt, D.R. *Physicians Observed*. Garden City, NY: Doubleday, 1987, p. 39.

Spiegel, David. The healing trance. *The Sciences*, March/April, 1987, pp. 34-40.

Szasz, Thomas. *The Untamed Tongue: A Dissenting Dictionary*. San Francisco: Laissez Faire Books, 1990.

Torrey, E.F. *Witchdoctors and Psychiatrists*. New York: Harper and Row, 1986, p. 168.

Walls, Claudia. Weeding out the incompetents. *Time*, May 26, 1986.

Werbach, Melvyn. *Third Line Medicine.* New York: Methuen, 1986.

Williams, Walter L. *The Spirit and The Flesh: Sexual Diversity in American Indian Culture.* Boston: Beacon Press, 1986.

Name Index

Subject Index

The Wisdom of Milton H. Erickson
Volume 2, Human Behavior & Psychotherapy

Ronald A. Havens, Editor

Milton H. Erickson was one of the most creative, dynamic, and effective hypnotherapists and psychotherapists of the twentieth century. Erickson's books have sold more than 250,000 copies. He used unconventional techniques with remarkable success. An indication of the respect Erickson gained from his peers are the words inscribed on his 1976 Benjamin Franklin Gold Medal, the highest award that the International Society of Clinical and Experimental Hypnosis can bestow: "To Milton H. Erickson, M.D.—innovator, outstanding clinician, and distinguished investigator whose ideas have not only helped create the modern view of hypnosis but have profoundly influenced the practice of all psychotherapy throughout the world."

Although he wrote hundreds of papers, articles, and books in his lifetime, Erickson himself never put his techniques and methods into a clear and centralized body of work. *The Wisdom of Milton H. Erickson, II: Human Behavior and Psychotherapy* is an effort to do just that. Along with its companion volume, *The Wisdom of Milton H. Erickson I: Hypnosis and Hypnotherapy*, this book is a collection of Erickson's methods and lessons, including his feelings on the uses of objective observation, the uniqueness of the conscious mind, the realities and abilities of the unconscious mind, the creation and use of a therapeutic environment, and many other aspects of the life and work of this remarkable thinker and teacher.

...a heroic effort to bring clarity to a hard-to-grasp theory...(This book) is a major reference for students and scholars who want to know what Erickson said and when and where he said it.
Contemporary Psychology

ISBN 0-8290-2414-X (Paper)
258 pages
$14.95

IRVINGTON PUBLISHERS, INC.
740 Broadway, New York, NY 10003

MC/Visa orders may be telephoned to (603) 669-5933.